D0146661

TECHNIQUES FOR CONSTRUCTION NETWORK SCHEDULING

McGraw-Hill Series in Construction Engineering and Project Management

Consulting Editor: Raymond E. Levitt, *Stanford University*

Barrie and Paulson: Professional Construction Management
Jervis and Levin: Construction Law: Principles and Practice
Koerner: Construction and Geotechnical Methods in Foundation Engineering
Levitt and Samelson: Construction Safety Management
Oglesby, Parker, and Howell: Productivity Improvement in Construction
Peurifoy and Ledbetter: Construction Planning, Equipment, and Methods
Peurifoy and Oberlender: Estimating Construction Costs
Shuttleworth: Mechanical and Electrical Systems for Construction
Stevens: Techniques for Construction Network Scheduling

TECHNIQUES FOR CONSTRUCTION NETWORK SCHEDULING

James D. Stevens

Department of Civil Engineering
University of Kentucky

McGRAW-HILL PUBLISHING COMPANY

New York St. Louis San Francisco Auckland Bogotá Caracas
Hamburg Lisbon London Madrid Mexico Milan Montreal New Delhi
Oklahoma City Paris San Juan São Paulo Singapore Sydney Tokyo Toronto

TECHNIQUES FOR CONSTRUCTION NETWORK SCHEDULING

Copyright © 1990 by McGraw-Hill, Inc. All rights reserved. Printed in the United States of America. Except as permitted under the United States Copyright Act of 1976, no part of this publication may be reproduced or distributed in any form or by any means, or stored in a data base or retrieval system, without the prior written permission of the publisher.

1 2 3 4 5 6 7 8 9 0   DOC   DOC   8 9 4 3 2 1 0 9

ISBN 0-07-061291-9

This book was set in Times Roman by the College Composition Unit in cooperation with Waldman Graphics, Inc.
The editors were B. J. Clark and Scott Amerman;
the production supervisor was Janelle S. Travers.
The cover was designed by Carla Bauer.
R. R. Donnelley & Sons Company was printer and binder.

Some material in Chapter 11 first appeared in "Modified CPM—A Scheduler's Best Friend." Vol. 30, No. 10 of *Cost Engineering*. (American Association of Cost Engineers; October 1988.)

Library of Congress Cataloging-in-Publication Data

Stevens, James (date).
   Techniques for construction network scheduling.

   Bibliography: p.
   Includes index.
   1. Building—Superintendence.   2. Scheduling
(Management) I. Title.
TH438.4.S74   1990   624'.068   89–8159
ISBN 0-07-061291-9

To Adrienne and Victor

CONTENTS

PREFACE

Network scheduling for construction was formalized in the 1950s with the development of the Critical Path Method (CPM) and Program Evaluation and Review Technique (PERT). Acceptance of network scheduling by the construction industry has since grown to where today it is a necessary management tool, partly because many buyers of construction services insist on its use, but more importantly, because proper use of network schedules can make the construction process more efficient. In today's highly competitive market not only owners and contractors, but all players in the construction game need an understanding of network schedules.

A formal course covering network scheduling, especially CPM, is required in most civil engineering and construction technology programs, and is available as an elective for most other engineering, architecture, and technology programs. Also, many construction organizations offer short courses to provide working knowledge of network scheduling to practitioners without prior training and/or as refresher courses.

This book is intended to assist students and practitioners in developing the necessary skills needed for practical network scheduling using CPM and PERT, and to provide an introduction to simulation.

Many fine texts are available which discuss network scheduling for various levels of management. This book, however, offers some features not found in most others. It is primarily aimed at "beginners." It is designed to be used by students in engineering, architecture, and construction technology, as well as practitioners desiring to understand network scheduling. No experience in construction is required and none is assumed by the author. Where this book differs from many other texts is in its conversational manner with often-asked questions posed and answered.

The pedagogical aspects of this book make the subject extremely easy for students and practitioners to understand. Typically, each chapter starts with "new words," followed by an introduction and explanation of new concepts; then an example is developed step by step, with numerous illustrations. At the end of the chapter several "practice" problems with solutions and several "supplemental" problems without solutions are provided. An actual project, JIMBEAU project, is developed throughout the book to demonstrate the entire network scheduling process. Also, most chapters contain reference to simple BASIC programs, provided in the appendix, which can assist in applying the techniques discussed in the chapter. The reader may use these programs "as is" to perform steps in the network scheduling process and/or to modify them as desired.

It is recommended that students using this book in an undergraduate course have an instructor present. Practitioners and students with some construction background, however, may find the material self-explanatory. The simple, straightforward approach and step-by-step instructions with numerous illustrations make this book ideal as a text for short courses where material must be covered quickly and as a reference book where one can grasp details easily.

This book deals primarily with network scheduling techniques themselves. There are many topics in construction management which are closely related to network scheduling, such as cost estimating and cost control, which are not covered; but sources for these topics are listed in the bibliography for the interested reader.

The discussion of network scheduling flows logically throughout the book.

Section 1 provides an introduction to network scheduling and gives answers to many "why" questions.

Sections 2, 3, and 4 cover the primary steps of creating simple network schedules: planning the project, creating the network, and determining project timing.

Section 5 discusses project control: monitoring, updating, and presenting the schedule in a useful fashion.

Sections 6 and 7 discuss the CPM extensions of least-cost scheduling and resource leveling at an elementary level.

Section 8 discusses precedence diagraming, a powerful network scheduling model just coming into wide acceptance.

Section 9 discusses PERT, a common network scheduling technique more suited to nonconstruction schedules such as design and research and development.

Section 10 discusses simulation, a technique utilizing Monte Carlo methods to simulate project duration.

Section 11 discusses some ancillary applications for network schedules which arise out of their use during a construction project.

Section 12 gives examples of several commercially available software packages.

McGraw-Hill and I would like to thank the following reviewers for their many helpful comments and suggestions: Lee Boyer, University of Illinois; Donn E. Hancher, Texas A&M University; Raymond E. Levitt, Stanford University; Jerald Rounds, Arizona State University; James Rowings, Iowa State University; and Gary R. Smith, Pennsylvania State University.

I would also like to express my thanks to the following companies for providing the commercially available network scheduling software discussed in Chapter 12: Microsoft Corporation, MICROSOFT PROJECT; Breakthrough Software Corporation, TIMELINE; and InstaPlan Corporation, INSTAPLAN.

Throughout the book, reference is made to computer programs that can be used to assist in network schedule development. Code listings for these programs are provided in the appendix. These code listings are "bare bones" in that while their functions may be performed accurately, they have few user-friendly features.

For readers desiring more, the BASIC programs listed in the appendix, with enhancements such as color and printing capabilities, plus additional programs which allow data input in both the arrow and node formats are available on 3.5- or 5.25-in disks in IBM PC format and on 3.5-in disk in Apple Macintosh format. These disks sell for $10.00 each and may be ordered from:

JIMBEAU CONSTRUCTION MANAGEMENT
P.O. Box 356
Dawson Springs, KY 42408

James D. Stevens

TECHNIQUES FOR CONSTRUCTION NETWORK SCHEDULING

INTRODUCTION

NEW WORDS

Activity   An amount of work that can be identified so that we know what it involves and can recognize when it starts and finishes

Bar chart   A non-network-scheduling technique for scheduling (also called a Gantt chart)

CPM (critical path method)   A deterministic network-scheduling technique

Deterministic process   Finding a total project duration based on the sum of known values

Network   A series of interconnected links with fixed logical relationships

PERT (program evaluation and review technique)   A stochastic network-scheduling technique

Schedule   A time-based arrangement of project activities

Simulation   A network-scheduling technique using Monte Carlo methods

Stochastic process   Finding a probable total project duration based on the sum of probable values

WHAT IS A SCHEDULE?

Webster's New Collegiate Dictionary tells us the noun "schedule" is "a written document," "a written or printed list, catalog, or inventory," and also "a timetable, program, proposal, agenda, or a body of items to be dealt with." It also says the verb "schedule" is "to appoint, assign, or designate for a fixed time."

In construction we usually use the term "schedule" to indicate a list of resources needed for a project, with or without relation to time, and for a time-based plan of work. For instance, a record of all windows needed, taken from the plans, is called the window schedule, which at first is merely a list but later may contain required delivery dates. There is also a project time schedule which shows when the various activities should take place, including window installation. So, in construction the word ''schedule'' can mean any list of resources needed for the project and/or any orderly arrangement of activities describing sequence and/or timing.

This text deals with, and refers to, ''the schedule'' as a time-based arrangement of activities planned to take place in order to efficiently complete the project.

WHY SCHEDULE CONSTRUCTION?

We use schedules to be more efficient in the construction process. In order to manage a construction project effectively, we must have a plan which includes what is to be accomplished, the technology involved, the resources needed, and the expected time for construction. A very crucial part of this plan is the time-based schedule which is so important for all concerned. The contractor needs such a schedule to know when and how much labor is needed; vendors need such a schedule to know when to deliver material; subcontractors need such a schedule to know when they can do their work; etc.

AIA (American Institute of Architects) A201-1987, ''The General Conditions to the Construction Contract,'' is a document commonly used in conjunction with the owner-contractor agreement for private construction. This is what it has to say about the schedule:

3.10 Contractor's Construction Schedules

3.10.1 The Contractor, promptly after being awarded the Contract, shall prepare and submit for the Owner's and Architect's information a Contractor's construction schedule for the Work. The schedule shall not exceed time limits current under the Contract Documents, shall be related to the entire Project to the extent required by the Contract Documents, and shall provide for expeditious and practicable execution of the Work.

WHAT IS NETWORK SCHEDULING?

Network scheduling is a method of scheduling activities by joining them in a series of interconnected links which reflect relationships of activities as assigned by the planner. These relationships may represent those dictated by technology such as building the foundation before the walls, those suggested by economics such as excavating for the septic tank while the equipment is on location for foundation work, and those based on common sense, policy, prejudice, or the whimsey of the planner.

The basic assumptions for creating a network schedule are:

1 The project can be broken down into a group of activities.
2 Each activity can be assigned a duration.

3 The logical relationships among activities are known and fixed in the network chains.

Networks are usually drawn using arrows and circles (or squares). While these diagrams are called by various names, their presentation is rather conventional. Figures 1-1 and 1-2 show the same project network schedule expressed by two different diagrams. The diagram in Fig. 1-1 is often called an "arrow" or "activity-on-arrow" diagram, and the diagram in Fig. 1-2 is often called a "node," "precedence," or "activity-on-node" diagram. In this text we will use the simplest terms, arrow and node, to refer to the diagrams.

WHY USE NETWORK SCHEDULING?

We use network scheduling as a tool for effective construction management. Network schedules have many things to offer us in construction. Their main use, and the impetus for their proliferation, is to provide a mathematical model to represent the construction process over time. It also provides a means to do "what if" analysis—try changing a part of the process and observe the effect on the total project. Network scheduling has also become very important in the settling of legal claims caused by delay, in simplifying determination of progress payments, in analyzing cash-flow analysis, and in controlling costs.

It is very important to learn to use network schedules because they are required by many owners. Most large U.S. government projects require network schedules (usually CPM) and many private projects do so as well. There are also more subtle reasons for using network schedules. The familiarity of the work plan gained while creating the network schedule enhances the ability of the project team to control the actual project. Also, network schedules provide a convenient way to tie scheduling in with cost accounting.

In order to better understand and appreciate network-scheduling techniques, you should know something about nonnetwork techniques. The most common nonnetwork technique is usually referred to as a bar chart, or some-

Figure 1-1
Arrow diagram.

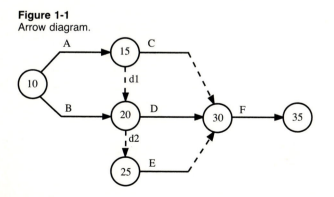

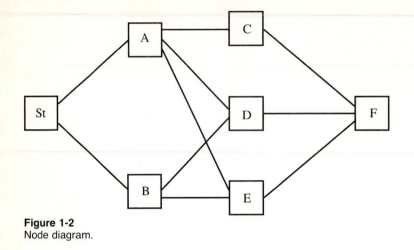

Figure 1-2
Node diagram.

times as a Gantt chart for the man, Henry Gantt, who introduced its use circa the early 1900s. A bar chart for a simple project is shown in Fig. 1-3.

The activities in Fig. 1-3, which are designated by letters for simplicity, represent parts of the project: excavation, forming, etc. Across the top of the bar chart is the calendar time line which shows the dates. The horizontal lines, or bars, show on what dates the corresponding activities are scheduled.

The bar chart is probably the easiest construction scheduling technique to understand and is used to some extent on most construction projects; however, when used alone, it has a serious drawback. If a project could be constructed exactly in accordance with the schedule then the bar chart alone might be sufficient. However, construction projects seldom go according to schedule for a variety of reasons. The main problem with the bar chart, or any

Figure 1-3
Bar chart.

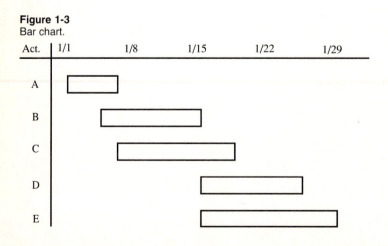

nonnetwork schedule, is that you cannot tell exactly what effect a delay today will have on the timing of future activities.

For instance, in Fig. 1-3 the scheduler has activities D and E starting when activity B completes, on 1/15. If B completes on schedule, everything is fine, but if B is delayed by 1 week, what effect does that have on D and E? This question cannot be answered by the bar chart alone. Perhaps D needs the same machine that is being used for B, so it must be delayed until B is completed and the machine is made available. Perhaps E is scheduled to start on 1/15 because of reasons unrelated to activities B and D and can proceed as planned. There are several other possibilities, but we don't know for sure without asking the person responsible for creating the bar chart.

Bar charts can be made more elaborate to include updated information such as in Fig. 1-4. Here the empty rectangular box is the activity as planned, the cross-hatching represents the estimated work-in-place for activities in progress, and the shading shows completed activities with the actual time required.

There has been some use of the bar chart as a network diagram by using various means to show the relationship among activities, but by and large other diagrams can better express a network schedule. The bar chart is commonly used as a means of displaying a network schedule in a time-phased fashion. This will be discussed in Chap. 5.

WHAT TYPES OF NETWORK SCHEDULES ARE USED?

The most common network schedules currently used in construction are CPM and PERT. Techniques using Monte Carlo simulation are becoming more popular with the widespread availability of low-cost, high-speed computers.

The most popular network-scheduling technique used in construction is the critical path method (CPM). CPM was developed in the mid-fifties by Morgan Walker of E. I. DuPont de Nemours & Company and James E. Kelly of

Figure 1-4
Bar chart.

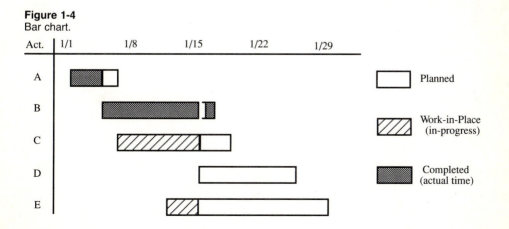

Remington Rand for managing the construction, overhaul, and shutdown of large chemical plants. It is a network technique where every activity is assigned a fixed duration. There is at least one path through the network, from start to finish, that controls the project length—it is called the critical path. By adding the durations of the activities on a critical path, the project duration is found. There is only one possible project duration, and hence the process is termed deterministic. Also, for those activities not on a critical path the amount of flexibility they have in starting and finishing (called float or slack) can be calculated.

Another network-scheduling method that is often used in planning and design applications is the program evaluation and review technique (PERT). PERT was developed in the mid-fifties—but not in connection with CPM—by the U.S. Navy for planning the research and development of the Polaris missile. PERT is a network technique similar to CPM but which has activity durations expressed as probability distributions rather than fixed values. PERT networks also have critical paths, and the project duration can be calculated. However, this duration being a sum of distributions is itself a probability distribution, and hence it is termed stochastic. PERT is the more general of the two techniques, but CPM is the one more widely used. CPM also has various and sundry cost and resource control capabilities.

A third technique, which has no formal name—we shall simply call it simulation—uses Monte Carlo simulation methods. Monte Carlo simulation is not new, but its practical use in network scheduling *is* new, due to the availability of fast, affordable computers. The technique utilizes simulation to predict a project duration by using random numbers to assign probable durations to activities and then solving the CPM algorithm for project duration. By repeating this process many times, one can produce a distribution for the probable project duration.

HOW ARE NETWORK SCHEDULES USED?

The primary use of network schedules is to schedule activities against time in order to predict when the various phases of a project should start and end in order to complete the project on a certain date. There are, however, several other valuable uses for network schedules, primarily CPM, that can assist the scheduler-estimator in cost control.

A CPM network reflecting the most efficient utilization of resources represents an optimum based on direct costs. When overhead costs are considered, a technique called least-cost scheduling can be applied to balance the two cost categories and indicate a schedule that will produce the least total project cost.

A CPM network can be treated by a technique called resource leveling in an attempt to level out the labor, or other resource, utilization. This situation promotes a more stable work force and reduces time lost to training new workers.

Precedence diagraming is a network-scheduling model that allows various logic relationships among activities. To express logic in the three networks already mentioned, a certain activity (or activities) must finish before another can start—this is called a finish-start relationship. Precedence diagraming allows multiple logic relationships: start-start, start-finish, finish-start, and finish-finish. It is a more realistic model of the construction process than either CPM or PERT but is unwieldy to use manually. It has not been widely used by the construction industry in the past, but it is quickly gaining acceptance as computers and software become available.

All network-scheduling techniques to be discussed can be performed manually. However, a computer is usually needed to make practical use of these techniques because of the many time-consuming calculations required for an actual project. There are many software packages available to facilitate network scheduling, but most require the user to have a good working knowledge of CPM. Source code listings and sample outputs for simple programs are provided in the Appendix to facilitate performing intermediate steps in network scheduling. Examples of commercially available software packages are presented in Chap. 12. A glossary of terms related to network scheduling, scheduling software, and general construction, and a bibliography listing other texts for network scheduling are also provided.

A sample project, called the JIMBEAU project, will be used throughout the text to illustrate the practical uses of network-scheduling techniques. Problems to be solved concerning the JIMBEAU project will be presented at the end of various sections. Also, most sections contain an example problem solved step by step, several practice problems with solutions, and unanswered supplementary problems.

CHAPTER **2**

PLANNING

NEW WORDS

Activity list A list of activities making up a project
Duration The time it takes for an activity to be completed
PA list A list of activities preceding any given activity
IPA list A list of activities immediately preceding any given activity

The secret to good construction scheduling is good planning. The planner must decide what work is to be done and how it will be done before a schedule can be created.

HOW DO WE START?

We start by creating a plan for constructing the project.

The planning process begins by defining the task to be accomplished, which in the case of construction is usually a project for which exist plans, specifications, and a time frame for completing the construction work.

There are five main resources the planner uses for planning the project. These are material, workers, equipment, money, and time. Each of these resources is required to some extent, but the amount of each needed depends somewhat on the availability of the others. For instance, the roof of a building can use either trusses or rafters and joists. Trusses cost more, and a crane is required to lift them into place, while more workers and time are required if rafters and joists are used. The planner must choose the option that is available or, if more than one option is available, choose the one which best fits the overall plan.

8

After a tentative plan is developed, the planner must schedule each of the resources. This can be very difficult if all resources are scheduled at once, so the usual procedure is to schedule resources one at a time, checking to see if the latest resource scheduled supports all previous schedules.

A typical process for creating a network schedule is as follows:

1 Create a *time* schedule for the construction of the project based on the assumption that all other resources needed will be available. (*Note:* "All other resources needed" means "resources needed within the normal total available"; it does not mean we can assume there are unlimited resources.) This will become the network schedule.

2 Create a *material* schedule showing delivery dates of needed material, and compare this schedule with the network schedule. If items of material are arriving later than shown on the network schedule, then the network schedule must be stretched to accommodate this change.

3 Create an *equipment* schedule, checking that necessary equipment is available when needed, and modify the network schedule, if necessary.

4 Create a *worker* schedule, checking that workers of proper trades are available when needed, and modify the network schedule, if necessary.

5 Create a *money* or cash-flow schedule, checking if money will be available to meet the expenses of construction when payments are due, and modify the network schedule, if necessary.

This process is required for all projects, but for now we'll concentrate on the time schedule.

HOW DO WE SELECT ACTIVITIES?

We select activities primarily from experience to reflect a unit of work that is easily distinguishable and fits our scheduling technique.

The first step in creating a network schedule is to select the activities and specify their logic relationships. After this step, each activity is listed and a list of activities that must logically precede it [a preceding activities (PA) list] is developed. This list is then reduced to an immediately preceding activities (IPA) list which shows only the activities immediately preceding any given activity. Figure 2-1 shows a PA and an IPA list with the corresponding arrow diagram.

Activities and their logic relationships are generated by the scheduler, who does this by experience, by asking others, or by making an educated guess. There is no one correct way to break a project down into activities, but there are three categories of activities that should be included in the activity list.

Procurement: This category includes all things that must be brought to the job that require time, such as permanent materials, temporary materials, workers, equipment, money, and utilities. Bills of material, work standards, and plans and specifications assist the scheduler in identifying activities in this category.

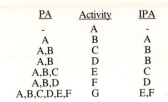

PA	Activity	IPA
-	A	-
A	B	A
A,B	C	B
A,B	D	B
A,B,C	E	C
A,B,D	F	D
A,B,C,D,E,F	G	E,F

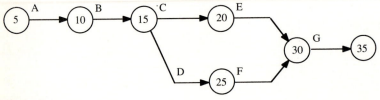

Figure 2-1
PA and IPA lists.

Construction: This category includes the activities necessary to assemble and erect the facility. Identifying activities in this category requires an understanding of the drawings and plans and specifications. Experience in the required technology is also very important.

Management: This category includes all items necessary for the project but not specifically identified in the first or second category. Experience is essential for this category, which addresses such items as safety, site access, and social concerns.

After the activities have been identified, their interrelationships must be defined. Most activities must precede some activities and succeed other activities, but there are also those that start or finish the project.

One factor we must keep in mind, at least for the time being, is that the most common network-scheduling techniques use a "finish-start" relationship, which means an activity must finish completely before its successors can start. Later, in Chap. 8, Precedence Diagraming, we will be able to relax this requirement. Actually, the finish-start constraint doesn't cause us any unsolvable problems, but it does require us to be very careful in defining our activities and generally causes a larger number of activities to be needed for a given project. Let's look at an example.

Suppose you are going to build the footing shown in Fig. 2-2 which requires the following items of work:

A Excavate using backhoe
B Build formwork
C Place rebar
D Place concrete

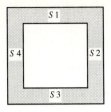

Figure 2-2
Overlapping activities.

If you are working alone, you can use A, B, C, and D as activities in your network schedule. However, if you have help, you will probably want to work on more than one item at a time. For instance, after side $S1$ is excavated, $S2$ can be excavated while $S1$ is being formed. Later, the reinforcing bars (rebar) can be placed for $S1$, $S2$ can be formed, and $S3$ can be excavated. If we want to overlap these items, we must define our activities in smaller units that will conform to the finish-start relationship. We can do this by calling our activities A1, A2,..., B1, B2,..., C1, C2,..., and D. Then we will first excavate $S1$ (activity A1), and then excavate $S2$ (activity A2) and build formwork $S1$ (activity B1), etc.

After the activities have been determined, we assign durations to each activity according to the time it should take to complete the activity. A scheduler may get these durations by any of several means, including:

1 Check past records
2 Check standards and/or cost guides, if available
3 Ask the workers who will do it
4 Make an educated guess

First, we must decide which time units work best for the project being scheduled.

WHAT DURATION UNITS SHOULD WE USE?

We should use units that best fit the majority of the activities on our schedule. ''Workdays'' usually work best for construction; shifts work well for manufacturing; and calendar days, weeks, or months may be used for design work. No matter what units you choose, some activities will naturally be expressed in other units. Since all durations must be expressed in the same units to facilitate the network calculations, this sometimes requires us to convert units. For instance, on a construction time schedule the CPM diagram uses workdays, but a supplier quotes a delivery of material in 30 days. This requires us to convert 30 calendar days to the proper number of workdays (which will depend on the number of days worked per week, the number of holidays, etc.).

WHAT DETERMINES THE ACTIVITY DURATION?

The proper activity duration is determined by considering several factors. For instance, how would we answer the question, ''How long does it take to paint a house?'' Well, it depends on the quantity of work (size and shape of the house), quantity of resources (number of painters and type of equipment), and technology (number of coats, drying time, etc.). In planning our project we choose activities such that the quantity of work is known. We then identify technological factors, some of which are relatively constant—like drying time—and some of which are selectable—such as what type of paint to use. For the quantity of resources, we generally start out with "normal" crews and "owned" equipment. For instance, if we had a crew consisting of three painters and one paint sprayer, we would first use these resources to determine the time required to paint the house. This can be done by finding the productivity of our painting crew on past jobs (square feet per hour, worker-hours per gallon, etc.) and calculating the time needed to do this job. Later, after all the activities are scheduled, if we need to shorten the activities, we can investigate adding more resources to decrease the time duration.

Another approach is to use "standard" activities. A standard activity might be called "paint walls" with a duration of 1 workday per 1000 square feet.

SHOULD THERE BE A LIMIT ON ACTIVITY DURATIONS?

Yes, most construction network schedules should have a minimum and maximum limit on durations to allow for effective monitoring.

Assigning durations to activities depends in large measure on how a particular activity is defined. For instance, an activity called "build foundation" may be assigned a duration of 60 days. While this would undoubtedly simplify the network diagram, it wouldn't be very helpful in controlling the work. At the other extreme, if "building foundation" was broken into many activities, one of which might be called "place rebar piece #1162, duration 0.01 h," the task of drawing the diagram would be horrendous and, in addition, the updating of the diagram might take more time than the construction work. In practice we look for a compromise that maximizes the usefulness of the schedule for control while minimizing the effort necessary to create and update the schedule. For most construction projects a maximum activity duration of 15 days should work well. Scheduling other types of work such as design and/or manufacturing might require maximum durations of greater or lesser amounts.

HOW CAN WE ACCOUNT FOR WEATHER AND CONTINGENCIES?

We account for weather and contingencies by adding or subtracting days for items such as (a) expected weather, (b) expectation of some particular interruption, and/or (c) other contingencies.

The process for adding or subtracting time for weather is tricky. For instance, if our project is to take about 1 year and our records show that in the past we have lost an average of 11 days of work per year due to bad weather, we will want to lengthen our schedule by 11 days. The problem with doing this is deciding where to add the 11 days. Of course, if we only want to know when the project will be completed, we can add the 11 days almost anywhere, but normally we want our CPM schedule to indicate when every activity should start and finish. If we add 11 days at the beginning of the project, we will appear to be ahead of schedule because the first real productive activity won't be scheduled to start until 11 days after the project starts. Conversely, if we add 11 days at the end of the project, each time we lose a day to weather during the project, it will seem to put us behind schedule when, in fact, we are not behind because we have that day reserved at the end. We could try to make several shorter activities, say 1 or 2 days each, and stagger them throughout the project; we could increase the durations of all activities by a percentage; or we could increase the durations of activities that would be most affected by bad weather (i.e., concrete work) and leave other activities (i.e., inside work) alone. Actually, in practice even the best CPM schedules need to be updated often, so perhaps the best way to handle schedules that are subject to weather is as follows:

1 Draw the CPM diagram and perform the calculations (discussed in Chap. 4).
2 Identify the critical activities—those that control the project's length.
3 Determine how the critical activities would be affected by bad weather: canceled, slowed by 50 percent, no effect, etc.
4 Roughly estimate the chance that those activities most affected by bad weather will fall during the annual period when that weather is likely to occur. By knowing when the project starts, you should know approximately when an activity will take place. For instance, if a building project in the United States starts in the summer and is expected to take 1 year, foundation work probably won't be affected by bad weather, but roofing or siding work may be affected since it will probably occur during the winter.
5 Increase the durations of those activities that control the project and are most likely to be affected during the life of the project to absorb the 11 days of expected delay.

For other contingencies, common sense is most useful. For instance, a delay often experienced is the shutting down of a project for vacations or for some social event which makes construction work hazardous or undesirable for a short period. In this case it's best to simply add an activity (you could call it "wait") in series with the controlling activities of the project. Remember, while you want your initial schedule to be as good as possible for planning purposes, you are going to be updating the schedule periodically and can move activities around as better information becomes available.

HOW DO WE DEFINE THE NETWORK LOGIC?

We define the network logic to reflect our construction plan in a cost-effective manner, considering our available resources.

There is no doubt that experience is very valuable to a planner, and some knowledge of the technology is absolutely required. There is, however, a very simple procedure that can assist in defining interrelationships; it entails creating a PA list. The procedure is to list all the activities, and then taking each activity one at a time, to ask the question of every other activity, "Must this other activity come first?" If the answer is yes, include it in the PA list next to the subject activity; if the answer is no, go on to the next activity. This process will result in a PA list as shown in Fig. 2-1.

It is necessary to know all the activities that must precede any particular activity, but to make practical use of this information we must reduce the PA list to an IPA list. An IPA list only shows the activities immediately preceding each activity since it eliminates those occurring before a certain activity in the schedule but not immediately preceding that activity. To reduce the PA list to the IPA list we identify, among those activities preceding a given activity, which activities are themselves predecessors to others. For instance, in Fig. 2-1, A, B, and C precede E, but since A and B precede C, they cannot immediately precede E. Therefore, only C immediately precedes E and appears in the IPA list, while A and B precede E but occur earlier in the network.

Computers can be very helpful in planning. In the creation of the activity list a computer can be used to recall activity lists stored from previous similar projects which can then be modified to incorporate the particular requirements of the current project. This historical data may also assist in creating the PA list. Creating the PA list requires experience, but knowledge-based systems are currently being developed that can assist in the task. Program PA, in the Appendix, is a simple program which, for each chosen activity, lists all other activities one at a time so that the user can respond by saying yes or no to whether the activity must precede the chosen activity or not. The output of this program is the PA list.

Reducing the PA list is a mechanical process and an ideal task for the computer. Program IPA, in the Appendix, performs this function.

Example

You are going to build a prefabricated steel warehouse according to the plans in Fig. 2-3 and using the activities in (2-1). The walls are primed, and the roof, doors, and windows are prepainted. You have the following constraints on the erection:

Figure 2-3
Warehouse plans.

Plan View   Front/Back (1 & 3)   Sides (2 & 4)

Technical Constraints

1 Items must be assembled in the following order: footing, walls, roof, lights.

2 Doors and windows can be installed after the corresponding sides are erected.

3 Both windows must be installed at the same time.

4 Walls can be painted only after all walls are erected.

Activities	Activities	Activities	
A Clear and grub	F Install wall 2	K Install windows	
B Excavate footing	G Install wall 3	2 and 4	
C Rebar footing	H Install wall 4	L Install roof	(2.1)
D Place footing	I Install door 1	M Install lights	
E Install wall 1	J Install door 3	N Paint walls	

First we'll make a PA list (2-2) indicating which activities must precede each given activity.

Activity	Preceding activities	
A	—	
B	A	
C	A,B	
D	A,B,C	
E	A,B,C,D	
F	A,B,C,D	
G	A,B,C,D	
H	A,B,C,D	
I	A,B,C,D,E	(2.2)
J	A,B,C,D,G	
K	A,B,C,D,F,H	
L	A,B,C,D,E,F,G,H	
M	A,B,C,D,E,F,G,H,L	
N	A,B,C,D,E,F,G,H	

Next, we'll reduce the PA list to an IPA list (2-3).

Act	IPA	Explanation
A	—	—
B	A	—
C	B	A comes before B

D	C	A,B come before C
E	D	A,B,C, come before D
F	D	A,B,C come before D
G	D	A,B,C come before D
H	D	A,B,C come before D
I	E	A,B,C,D, come before E
J	G	A,B,C,D come before G
K	F,H	A,B,C,D, come before F,H
L	E,F,G,H	A,B,C,D, come before E,F,G,H
M	L	A,B,C,D,E,F,G,H come before L
N	E,F,G,H	A,B,C,D come before E,F,G,H

(2-3)

Later this IPA information will help us in drawing the network diagram.

Throughout the text an actual project, JIMBEAU, will be used to practice the skills and techniques of network scheduling. The JIMBEAU project is to build a small wood-frame workshop which will have heating, ventilation, and air conditioning (HVAC), in addition to workbenches and electrical outlets.

The initial steps in scheduling a construction project deal with identifying activities and their interrelationships. Since there is no one correct way to do this, we'll assume a set of activities and logical relationships for the JIMBEAU project so that we can proceed. Later in the book, after we're familiar with the whole process, we will look at some hints to help us in the beginning phases.

We will use the activities listed in (2-4) for the JIMBEAU project.

Act	Dur	Description
A	2	Get building permit
B	2	Prepare site
C	3	Order forming materials for utility ways
D	2	Order and arrange for concrete delivery
E	3	Form and lay utility ways
F	3	Place and cure concrete
G	10	Order utility service to site
H	7	Order HVAC and electrical items
I	4	Install and connect HVAC and electrical items
J	1	Inspect HVAC and electrical items
K	8	Order lumber, fasteners, doors, windows, siding
L	6	Frame walls
M	6	Frame roof
N	4	Install doors and windows

(2-4)

O	5	Order insulation, plasterboard, ceiling, flooring
P	3	Attach siding
Q	5	Attach roof
R	3	Insulate walls and ceiling
S	4	Install plasterboard and ceilings
T	2	Install flooring
U	10	Order workbenches and paint
V	2	Install workbenches
W	5	Paint and trim exterior
X	4	Paint and trim interior
Y	1	Final inspection

PRACTICE PROBLEMS

P1 See (2-5).

PA	Activity	IPA
—	A	
—	B	
—	C	
A,B	D	
B	E	
A,B,D	F	
A,B,D,E	G	
A,B,C,D,E,F,G	H	
A,B,C,D,E,G	I	

(2-5)

P2 See (2-6).

PA	Activity	IPA
—	A	
A	B	
A,B	C	
A,B,C	D	
A,B,C	E	
A,B,C,D,E	F	
A,B,C,D	G	
A,B,C,D,E,F,G	H	
A,B,C,D,E,F,G,H	I	
A,B,C,D,E,F,G,H,I	J	

(2-6)

P3 See (2-7).

PA	Activity	IPA
—	A	
A	B	
A	C	
A	D	
A,B,C	E	
A,C	F	
A,D	G	
A,C,F	H	
A,C,D,F,G	I	
A,B,C,D,E,F,G,H,I	J	

(2-7)

P4 You are planning for the tennis court shown in Fig. 2-P1. You have identified the activities listed in (2-8).

Act description	Act description
A Get permit	N Place court pavement
B Order all paint	O Cure court pavement
C Order court pavement	P Place court overlay
D Order bleacher pavement	Q Cure court overlay
E Order court overlay	R Paint court
F Order fencing	S Erect fence
G Order judge's stand and nets	T Erect judge's stand and nets
H Order bleacher material	U Place bleacher pavement
I Order stand material	V Cure bleacher pavement
J Order stand equipment	W Erect bleachers
K Mobilize	X Erect stand
L Clear and grub	Y Paint stand
M Level and compact	Z Install stand equipment

(2-8)

Sequence of events

 1 The permit is required prior to starting any *construction* activities.

 2 The entire area must be prepared first.

 3 The court area must be paved, overlaid, and cured; then painting, fencing, and installing the judge's stand and nets can be done in any order, at any time.

 4 The bleacher area must be paved after the court is paved (court curing is not required to be done); then bleachers and stand can be built in any order, at any time.

 5 Stand equipment must be installed after stand is painted.

    a Tell whether each activity is management (M), procurement (P), or construction (C).

    b Show the PA and IPA lists.

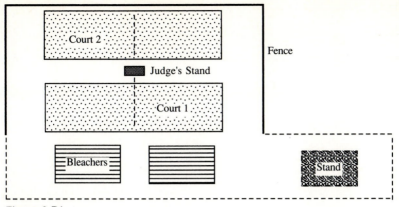

Figure 2-P1
Tennis court plans.

ANSWERS TO PRACTICE PROBLEMS

P1 See (2-9).

PA	Activity	IPA	
—	A	—	
—	B	—	
—	C	—	
A,B	D	A,B	(2-9)
B	E	B	
A,B,D	F	D	
A,B,D,E	G	D,E	
A,B,C,D,E,F,G	H	C,F,G	
A,B,C,D,E,G	I	C,G	

P2 See (2-10).

PA	Activity	IPA	
—	A	—	
A	B	A	
A,B	C	B	
A,B,C	D	C	
A,B,C	E	C	(2-10)
A,B,C,D,E	F	D,E	
A,B,C,D	G	D	
A,B,C,D,E,F,G	H	F,G	
A,B,C,D,E,F,G,H	I	H	
A,B,C,D,E,F,G,H,I	J	I	

P3 See (2-11).

PA	Activity	IPA	
—	A	—	
A	B	A	
A	C	A	
A	D	A	(2-11)
A,B,C	E	B,C	
A,C	F	C	
A,D	G	D	
A,C,F	H	F	
A,C,D,F,G	I	F,G	
A,B,C,D,E,F,G,H,I	J	E,H,I	

P4 The categories are management (M), procurement (P), and construction (C).
   a See (2-12).
   b See (2-13).

Act	Cat	Act	Cat	Act	Cat	Act	Cat	
A	M	H	P	O	C	V	C	
B	P	I	P	P	C	W	C	
C	P	J	P	Q	C	X	C	(2-12)
D	P	K	M	R	C	Y	C	
E	P	L	C	S	C	Z	C	
F	P	M	C	T	C			
G	P	N	C	U	C			

PA	Act	IPA	PA	Act	IPA	
—	A	—	A,C,K,L,M	N	C,M	
—	B	—	A,C,K,L,M,N	O	N	
—	C	—	A,C,E,K,L,M,N,O	P	E,O	
—	D	—	A,C,E,K,L,M,N,O,P	Q	P	
—	E	—	A,B,C,E,K,L,M,N,O,P,Q	R	B,Q	
—	F	—	A,C,E,F,K,L,M,N,O,P,Q	S	F,Q	(2-13)
—	G	—	A,C,E,G,K,L,M,N,O,P,Q	T	G,Q	
—	H	—	A,C,D,K,L,M,N	U	D,N	
—	I	—	A,C,D,K,L,M,N,U	V	U	
—	J	—	A,C,D,H,K,L,M,N,U,V	W	H,V	
—	K	—	A,C,D,I,K,L,M,N,U,V	X	I,V	
A,K	L	A,K	A,B,C,D,I,K,L,M,N,U,V,X	Y	B,X	
A,K,L	M	L	A,B,C,D,I,J,K,L,M,N,U,V,Y	Z	J,Y	

JIMBEAU PROJECT

J1 Indicate which of the activities are construction (C), procurement (P), and management (M).

J2 Use the technical constraints given, and common sense, to create a preceding activity list. To do this, for each activity, list all the other activities that *must* be completed before it can start.

Technical Constraints

1 We must get a building permit before we commence work at the site.

2 Durations given for ordering activities are for material on site.

3 Utility ways are under slab.

4 Construction sequence is frame, install and inspect utilities, insulate, cover, and paint.

5 Doors and windows must be installed after wall framing and before painting.

6 Flooring can go in after HVAC and electrical inspection.

7 Workbenches can go in after the floor is put in and the interior is painted.

8 Interior painting comes after all interior work and installation of doors and windows are completed.

9 Exterior painting comes after siding and doors and windows are installed.

10 Final inspection is made after all work is completed.

To facilitate this process, just fill in the PA list in (2-14).

Act	Description	PA	IPA
A	Get building permit		
B	Prepare site		
C	Order forming materials for utility ways		
D	Order and arrange for concrete delivery		
E	Form and lay utility ways		
F	Place and cure concrete		
G	Order utility service to site		
H	Order HVAC and electrical items		
I	Install and connect HVAC and electrical items		
J	Inspect HVAC and electrical items		
K	Order lumber, fasteners, doors, windows, siding		
L	Frame walls		
M	Frame roof		
N	Install doors and windows		
O	Order insulation, plasterboard, ceiling, flooring		
P	Attach siding		
Q	Attach roof		
R	Insulate walls and ceiling		
S	Install plasterboard and ceilings		
T	Install flooring		
U	Order workbenches and paint		
V	Install workbenches		

(2-14)

W   Paint and trim exterior
X   Paint and trim interior
Y   Final inspection

Note: It is possible that you can produce more than one correct PA list because of different experiences or "common sense" approaches.

J3 Use program PA in the Appendix, to generate the PA list.
J4 Develop the IPA list for the JIMBEAU project based on your PA list.
J5 Use Program IPA, in the Appendix, to create the IPA list.

SUPPLEMENTARY PROBLEMS

S1 Think of something you know how to do that would consist of 15 to 25 activities. Make an activity list, a PA list, and an IPA list. (*Note:* Try to have some activities going on in parallel.) This will be called the personal project.
S2 Develop an IPA list from the PA list of (2-15).

PA	Activity	IPA
L	A	
A,C,F,H,L	B	
L	C	
C,F,K,L	D	
A,B,C,F,G,H,J,L	E	
C,L	F	
A,H,L	G	
A,L	H	
A,B,C,F,H,I,L	I	
A,G,H,L	J	
C,F,L	K	
—	L	
A,B,C,D,E,F,G,H,I,J,K,L	M	

(2-15)

S3 Develop an IPA list from the PA list of (2-16).

PA	Activity	IPA
J	A	
C,H,I,J,L,M,O	B	
J	C	
A,E,I,J	D	
J	E	
A,B,C,D,E,G,H,I,J,K,L,M,N,O	F	
A,D,E,I,J,K,N	G	
C,J	H	
J	I	

(2-16)

—	J
E,J	K
C,J,H	L
I,J	M
E,J,K	N
C,I,J,M	O
A,D,E,G,I,J,K,N	P

S4 Develop an IPA list for the swimming pool project shown in Fig. 2-P2. Assume all needed resources are available (i.e., materials, labor, and equipment) so that only technical constraints must be considered. *Some* of the constraints are shown in the following list:

Technical Constraints

1 Site must be cleared.
2 Equipment:
  a Pad must be formed, poured, and cured before equipment is installed.
  b Electrical service must be brought to the site.
3 Piping must be placed in trench and covered.
4 Swimming pool:
  a Assemble frame.
    (1) Install panels (D section first); then install sides (L and R sections); install S section last.
    (2) Align panels and panel supports; set panel supports in concrete.
    (3) Install attachment ridge on panels.
  b Finish bottom: Shape bottom and apply and cure vermiculite.

Figure 2-P2
Swimming pool plans.

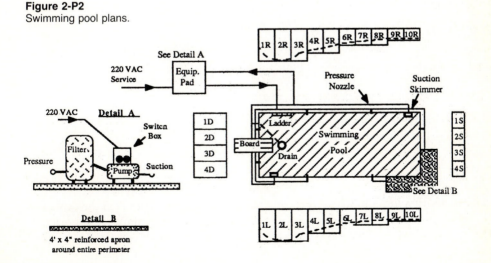

CPM DIAGRAMS

NEW WORDS

Arrow diagram   A method of drawing network schedules using arrows to represent activities, sometimes called an activity-on-arrow diagram

Dummy   An activity with zero time duration used to express logic, to provide a unique numbering for each activity, and to start or finish a network schedule

Event   A connection between two or more activities and at the start and/or finish of a diagram—an event has no duration

Milestone   An event that has some special significance

Node diagram   A method of drawing network schedules using circles or squares, called nodes, to represent activities, sometimes called an activity-on-node or precedence diagram

Sequence steps   A method to simplify drawing node diagrams

WHAT TYPES OF CPM DIAGRAMS ARE USED?

CPM schedules are usually drawn as either arrow (activity-on-arrow) or node (activity-on-node) diagrams.

Arrow Diagrams

Using the IPA list, an arrow diagram can be drawn. The arrow can be any continuous line, but in this text we will use straight-line segments. A generic activity is represented as shown in Fig. 3-1. The nodes at the ends of the activ-

Figure 3-1
Generic activity.

ities are called events. The node at the tail of the arrow is called *i* and the node at the point is called *j* so an activity can be called by its (*i, j*) pair. As shown in Fig. 3-2, A is (5, 10), B is (10, 15), C is (15, 20), etc. Some events may be called "milestones," which indicates they have some particular significance to the scheduler. Usually the start, the finish, and the completion of major phases of a project will be called milestones. These milestones may have a special meaning to company management, but to the CPM model they are just the same as other events.

CPM uses a "finish-start" relationship between dependent activities. This means that if activity B depends on activity A, then A must finish before B can start; or in other words, when all arrows entering a node are complete, all arrows leaving may start. Some typical configurations for activities are shown in Fig. 3-3. Figure 3-3*a* shows that D depends on A, B, and C, so D cannot start until the others are completed; Fig. 3-3*b* shows that B, C, and D can start when A is finished; and Fig. 3-3*c* shows that C and D can start only when both A and B are finished.

Now an arrow diagram can be drawn, almost. Unfortunately, there are some relationships among activities that cannot be expressed by activity arrows alone. This difficulty is overcome by using "dummies" which have a duration of 0. Dummies used to express relationships are called "logic dummies." For example see (3-1).

Activity	IPA
A	—
B	—
C	A
D	A,B

(3-1)

Since there is only one each of A, B, C, and D, we cannot represent the logic with four arrows alone. *Try it.* With a dummy, however, it's easy, as shown in Fig. 3-4.

The logic dummy is the only dummy absolutely required for the arrow diagram, but there are two other types of dummies that make life easier. One of

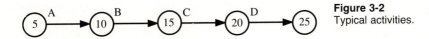

Figure 3-2
Typical activities.

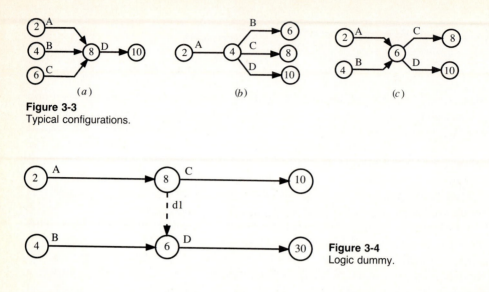

Figure 3-3
Typical configurations.

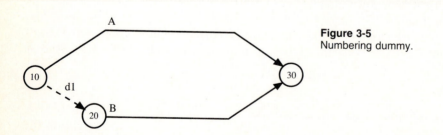

Figure 3-4
Logic dummy.

these is called a "numbering dummy," shown in Fig. 3-5, which is used to prevent two or more activities from having the same *i* and *j* numbers. This is necessary when a computer is used to perform the calculations.

Another dummy we sometimes use is called a "start or finish" dummy, shown in Fig. 3-6. This dummy is used to ensure a single start and/or finish activity. This is necessary in certain methods of performing network calculations and is a requirement of some older computer programs. We won't consider it a requirement just now, but we may want to do so later on.

Now we should be able to draw an arrow diagram for any IPA list. However, we may be the only ones (or things) that can understand it. So, we'll use the following rules and, we hope, be understood by human and machine alike.

1 Draw all activities pointing to the right or vertical. Forward is left to right. Don't have arrows pointing backward.
2 Draw arrows long enough to write eight characters along the arrow.
3 Designate activities with letters A to Z, AA to ZZ, etc.
4 Designate dummies d1, d2, etc.

Figure 3-5
Numbering dummy.

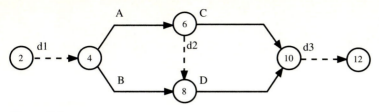

Figure 3-6
Start or finish dummy.

5 Number events such that the *i* for each activity is less than its *j*.
6 Don't cross arrows or use dummies unless necessary.
7 Ensure that each activity has a unique (*i, j*) pair.

Notes

1 Most newer computer programs allow for nonconsecutive numbers (*i < j* or *j < i*); however, consecutive events (*i < j*) are preferable for several reasons. First, it is much easier to locate a particular activity on a CPM arrow diagram if you know that event numbers increase from left to right. Also, if we stick to *i < j*, it is much easier to detect a logical loop, where for instance, A follows B, B follows C, and C follows A (which is not allowed in CPM). In this text we'll always use *i < j*.

2 In an arrow diagram for an actual project it is often better to label activities with a brief description of the work than to use letter codes, but sometimes there just isn't enough room on the paper. If you do use letter codes, try to have the table showing the work each code represents readily accessible—on the same paper, if possible. Also, if you use letter codes, try to use a system such as left to right or top to bottom to facilitate locating a particular activity on the diagram.

3 When drawing an arrow diagram, we have to contend with the problem of crossing lines. While it is always a goal to avoid crossing lines, there is no guarantee that it is possible. In practice we try to reduce the number of crossings to a minimum, and then draw the lines in such a way as to avoid confusing the user. Some common ways are shown in Fig. 3-7.

4 Another similar problem is how to show continuation for diagrams that require multiple sheets. Some common techniques are shown in Fig. 3-8. In any case, it is best to break the sheet at milestones or major events and, if possible, at places where a minimum of activities continue on to other sheets. Again, these goals are not always possible but should be kept in mind to be used where applicable.

5 Arrows representing activities should have direction points so that we can follow the logic flow, but if we agree that time flows from left to right on the

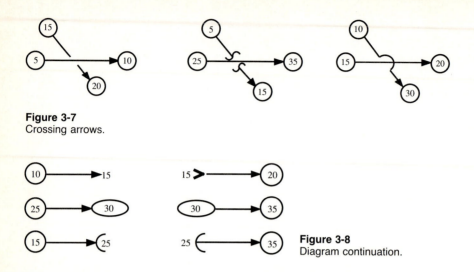

Figure 3-7
Crossing arrows.

Figure 3-8
Diagram continuation.

diagram and that no arrows can go backward, then we can eliminate the direction points except where there might be confusion, such as arrows that are drawn vertically or almost vertically. Also, dummies which have no time dimension should have arrows.

HOW DO WE DRAW AN ARROW DIAGRAM?

We draw an arrow diagram with patience and a fair amount of paper, lead, and erasers. As you will soon be aware, it is almost impossible to draw an arrow diagram that complies with the above rules on the first try. The best way to draw the early drafts of the diagram is to use "butcher" paper, 15-in continuous-feed computer paper, or other large inexpensive sheets. On the first draft of the arrow diagram simply try to get the logic correct. Since you'll probably have some arrows going backward, be sure to put the direction points on them at this time. Don't worry about numbering the nodes yet.

One arrow diagraming technique is to draw the last activity on the right side of the page and then to draw the activities that are on its IPA list. You then work backward, right to left, drawing the IPAs and connecting them to the proper activities. This method can produce a fairly neat drawing on the first draft but requires a lot of erasing and redrawing. This is because any given activity may be on the IPA list several times, while there can be only one arrow to represent it. Therefore, you must figure out where to put dummies as you go. Figure 3-9 illustrates this technique.

For the given project (Fig. 3-9a and b), activities D, E, and F do not appear on the IPA list, so they must be at the end of the project. Draw them to the right (Fig. 3-9a); then draw in their IPAs (Fig. 3-9b). Since activity C is an IPA for three activities and only one arrow can represent each activity, a logic dummy must be used. You often have a choice of how to orient a logic dummy, so just

IPA	ACT
-	A
A	B
A	C
B,C	D
C	E
C	F

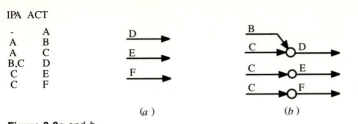

(a)   (b)

Figure 3-9a and b
Drawing the arrow diagram—right to left.

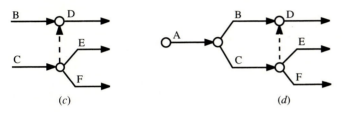

(c)   (d)

Figure 3-9c and d
Drawing the arrow diagram—logic dummies.

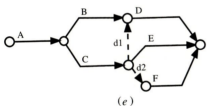

(e)

Figure 3-9e
Drawing the arrow diagram—numbering dummies.

select one that looks neat (Fig. 3-9c). Continue by adding the next group of IPAs (Fig. 3-9d). Finally, add numbering dummies, if needed, and label the dummies—normally left to right, top to bottom (Fig. 3-9e).

The second technique produces a diagram much faster but not as neatly. For this method you draw every activity as a single activity (i.e., one arrow and two nodes). Those activities that obviously occur early in the project should be drawn toward the left of the sheet, and those that occur late in the project should be drawn to the right. The majority of activities, which are somewhere in the middle of the project, should just be spread around. After all the activities are drawn, connect the i node of each activity to the j node of each IPA by using a dummy. When this is done, you have an arrow diagram that is perfectly logical but rather hard to use. The next step is to clean up the diagram by getting rid of unnecessary dummies. Do this by taking one dummy at a time and asking the question, "If I shrink this dummy, combining the nodes at either end, will it change the logic?" If the answer is yes, then leave

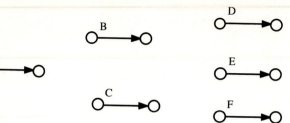

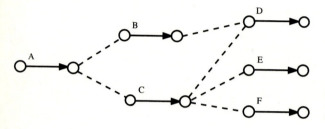

Figure 3-10a
Drawing the arrow diagram—placing activities.

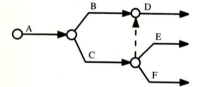

Figure 3-10b
Drawing the arrow
diagram—connecting dummies.

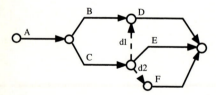

Figure 3-10c
Drawing the arrow diagram—eliminating redundant
dummies.

Figure 3-10d
Drawing the arrow diagram—dummies.

it in; if the answer is no, just shrink and combine the j node of the preceding activity with the i node of the succeeding activity. After this reduction process, redraw the diagram, trying to follow the rules given. Don't get discouraged—it usually takes several drafts to get a very neat diagram that you would be proud to show a client. Figure 3-10, using the data of Fig. 9a and b, illustrates this technique.

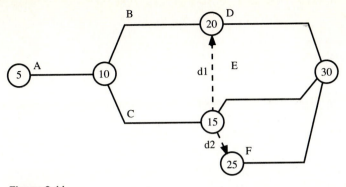

Figure 3-11
Numbering nodes.

Activity A has no IPAs, so it is obviously a starting activity—put it to the left. Activities D, E, and F are not IPAs of other activities, so they are finishing activities—put them to the right. Other activities should just be placed somewhere in the middle (Fig. 3-10a). Next, use dummies to connect the activities in accordance with the logic expressed by the IPA list (Fig. 3-10b). Next, eliminate the dummies one at a time by asking, "If I shrink this dummy, combining the nodes at either end, will it change the logic?" (Fig. 3-10c). Finally, add numbering dummies as needed, and then label the dummies (Fig. 3-10d).

After you get an arrow diagram drawn in accordance with the rules, you must number the nodes, unless you are going to do the calculations manually. When numbering the nodes, the only rule is that the i node for every activity be lower than its j node. However, here are some suggestions that make arrow diagraming easier. The first is don't number nodes consecutively (unless you have a computer program that requires it), but number by 2s, 5s, 10s or some other small interval. The reason for skipping numbers is so you can add activities later without having to renumber the entire schedule. The second suggestion is to use small numbers. The reason is simply to avoid having to draw large circles. Instead of using small numbers, some schedulers use node numbers that comply with a cost code, work code, etc., to give additional information about activities, but the numbers still must follow the rule ($i < j$). Also, most computer programs limit the activity number to no more than six places. Figure 3-11 illustrates an acceptable numbering scheme for the arrow diagram just drawn.

Example

This example shows step by step the procedures for drawing an arrow diagram. See (3-2) for the IPA list.

IPA	Activity	IPA	Activity	
—	A	A,B,C	F	
—	B	E,F	G	(3-2)
—	C	D,G	H	
A	D	D,G	I	
A,B,C	E			

For the first technique, drawing the diagram right to left, first show the activities at the end of the project (those that are not IPAs for any other activity), as illustrated in Fig. 3-12a. Next, add the IPAs for these ending activities, as shown in Fig. 3-12b. Then, keep adding IPAs right to left, as shown in Fig. 3-12c. Now, clean up the diagram, making the backward arrow go forward and bringing together the start and finish nodes, as shown in

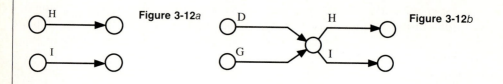

Figure 3-12a **Figure 3-12b**

Figure 3-12c

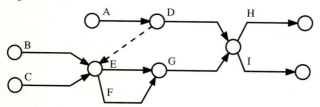

Figure 3-12d

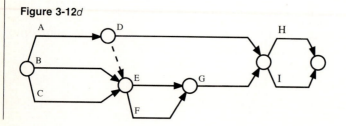

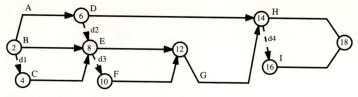

Figure 3-12e

Fig. 3-12d. Finally, check for redundant dummies that are not needed and for numbering dummies that are needed. We can then draw the completed diagram, as shown in Fig. 3-12e.

For the second technique, first let's place the activities on the paper—starting activities to the left, ending activities to the right, and the others sprinkled around between, as shown in Fig. 3-13a. Then, let's connect the activities with *logic* dummies, which we will arbitrarily number, to show the correct logic, as shown in Fig. 3-13b. Now, let's ask the question, for each dummy, "If I shrink this dummy, combining the nodes at either end, will it change the network logic?"

Figure 3-13a

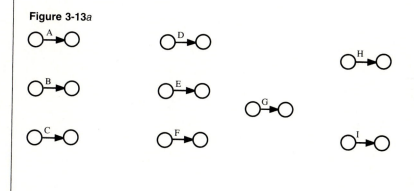

Figure 3-13b

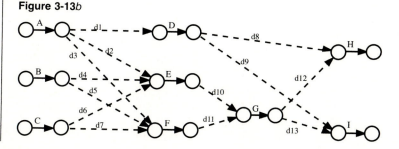

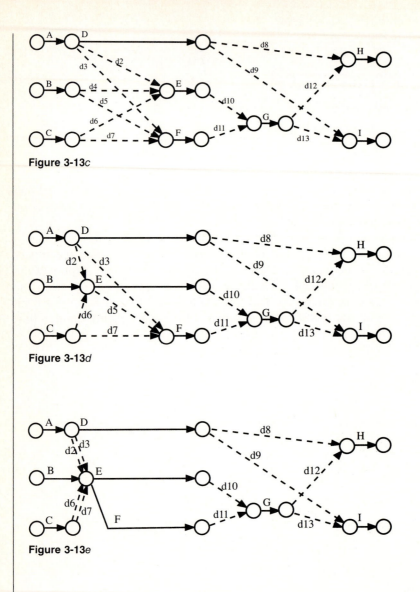

Figure 3-13c

Figure 3-13d

Figure 3-13e

d1: No, A is still the only IPA for D—shrink the dummy (Fig. 3-13c).
d2: Yes, it would cause B and C to become IPAs for D—leave it in.
d3: Yes, it would cause B and C to become IPAs for D—leave it in.
d4: No, A, B, and C are still the only IPAs for E—shrink it (Fig. 3-13d).
d5: No, A, B, and C are still the only IPAs for F—shrink it (Fig. 3-13e).
d2 and d3: These are redundant; let's keep d3.
d6 and d7: These are redundant; let's keep d7 (Fig. 3-13f).

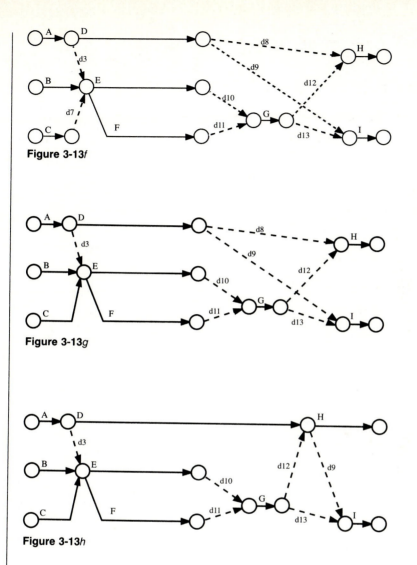

Figure 3-13f

Figure 3-13g

Figure 3-13h

d7: No, d3 is a logic dummy in series—shrink it (Fig. 3-13*g*).
d8: No, same logic exists—shrink it (Fig. 3-13*h*).
d9: No, same logic exists—shrink it (Fig. 3-13*i*).
d12 and d13: These are redundant, let's keep d13 (Fig. 3-13*j*).
d10: No, the same logic exists—shrink it (Fig. 3-13*k*).
d11: No, the same logic exists—shrink it (Fig. 3-13*l*).
d13: No, the same logic exists—shrink it (Fig. 3-13*m*).

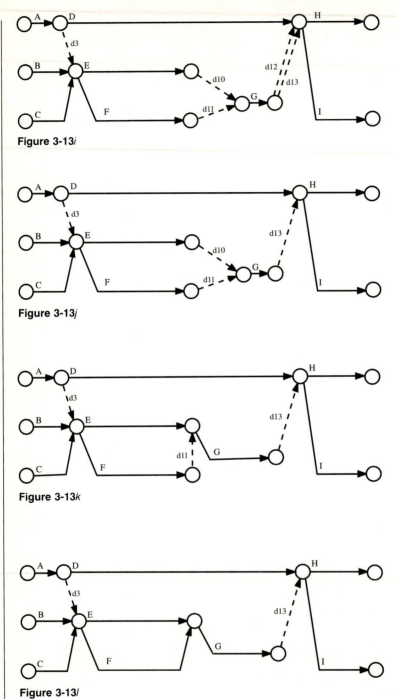

Figure 3-13*i*

Figure 3-13*j*

Figure 3-13*k*

Figure 3-13*l*

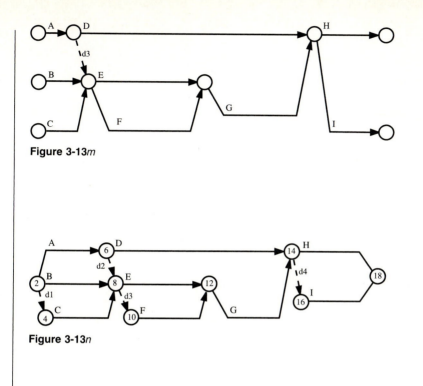

Figure 3-13*m*

Figure 3-13*n*

Finally, we'll add and label the numbering dummies which will give us the completed arrow diagram, as shown in Fig. 3-13*n*.

Once we become more familiar with this process, we can leave some of the dummies in as numbering dummies, but in the beginning it is simpler to consider only logic dummies until the basic logic network is developed and then go back to add the other dummies and labeling later.

Note that in this example the completed arrow diagrams developed by the two methods look the same. This was accomplished by a judicious placing of numbering dummies and by drawing the activities in the same relative positions. Actually, there are many ways any particular diagram may be drawn graphically, but they must all express the same logic. Figure 3-14 shows a different way of drawing the diagram, but it still has the same logic.

A practice that makes a network diagram easier to use is to draw the critical path(s) left to right near the centerline. Of course, this isn't always possible because some schedules have many critical paths and on many projects the critical path(s) change with updating. In any event, this is a goal to keep in mind.

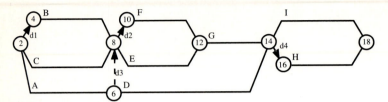

Figure 3-14

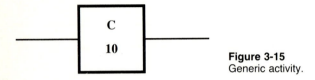

Figure 3-15
Generic activity.

Node Diagram

In a node diagram an activity is represented as shown in Fig. 3-15. The "box" is the activity, the "links" connect two activities, "C" is the activity name, and "10" is the activity duration.

Now a node diagram can be drawn. Also, dummies can be forgotten, almost. Only a starting or ending dummy will be used, if needed, to ensure that we have a single start and finish activity. We'll call a start dummy "St" and a finish dummy "Fn." The practice of requiring a single starting and finishing activity isn't mandatory, but since some computer programs and the matrix calculation method discussed in Chap. 4 require the network to start and finish with a single activity, we'll consider it a requirement for node diagrams for the time being. Figure 3-16 shows a simple example.

Sequence Steps

There is a neat way of finding out where to place activities in a node diagram that makes drawing the node diagram easy. This method uses "sequence steps" (SS).

If you knew activity B followed activity A and A was on step 1, then you would guess B was on step 2. Right? Good! Therefore, any activity must be on a step higher than any of its IPAs.

Let's look at Fig. 3-16. The IPAs and SS are listed in (3-3).

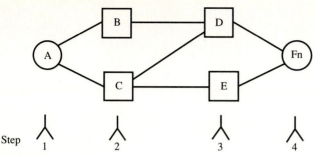

Figure 3-16
Typical node diagram.

IPA	Activity	SS	
—	A	1	
A	B	2	
A	C	2	
B,C	D	3	(3-3)
B,C	E	3	
D,E	Fn	4	

HOW DO WE DRAW A NODE DIAGRAM?

We also draw a node diagram with patience, but not as much is needed as for an arrow diagram.

Example

Let's use the same network (3-4) as we used for the arrow diagram and look at a step-by-step procedure for drawing the node diagram.

IPA	Activity	IPA	Activity	
—	A	A,B,C	F	
—	B	E,F	G	(3-4)
—	C	D,G	H	
A	D	D,G	I	
A,B,C	E			

First, let's see if we need either a starting or ending dummy to ensure that the network starts and finishes with a single activity. A, B, and C have no

IPAs, so they must be starting activities; H and I are not IPAs for any other activity, so they must be finishing activities. Since there are multiple starting activities and multiple finishing activities, we must use a start dummy and a finish dummy.

Let's add the new dummy activities St and Fn to our IPA list [see (3-5)].

IPA	Activity		IPA	Activity	
—	St		A,B,C	F	
St	A		E,F	G	(3-5)
St	B		D,G	H	
St	C		D,G	I	
A	D		H,I	Fn	
A,B,C	E				

Sequence Steps

St starts the diagram, so it is SS1.
A depends only on St (SS1), so it is SS2.
B depends only on St (SS1), so it is SS2.
C depends only on St (SS1), so it is SS2.
D depends on A (SS2), so it is SS3.
E depends on A, B, and C (SS1), so it is SS3.
F depends on A, B, and C (SS1), so it is SS3.
G depends on E and F (SS3), so it is SS4.
H depends on D (SS3) and G (SS4), so it is SS5.
I depends on D (SS3) and G (SS4), so it is SS5.
Fn depends on H and I (SS5), so it is SS6.

The sequence steps are summarized in (3-6).

IPA	Activity	SS		IPA	Activity	SS	
—	St	1		A,B,C	F	3	(3-6)
St	A	2		E,F	G	4	
St	B	2		D,G	H	5	
St	C	2		D,G	I	5	
A	D	3		H,I	Fn	6	
A,B,C	E	3					

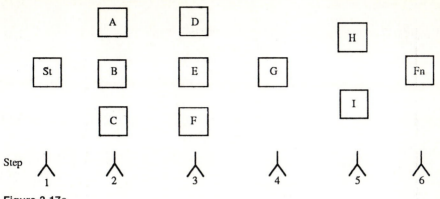

Figure 3-17a
Sequence steps.

Now we can start the diagram by placing the sequence steps across the page and arranging the activities vertically above the proper step, as shown in Fig. 3-17a.

We then connect the activities with straight lines, according to their IPAs. The activities will always stay on the same sequence steps, but sometimes we may want to rearrange them vertically to make the diagram clearer (i.e., to reduce line crossings, etc.). The completed node diagram is shown in Fig. 3-17b. Don't you wish arrow diagrams were so easy? Program SS, in the Appendix, can be used to find the sequence steps.

Figure 3-17b
Sequence steps.

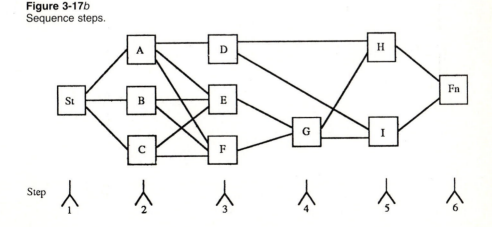

PRACTICE PROBLEMS

Draw arrow diagrams and node diagrams for the following:

P1 See (3-7).

IPA	Activity	IPA	Activity	
—	A	B	D	(3-7)
A	B	B,C	E	
A	C			

P2 See (3-8).

IPA	Activity	IPA	Activity	
—	A	B,C	E	(3-8)
A	B	D	F	
A	C	E,F	G	
A	D			

P3 See (3-9).

IPA	Activity	IPA	Activity	
—	A	A	D	(3-9)
—	B	C,D	E	
A	C	B,C,D	F	

P4 See (3-10).

IPA	Activity	IPA	Activity	
—	A	D	F	(3-10)
—	B	D,E	G	
—	C	C,F,G	H	
A,B	D	C,G	I	
B	E			

P5 See (3-11).

IPA	Activity	IPA	Activity	
—	A	C	F	(3-11)
—	B	D,E	G	
—	C	D,E	H	
A	D	D,E,F	I	
A,B,C	E			

P6 See (3-12).

IPA	Activity	IPA	Activity	IPA	Activity	
—	A	B	F	D	K	
—	B	A,C	G	G,H,K	L	(3-12)
—	C	A,C,E	H	J	M	
A	D	A,C,E	I	F	N	
B	E	D	J	F,I	O	

P7 The tennis court project, Prob. 2-P4. See (3-13).

IPA	Activity	IPA	Activity	IPA	Activity	
—	A	—	J	F,N	S	
—	B	—	K	G,Q	T	
—	C	K	L	D,N	U	
—	D	A,L	M	U	V	(3-13)
—	E	C,M	N	H,V	W	
—	F	N	O	I,V	X	
—	G	E,O	P	B,X	Y	
—	H	P	Q	J,Y	Z	
—	I	D,Q	R			

P8 See (3-14).

IPA	Activity	IPA	Activity	IPA	Activity	
J,I,P	A	O	G	D	M	
H	B	—	H	F	N	
B,G	C	N,Q	I	—	O	(3-14)
H,L	D	B,N	J	H,N	P	
A,C,K	E	J,M,P	K	F	Q	
—	F	—	L			

P9 See (3-15).

IPA	Activity	IPA	Activity	IPA	Activity	
—	A	V	I	—	Q	
S	B	W	J	—	R	
S	C	W	K	P	S	(3-15)
A,O	D	H,Q	L	—	T	
—	E	G,U	M	—	U	
B,C	F	G,U	N	J,K,L,N	V	
D,F,R,T	G	S	O	H,Q	W	
E,M	H	—	P			

P10 See (3-16).

IPA	Activity	IPA	Activity	IPA	Activity
—	A	J,N	I	A	Q
E,R,U	B	O,Q	J	S	R
H	C	L	K	H	S
L	D	—	L	J,N	T
C,X	E	D,K,S	M	C	U
O,P,Q,W	F	F	N	—	V
—	G	A	O	V	W
—	H	G	P	O,P,Q,W	X

(3-16)

ANSWERS TO PRACTICE PROBLEMS

P1 See Fig. 3-Ps1*a* and *n*.

P2 See Fig. 3-Ps2*a* and *n*.

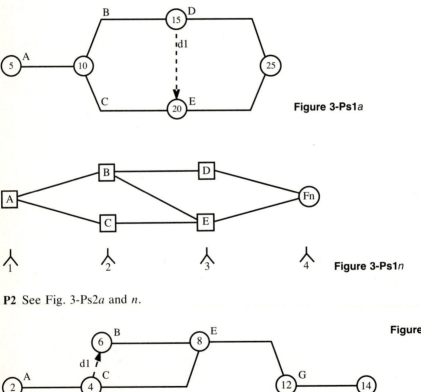

Figure 3-Ps1a

Figure 3-Ps1n

Figure 3-Ps2a

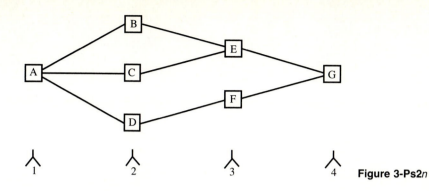

Figure 3-Ps2*n*

P3 See Fig. 3-Ps3*a* and *n*.

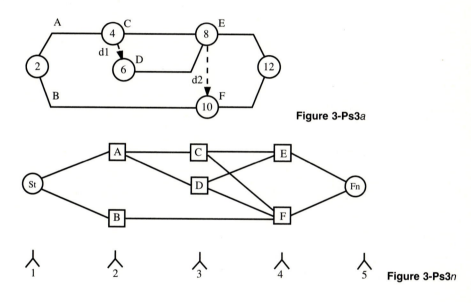

Figure 3-Ps3*a*

Figure 3-Ps3*n*

P4 See Fig. 3-Ps4*a* and *n*.

Figure 3-Ps4*a*

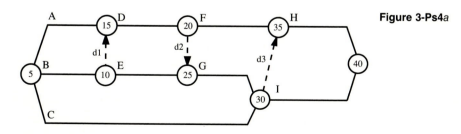

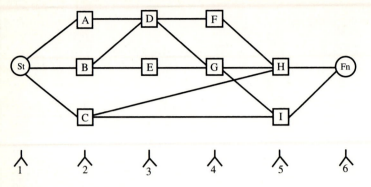

1   2   3   4   5   6   **Figure 3-Ps4n**

P5 See Fig. 3-Ps5a and n.

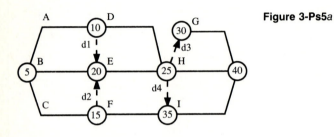

Figure 3-Ps5a

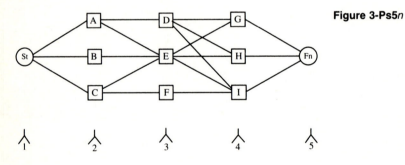

Figure 3-Ps5n

1   2   3   4   5

P6 See Fig. 3-Ps6*a* and *n*.

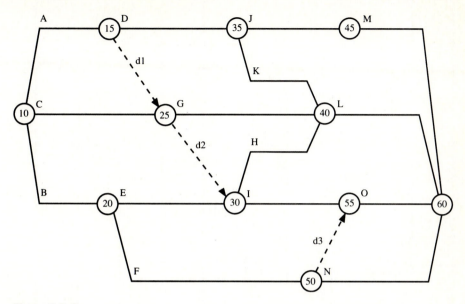

Figure 3-Ps6*a*

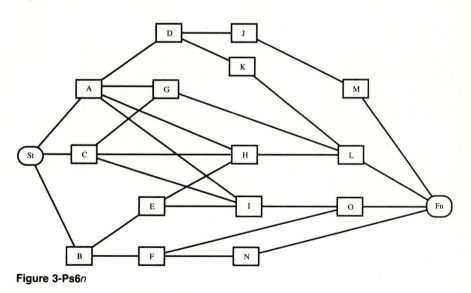

Figure 3-Ps6*n*

P7 See Fig. 3-Ps7*a* and *n*.
P8 See Fig. 3-Ps8*a* and *n*.

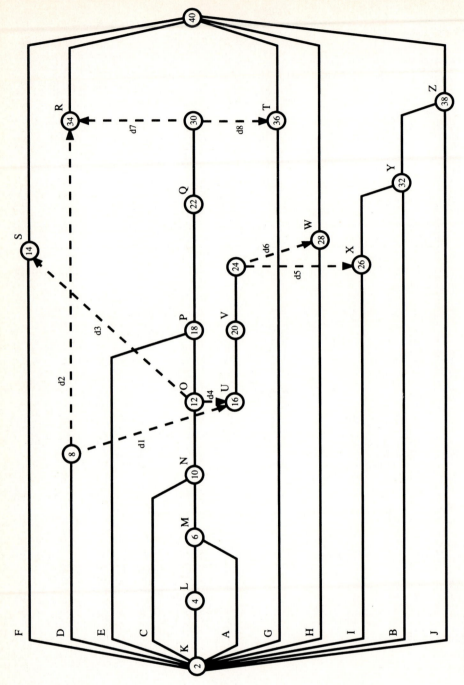

48

Figure 3-Ps7a

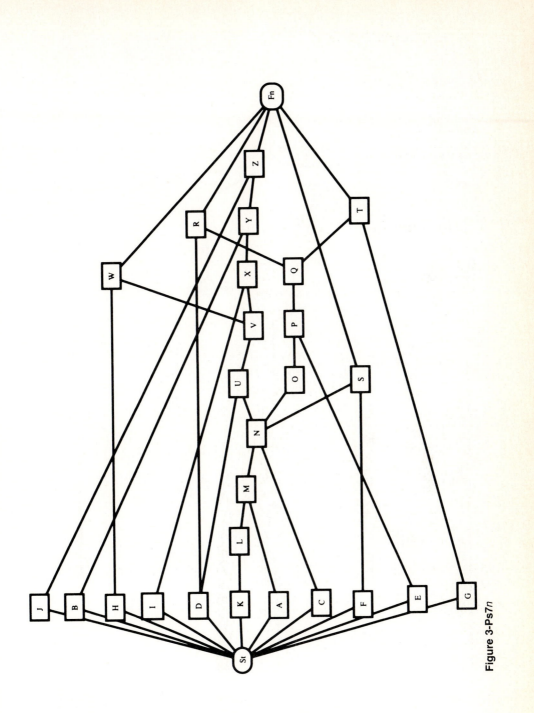

Figure 3-Ps7n

49

50

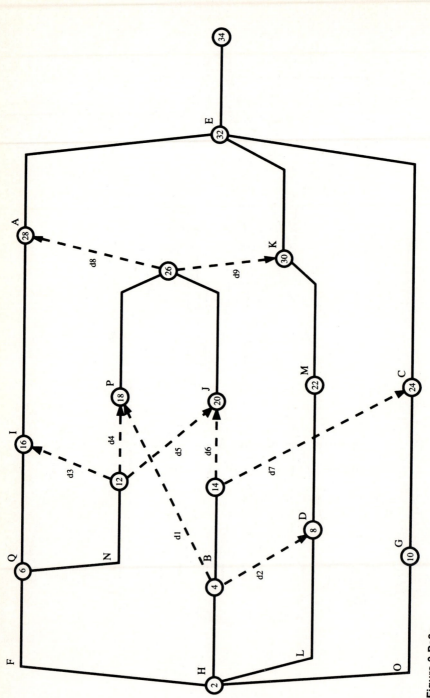

Figure 3-Ps8a

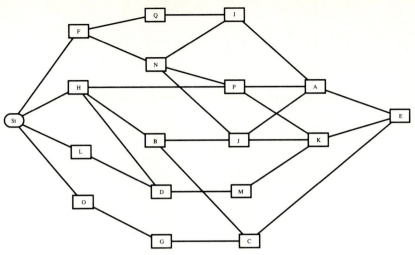

Figure 3-Ps8*n*

P9 See Fig. 3-Ps9*a* and *n*.

Figure 3-Ps9*a*

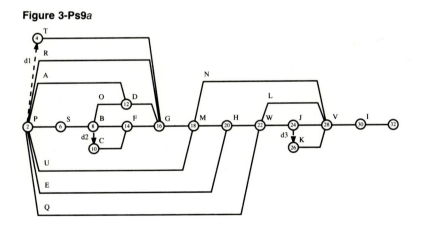

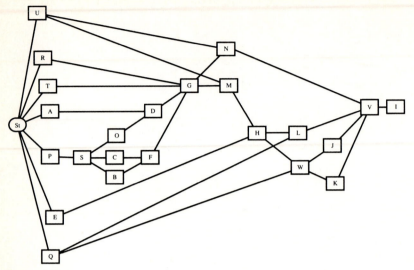

Figure 3-Ps9*n*

P10 See Fig. 3-Ps10*a* and *n*.

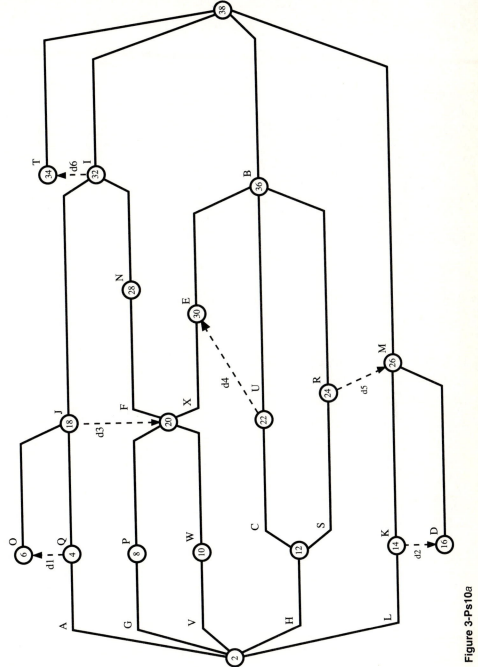

Figure 3-Ps10a

53

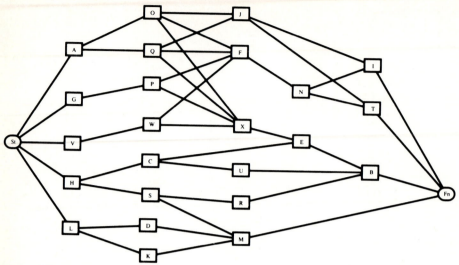

Figure 3-Ps10n

JIMBEAU PROJECT

J1 Using the IPA list of (3-17), draw the arrow diagram for the JIMBEAU project.

IPA	Activity	IPA	Activity	
—	A	L	N	
A	B	A	O	
A	C	L	P	
A	D	M	Q	
B,C	E	O,P,Q	R	
D,E	F	J,R	S	(3-17)
A	G	J	T	
A	H	A	U	
G,H,M	I	T,X	V	
I	J	N,P,U	W	
A	K	N,S,U	X	
F,K	L	W,V	Y	
L	M			

J2 Using the same IPA list as for Prob. J1, list the sequence steps and draw the node diagram for the JIMBEAU project.

J3 Use program SS in the Appendix to find the sequence steps for the IPA list used for Prob. 3-J1.

SUPPLEMENTARY PROBLEMS

Draw arrow and node diagrams for the following:

S1 See (3-18).

IPA	Activity	IPA	Activity	IPA	Activity	
—	A	A,B	D	D,E,F	G	
—	B	B	E	D,E,F	H	(3-18)
—	C	B,C	F	F	I	

S2 See (3-19).

IPA	Activity	IPA	Activity	IPA	Activity	
—	A	B,C	E	F,G	I	
A	B	C	F	B,H,I	J	(3-19)
A	C	D	G			
A	D	F	H			

S3 See (3-20).

IPA	Activity	IPA	Activity	IPA	Activity	
L	A	C	F	F	K	
F,H	B	H	G	—	L	(3-20)
L	C	A	H	D,E	M	
K	D	B	I			
I,J	E	G	J			

S4 See (3-21).

IPA	Activity	IPA	Activity	IPA	Activity	
J	A	D,N	G	I	M	
L,O	B	C	H	K	N	
J	C	J	I	C,M	O	(3-21)
A,E,I	D	—	J	G	P	
J	E	E	K			
B,G	F	H	L			

S5 See (3-22).

IPA	Activity	IPA	Activity	IPA	Activity	
B,J	A	D,O	G	E	M	
Q	B	Q	H	K,L	N	
M,N	C	B	I	A	O	(3-22)
K,L	D	F	J	K,L	P	
L	E	I	K	—	Q	
Q	F	H	L			

S6 See (3-23).

IPA	Activity	IPA	Activity	IPA	Activity	
—	A	C,D	F	H	K	
—	B	C	G	I,J	L	
A	C	E	H	I,J	M	(3-23)
B	D	G	I	L	N	
B	E	E,F	J	L,M	O	

S7 See (3-24).

IPA	Activity	IPA	Activity	IPA	Activity	
E	A	A,I	G	J	M	
—	B	—	H	C,F,J,P	N	
D	C	E	I	I	O	(3-24)
B,H	D	D	J	B,H,K	P	
H	E	—	K	L,M,N	Q	
B,H,K	F	F,P	L			

S8 See (3-25).

IPA	Activity	IPA	Activity	IPA	Activity	
—	A	H	I	M	Q	
A	B	I	J	Q	R	
—	C	I	K	P	S	
B	D	J,K	L	R,S	T	
A	E	L	M	T	U	(3-25)
E	F	M	N	D,F,O	V	
F	G	N	O	C,D	W	
A	H	O	P	T	X	

CPM CALCULATIONS

NEW WORDS

Backward pass   A process to find latest start times and latest finish times for all activities

Critical path   The longest path or paths from project start to finish

Early-event time   The earliest an event can occur

Early finish   The earliest an activity can finish

Early start   The earliest an activity can start

Forward pass   A process to find earliest start times and earliest finish times for all activities

Free float   The maximum time an activity can be delayed without delaying the start of any succeeding activity

Late-event time   The latest an event can occur

Late finish   The latest an activity can finish without delaying project completion

Late start   The latest an activity can start without delaying project completion

Time zero   The one time of day when work is considered to start and finish

Total float   The maximum time an activity can be delayed without delaying completion of the project

CPM network calculations enable us to determine when each activity must take place in order to finish the project in the least amount of time. They also allow us to identify critical activities which must start and finish on exact dates and noncritical activities whose start and finish times can vary somewhat.

WHAT IS FLOAT?

Float (sometimes called ''slack'') is the amount of discretionary time in which an activity must start and/or finish, or said another way, it's the time frame in which an activity can take place without interfering with future events. In construction we are primarily concerned with two types of float, total float and free float, even though other types can be defined.

Total float is defined as the maximum amount of time an activity can be delayed without delaying project completion. In the simple case shown in Fig. 4-1a, the time between project start and project completion is 20 days, and the only activity takes 10 days. Therefore, the number of days in which the activity may be started and still be completed in 20 days is 10 (i.e., it may go for days 1 to 11, 3 to 13, 10 to 20, etc.); therefore, total float = 10.

In Fig. 4-1b we have two activities in series, each taking 5 days, to accomplish during the 20-day window. Again we have 10 days total float, but now there's a difference: If the first activity takes up some of the total float by not starting on the first day, then the second activity no longer has 10 days discretionary time but instead has 10 days less the amount the first activity used. So, here we have what at first seems like a mathematical oddity, that is, the first activity has 10 days total float, the second activity has 10 days total float, and the total float for both activities is 10 days. The reason for this is that total float does not belong to any single activity but rather is the maximum amount available to an activity if other activities don't claim any of it.

Free float is defined as the maximum amount of time that an activity can be delayed without delaying the earliest time any succeeding activity can start. In Fig. 4-1b the first activity can't move without interfering with the second activity, so it has a free float of 0. The second activity, however, can delay 10 days without affecting any other activity. Suppose that the second activity can only start on or after day 11 *and* must follow the first activity, as shown in Fig. 4-1c. The first activity and the second activity now each have 5 days free float. This notion of float will soon become clearer as we learn to do network calculations.

HOW DO WE DO ARROW DIAGRAM CALCULATIONS?

First, we will learn to do CPM calculations on an arrow diagram. The notation we'll use is as follows (see Fig. 4-2):

Act: Activity designator
Dur: Duration in workdays
i: Beginning node of activity
j: Ending node of activity
ES: Early start (ES = latest EF of all IPAs)
EF: Early finish (EF = ES + Dur)
LS: Late start (LF − Dur)
LF: Late finish (LF = earliest LS of all succeeding ACTs)
FF: Free float [(earliest ES of succeeding ACTs) − EF]
TF: Total float of activity (LS − ES)

Figure 4-3 shows the completed calculations on a simple arrow diagram.

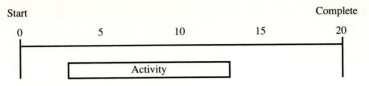

Figure 4-1a
Total float—single activity.

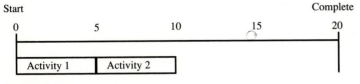

Figure 4-1b
Total float—multiple activities.

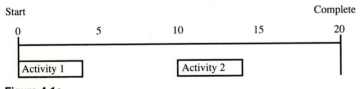

Figure 4-1c
Free float.

Figure 4-2
Arrow diagram notation.

Figure 4-3
Arrow diagram calculations.

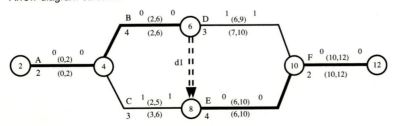

The bold print and double arrows indicate the critical path. Let's learn by looking at a more complex example.

Example

Find ES, EF, LS, LF, FF, and TF for the arrow diagram in Fig. 4-4*a*.

   We start our project at *time zero,* which we will let be the end of the working day; therefore, the project will start at the end of day 0. While this may seem strange, it makes the calculations work nicely. Let ES = 0 for all beginning activities, and use the formulas just given. It really is quite easy.

   The forward pass will give us an early-start schedule—the earliest the project can finish with the given logic and activity durations. Don't forget! All activities going into a node must be complete before activities leaving the node can begin.

Forward Pass

   1 A starts on day 0 (ES of A) and finishes on day 3 (ES + Dur).
   2 B, C, and D start on day 3 and finish on days 6, 8, and 10, respectively.
   3 E, F, and d1 start on day 6 and finish on days 10, 12, and 6, respectively.
   4 G starts on day 8 (after C and D) and finishes on day 12.
   5 I and d3 start on day 10 and finish on days 10 and 19, respectively.

Figure 4-4*a*
Example—arrow diagram.

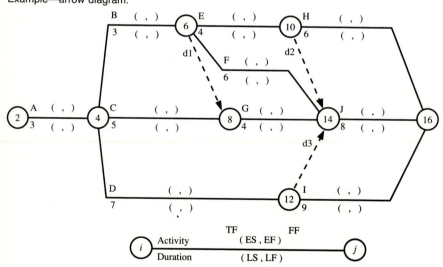

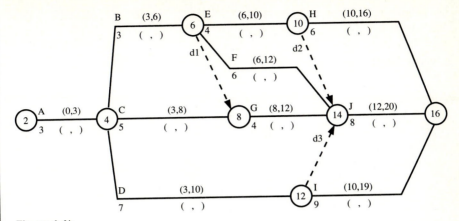

Figure 4-4*b*
Forward pass—arrow diagram.

6 H and d2 start on day 10 and finish on days 16 and 10, respectively.
7 J starts on day 12 (after d2, F, G, and d3) and finishes on day 20.

The earliest the last activity J can finish is day 20; therefore, the shortest time needed to complete the project is 20 days. Figure 4-4*b* shows the results of the forward pass.

The backward pass will give us a late-finish schedule—the latest each activity can finish if the project is to be finished in the shortest possible time, in this case on day 20. *Note:* For now we'll assume that we want to finish the project as soon as possible, which is usually the case. We will discuss other possibilities later in this section.

Backward Pass

1 H, I, and J must finish on day 20 (LF of J) in order for the project to finish on day 20, so they must start on days 14, 12, and 11, respectively (LF − Dur).

2 d2, F, G, and d3 must finish by day 12, so they must start by days 12, 6, 8, and 12, respectively.

3 E must finish by day 12 (before H and d2), so it must start by day 8.

4 D must finish by day 11 (before d3 and I), so it must start by day 4.

5 C and d1 must finish by day 8, so they must start by days 3 and 8, respectively.

6 B must finish by day 6 (before E, F, and d1), so it must start by day 3.

7 A must finish by day 3 (before B, C, and D), so it must start by day 0.

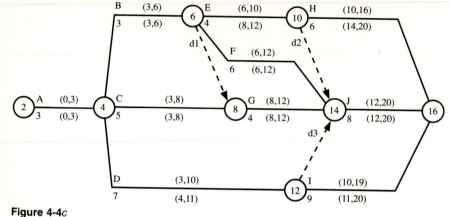

Figure 4-4c
Backward pass—arrow diagram.

Figure 4-4c shows the results of the backward pass.

A check shows that we started the first activity A on day 0 and our forward and backward passes brought us back to day 0. If this were not the case, then we would have an error. Why? We'll soon see.

Next, we will find the total float which is the maximum number of days an activity can "move"—that is, the number of days the start can be delayed—without extending the total project time. We know that for each activity, ES is the earliest and LS is the latest the activity can start in order for the project to be finished as soon as possible—so TF must be the difference. To find TF for each activity we simply subtract ES from LS. *Note:* We could also take the difference between EF and LF, which would give us the same value, but since we wrote TF on our arrow diagram near ES, it seems easier to use LS − ES to find TF.

Total Float

1 A: 0(LS) − 0(ES) = 0(TF)
2 B: 3 − 3 = 0; C: 3 − 3 = 0; D: 4 − 3 = 1
3 Continue for the remainder of the activities

WHAT IS A CRITICAL PATH?

Once we know the TF for each activity, we can determine the critical path(s). Any continuous path, from the starting node to the finishing node, that contains only activities with TF = 0 is a critical path. We *must have at least one critical path* and *may have many critical paths*—in fact, all activities and all paths may be critical. Figure 4-4*d* shows the critical paths in bold type. A check shows that all activities with TF = 0 are located on a critical path. If such were not the case, we would have an error. We can now find the free float, which is the maximum number of days an activity can delay its start without interfering with the ES of a succeeding activity. To find FF we subtract an activity's EF from the ES of each succeeding activity—whichever difference is less is the FF.

Free Float

1 A: ES(B) − EF(A) = 0; ES(C) − EF(A) = 0; ES(D) − EF(A) = 0. The lesser difference is 0, so FF of A = 0.
2 Continue for the remainder of the activities.

Figure 4-4*e* shows the complete arrow diagram calculations. *Note:* Even though d1 goes between critical paths, it is not critical because its ES = 6 and its LS = 8.

Hint: When using the procedure demonstrated, you can check your CPM network calculations as follows:

1 A start and finish activity must be on a critical path.
2 All critical paths must be continuous from start to finish.
3 Total float must be greater than or equal to free float for every activity.
4 Any activity with TF = 0 must be on a critical path.

Figure 4-4*d*
Total float—arrow diagram.

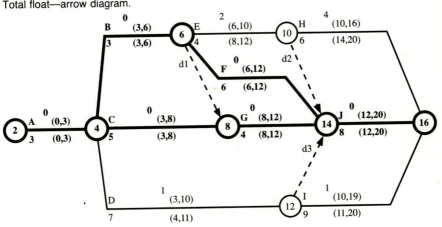

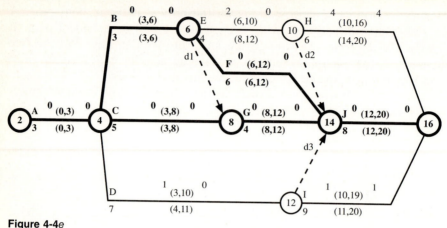

Figure 4-4e
Free float—arrow diagram.

Note: Variations of this procedure, which will be discussed later in this chapter under "Negative Total Float," will make checks 3 and 4 invalid.

There are two other types of float we can determine. The first type is interfering float and is the difference between TF and FF (noninterfering float). The second type is independent float and is the "safe" float that cannot be taken away by another activity. It is the difference of the latest of the preceding activities (LFs) and the earliest of the succeeding activities (ESs), minus the activity's duration. These two floats aren't of much practical use, so we won't consider them further.

NEGATIVE TOTAL FLOAT

In performing the network calculations on the arrow diagram we used the forward pass to find the earliest the project could finish, then we used that value to start our backward pass, which caused all critical activities to have TF = FF = 0. This procedure makes the calculations easy to check for errors and most often is the best procedure to use; however, total float can actually take on any real value. For instance, we may have a contract that calls for a total time of 180 workdays. We start our forward pass at day 0 and find that the earliest the project can finish is day 190. If we start our backward pass at day 180 (contractual completion date), we arrive back at project start on day −10, and all critical activities have TF = − 10 and noncritical activities have TF > − 10. This, of course, indicates that 10 days must be saved somehow if we are to finish on time. Another case is where the contract time is 210 workdays and our forward pass shows an early completion on day 190. If we start the backward pass on day 210, we end up with critical activities having

TF = 20 and noncritical activities having TF > 20. Such total float indicates that we can finish in 20 days less than is contractually allotted.

Since total float can be either negative, zero, or positive, the critical activities are those with the lowest TF, and no matter what the value is, all critical activities have the same TF.

HOW DO WE DETERMINE EVENT TIMES?

As discussed in Chap. 3, an event has no time dimension. Events are usually called "start...," "finish...," or something similar. Often upper management isn't interested in what activities are critical or how much float other activities have but are very interested in milestones such as when major phases of the project will start or finish. In order to provide this information, it is not necessary to perform the entire CPM calculation. To find the early-event time (EET) you just determine which activity entering the node finishes last and that is the EET. The late-event time (LET) is the earliest LS of activities leaving the node.

An event window (EW) can be defined as the number of days in which an event can occur, EW = LET − EET. *Note:* Events connecting critical activities must have EW = 0.

For the example above the event times are given in (4-1).

Node	EET	LET	EW	
2	0	0	0	
4	3	3	0	
6	6	6	0	
8	8	8	0	(4-1)
10	10	12	2	
12	10	11	1	
14	12	12	0	
16	20	20	0	

HOW DO WE DO NODE DIAGRAM CALCULATIONS?

One method for performing network calculations on a node diagram is to use the same approach as for the arrow diagram, i.e., calculate forward and backward passes on the node diagram as shown in Fig. 4-5.

Another method is to use a matrix. The advantage of the matrix is that neither the arrow diagram nor the node diagram need be drawn. However, a requirement is that there be only one starting and one finishing activity. If our schedule has more than one starting and/or finishing activity, we simply add a start and/or finish dummy as we did to the node diagram in Chap. 3. Figure 4-6 shows the completed matrix for the simple network of Fig. 4-3.

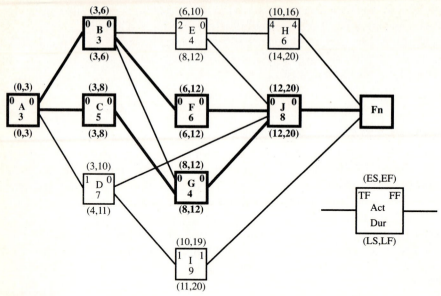

Figure 4-5
Node diagram calculations.

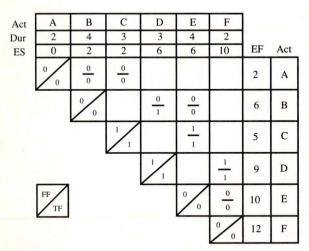

Figure 4-6
Matrix method—simple network.

Example

To draw a matrix and perform the network calculations for the data given in (4-2) (the same as for the arrow diagram example), we perform the following steps:

Act	Dur	IPA	SS		Act	Dur	IPA	SS
A	3	—	1		G	4	B,C	3
B	3	A	2		H	6	E	4
C	5	A	2		I	9	D	3
D	7	A	2		J	8	D,E,F,G	4
E	4	B	3		Fn	0	H,I,J	5
F	6	B	3					

(4-2)

Note: Network calculations require that there be single starting and finishing activities, hence the use of Fn.

1 Arrange the activities and durations in sequence step order, left to right, as shown in Fig. 4-7*a*, and leave a blank row for early start.

2 Arrange the activities in sequence step order, top to bottom, and leave a blank column for early finish.

3 Draw a matrix with the same number of columns and rows as there are activities; then draw in the inside boxes only. Draw a diagonal line in the

Figure 4-7*a*
Setup—matrix.

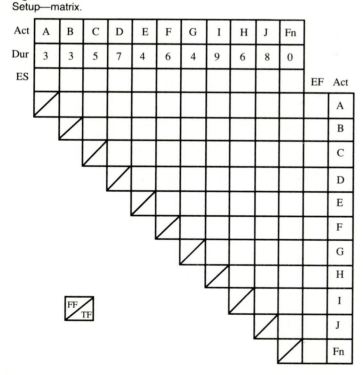

left-most box on each row (these boxes will contain the total float and free float).

Now we can calculate the early start, early finish, total float, and free float, and determine the critical path(s) by performing the following steps:

1 Draw a horizontal line in the center of each box of the matrix where a dependency exists between the column activity and the row activity. For example, activity A is an IPA of activity B, so a line must be drawn in row A and column B. After doing this for all activities, the matrix should look as shown in Fig. 4-7b.

2 We know that the starting activity, which has no IPA, had an early start of 0. We can then fill in the ES row for this activity A. We now add the duration to the early start in the A column to get the early finish for the A row [3(Dur) + 0(ES) = 3(EF)]. Since B, C, and D only depend on A, their ES is the same as A's EF. Therefore, ES(B), ES(C), and ES(D) = 3; EF(B) = 6(3 + 3), EF(C) = 8, and EF(D) = 10. E and F depend only on B, so ES(E) and ES(F) = 6, EF(E) = 10, EF(F) = 12. G depends on both B

Figure 4-7b
Logic relationship—matrix.

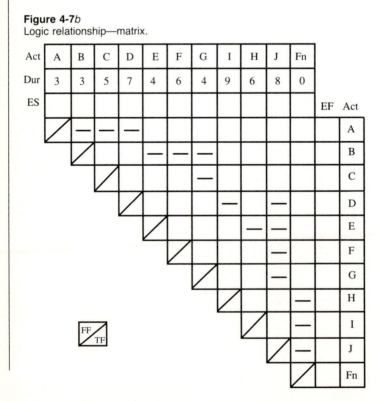

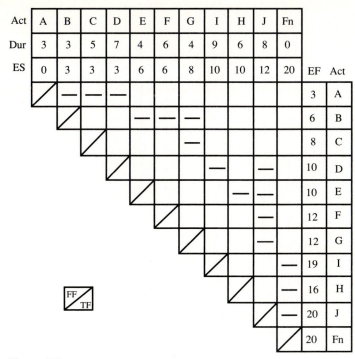

Act	A	B	C	D	E	F	G	I	H	J	Fn		
Dur	3	3	5	7	4	6	4	9	6	8	0		
ES	0	3	3	3	6	6	8	10	10	12	20	EF	Act
		—	—	—								3	A
			—	—	—							6	B
					—							8	C
					—		—					10	D
						—	—					10	E
							—					12	F
							—					12	G
								—				19	I
		FF						—				16	H
		TF							—			20	J
												20	Fn

Figure 4-7c
Early start and early finish—matrix.

and C and can only start when both are completed. Since EF(E) is 6 and EF(F) is 8, then ES(G) = 8. I depends only on D, so ES(I) = 10 and EF(I) = 19. H depends only on E, so ES(H) = 10 and EF(H) = 16. J depends on D, E, F, and G, so ES(J) equals the latest EF of these, or ES(J) = 12 and EF(J) = 20. Fn depends on I, H, and J, so ES(Fn) = 20 and EF(Fn) = 20.

Note: We must start at the top left and work down in order to get the values required in succeeding steps. Our matrix should now look as shown in Fig. 4-7c.

To find the free float for each activity, first find the difference ES − EF for each dependency, and then write this value on top of the dependency line. The FF for each activity is the minimum value of the FF of each dependency and should be recorded in the upper triangles on the left side of the matrix, as shown in Fig. 4-7d. *Note:* To find the total float we must start in the lower right corner and work up and toward the left.

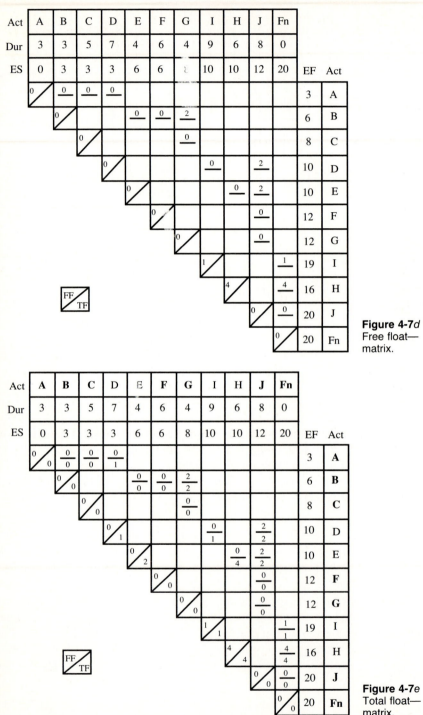

Figure 4-7d
Free float—matrix.

Figure 4-7e
Total float—matrix.

First, we know the TF of the last activity must be 0 because we ensure this by having only one finishing activity, which must be on a critical path. The value that goes below each dependency line is the value above the line plus the TF of the succeeding activity (found in the lower triangle at the bottom of the column). TF(Fn) = 0, so below the dependency line for J we write 0 [the value above the line, plus TF(Fn), the sum of which is 0]. The TF for J is the minimum horizontal value below the dependency line for J, which in this case is only 0. Working up and toward the left gives us TFs as shown in Fig. 4-7e. The critical activities are identified by TF = FF = 0. LS and LF are not calculated when using the matrix method but can be readily determined for each activity as LS = ES + TF and LF = LS + TF.

Microcomputer Solutions

As we have seen, CPM calculations are easy to perform but do take a lot of time if our schedule has a large number of activities, which is usually the case for a real project. Luckily, microcomputers can easily handle the calculations in minutes, requiring us only to type in the activity data. There are CPM programs available for almost all computers on the market. The CPM software you purchase usually has a lot of "bells and whistles" such as color, sound, a flashing screen, etc., and is often integrated with cost accounting or other functions. Two simple CPM programs, without frills, written in BASIC are provided in the Appendix.

Program CPM-A accepts input data in arrow diagram format (i.e., activity designator, i node number, j node number, and duration), and program CPM-N accepts input data in node diagram format (i.e., activity designator, duration, and IPA list). The CPM-N program requires that the activities be entered in sequence-step order.

Examples using commercial microcomputer software to solve network calculations are provided in Chap. 12, Microcomputer Applications.

PRACTICE PROBLEMS

Perform the CPM calculations for the following problems

P1 Prob. 3-P1 with the activity durations in (4-3).

Act	Dur	Act	Dur	Act	Dur	
A	5	C	3	E	4	(4-3)
B	4	D	2			

P2 Prob. 3-P2 with the activity durations in (4-4).

Act	Dur	Act	Dur	Act	Dur	
A	4	D	4	F	2	(4-4)
B	3	E	6	G	3	
C	3					

P3 Prob. 3-P3 with the activity durations in (4-5).

Act	Dur	Act	Dur	Act	Dur	
A	5	C	1	E	2	(4-5)
B	4	D	2	F	3	

P4 Prob. 3-P4 with the activity durations in (4-6).

Act	Dur	Act	Dur	Act	Dur	
A	5	D	4	G	6	
B	3	E	6	H	7	(4-6)
C	7	F	4	I	4	

P5 Prob. 3-P5 with the activity durations in (4-7).

Act	Dur	Act	Dur	Act	Dur	
A	5	D	3	G	2	
B	4	E	6	H	3	(4-7)
C	5	F	4	I	4	

P6 Prob. 3-P6 with the activity durations in (4-8).

Act	Dur	Act	Dur	Act	Dur	Act	Dur	
A	4	E	3	I	4	M	1	
B	5	F	7	J	1	N	1	(4-8)
C	7	G	2	K	1	O	2	
D	5	H	3	L	2			

P7 Prob. 3-P7 with the activity durations in (4-9).

Act	Dur	Act	Dur	Act	Dur	Act	Dur
A	1	H	1	O	2	V	2
B	1	I	1	P	1	W	2
C	1	J	1	Q	2	X	2
D	1	K	1	R	1	Y	1
E	1	L	1	S	2	Z	1
F	1	M	2	T	1		
G	1	N	1	U	1		

(4-9)

P8 Prob. 3-P8 with the activity durations in (4-10).

Act	Dur	Act	Dur	Act	Dur	Act	Dur
A	8	F	8	K	8	P	6
B	2	G	2	L	1	Q	6
C	10	H	6	M	11		
D	4	I	5	N	9		
E	7	J	12	O	5		

(4-10)

Perform the CPM calculations, and list the event times for the following problems:

P9 Prob. 3-P9 with the activity durations in (4-11).

Act	Dur	Act	Dur	Act	Dur	Act	Dur
A	5	G	5	M	4	S	1
B	3	H	3	N	2	T	1
C	2	I	2	O	2	U	7
D	4	J	2	P	3	V	3
E	10	K	1	Q	15	W	2
F	2	L	2	R	5		

(4-11)

P10 Prob. 3-P10 with the activity durations in (4-12).

Act	Dur	Act	Dur	Act	Dur	Act	Dur
A	3	G	5	M	5	S	5
B	9	H	2	N	8	T	3
C	3	I	9	O	3	U	8
D	6	J	4	P	7	V	6
E	8	K	9	Q	8	W	3
F	7	L	4	R	3	X	7

(4-12)

ANSWERS TO PRACTICE PROBLEMS

Note: * Indicates activities on a critical path.

P1 See (4-13).

Act	Dur	ES	EF	LS	LF	TF	FF	Cr
A	5	0	5	0	5	0	0	*
B	4	5	9	5	9	0	0	*
C	3	5	8	6	9	1	1	

Act	Dur	ES	EF	LS	LF	TF	FF	Cr
D	2	9	11	11	13	2	2	
E	4	9	13	9	13	0	0	*

(4-13)

P2 See (4-14).

Act	Dur	ES	EF	LS	LF	TF	FF	Cr
A	4	0	4	0	4	0	0	*
B	3	4	7	4	7	0	0	*
C	3	4	7	4	7	0	0	*
D	4	4	8	7	11	3	0	

Act	Dur	ES	EF	LS	LF	TF	FF	Cr
E	6	7	13	7	13	0	0	*
F	2	8	10	11	13	3	3	
G	3	13	16	13	16	0	0	*

(4-14)

P3 See (4-15).

Act	Dur	ES	EF	LS	LF	TF	FF	Cr
A	5	0	5	0	5	0	0	*
B	4	0	4	3	7	3	3	
C	1	5	6	6	7	1	1	

Act	Dur	ES	EF	LS	LF	TF	FF	Cr
D	2	5	7	5	7	0	0	*
E	2	7	9	8	10	1	1	
F	3	7	10	7	10	0	0	*

(4-15)

P4 See (4-16).

Act	Dur	ES	EF	LS	LF	TF	FF	Cr
A	5	0	5	0	5	0	0	*
B	3	0	3	0	3	0	0	*
C	7	0	7	8	15	8	8	
D	4	5	9	5	9	0	0	*
E	6	3	9	3	9	0	0	*

Act	Dur	ES	EF	LS	LF	TF	FF	Cr
F	4	9	13	11	15	2	2	
G	6	9	15	9	15	0	0	*
H	7	15	22	15	22	0	0	*
I	4	15	19	18	22	3	3	

(4-16)

P5 See (4-17).

Act	Dur	ES	EF	LS	LF	TF	FF	Cr
A	5	0	5	0	5	0	0	*
B	4	0	4	1	5	1	1	
C	5	0	5	0	5	0	0	*
D	3	5	8	8	11	3	3	
E	6	5	11	5	11	0	0	*

Act	Dur	ES	EF	LS	LF	TF	FF	Cr
F	4	5	9	7	11	2	2	
G	2	11	13	13	15	2	2	
H	3	11	14	12	15	1	1	
I	4	11	15	11	15	0	0	*

(4-17)

P6 See (4-18).

Act	Dur	ES	EF	LS	LF	TF	FF	Cr
A	4	0	4	2	6	2	0	
B	5	0	5	0	5	0	0	*
C	7	0	7	1	8	1	0	
D	5	4	9	6	11	2	0	
E	3	5	8	5	8	0	0	*
F	7	5	12	5	12	0	0	*
G	2	7	9	10	12	3	2	
H	3	8	11	9	12	1	0	

Act	Dur	ES	EF	LS	LF	TF	FF	Cr
I	4	8	12	8	12	0	0	*
J	1	9	10	12	13	3	0	
K	1	9	10	11	12	2	1	
L	2	11	13	12	14	1	1	
M	1	10	11	13	14	3	3	
N	1	12	13	13	14	1	1	
O	2	12	14	12	14	0	0	*

(4-18)

P7 See (4-19).

Act	Dur	ES	EF	LS	LF	TF	FF	Cr
A	1	0	1	1	2	1	1	
B	1	0	1	9	10	9	9	
C	1	0	1	3	4	3	3	
D	1	0	1	4	5	4	4	
E	1	0	1	7	8	7	7	
F	1	0	1	9	10	9	4	
G	1	0	1	10	11	10	10	
H	1	0	1	9	10	9	9	
I	1	0	1	7	8	7	7	
J	1	0	1	10	11	10	10	
K	1	0	1	0	1	0	0	*
L	1	1	2	1	2	0	0	*
M	2	2	4	2	4	0	0	*

Act	Dur	ES	EF	LS	LF	TF	FF	Cr
N	1	4	5	4	5	0	0	*
O	2	5	7	5	7	1	0	
P	1	7	8	8	9	1	0	
Q	2	8	10	9	11	1	0	
R	1	10	11	11	12	1	1	
S	2	5	7	10	12	5	5	
T	1	10	11	11	12	1	1	
U	1	5	6	5	6	0	0	*
V	2	6	8	6	8	0	0	*
W	2	8	10	10	12	2	2	
X	2	8	10	8	10	0	0	*
Y	1	10	11	10	11	0	0	*
Z	1	11	12	11	12	0	0	*

(4-19)

P8 See (4-20).

Act	Dur	ES	EF	LS	LF	TF	FF	Cr
A	8	29	37	29	37	0	0*	
B	2	6	8	15	17	9	9	
C	10	8	18	27	37	19	19	
D	4	6	10	14	18	8	0	
E	7	37	44	37	44	0	0	*
F	8	0	8	0	8	0	0	*
G	2	5	7	25	27	20	1	
H	6	0	6	8	14	8	0	
I	5	17	22	24	29	7	7	

Act	Dur	ES	EF	LS	LF	TF	FF	Cr
J	12	17	29	17	29	0	0	*
K	8	29	37	29	37	0	0	*
L	1	0	1	13	14	13	5	
M	11	10	21	18	29	8	8	
N	9	8	17	8	17	0	0	*
O	5	0	5	20	25	20	0	
P	6	17	23	23	29	6	6	
Q	6	8	14	18	24	10	3	

(4-20)

P9 See (4-21) for the CPM calculations and (4-22) for the event times.

Act	Dur	ES	EF	LS	LF	TF	FF	Cr
A	5	0	5	1	6	1	1	
B	3	4	7	5	8	1	0	
C	2	4	6	6	8	2	1	
D	4	6	10	6	10	0	0	*
E	10	0	10	9	19	9	9	
F	2	7	9	8	10	1	1	
G	5	10	15	10	15	0	0	*
H	3	19	22	19	22	0	0	*
I	2	29	31	29	31	0	0	*
J	2	24	26	24	26	0	0	*
K	1	24	25	25	26	1	1	
L	2	22	24	24	26	2	2	

Act	Dur	ES	EF	LS	LF	TF	FF	Cr
M	4	15	19	15	19	0	0	*
N	2	15	17	24	26	9	9	
O	2	4	6	4	6	0	0	*
P	3	0	3	0	3	0	0	*
Q	15	0	15	7	22	7	7	
R	5	0	5	5	10	5	5	
S	1	3	4	3	4	0	0	*
T	1	0	1	9	10	9	9	
U	7	0	7	8	15	8	8	
V	3	26	29	26	29	0	0	*
W	2	22	24	22	24	0	0	*

(4-21)

Node	EET	LET	EW
2	0	0	0
4	0	9	9
6	3	3	0
8	4	4	0
10	4	6	2
12	6	6	0

Node	EET	LET	EW
14	7	8	1
16	10	10	0
18	15	15	0
20	19	19	0
22	22	22	0

Node	EET	LET	EW
24	24	24	0
26	24	25	1
28	26	26	0
30	29	29	0
32	31	31	0

(4-22)

P10 See (4-23) for the CPM calculations and (4-24) for the event times.

Act	Dur	ES	EF	LS	LF	TF	FF	Cr
A	3	0	3	1	4	1	0	
B	9	27	36	27	36	0	0	*
C	3	2	5	16	19	14	0	
D	6	4	10	25	31	21	3	
E	8	19	27	19	27	0	0	*
F	7	12	19	12	19	0	0	*
G	5	0	5	0	5	0	0	*
H	2	0	2	14	16	14	0	
I	9	27	36	27	36	0	0	*
J	4	11	15	23	27	12	12	
K	9	4	13	22	31	18	0	
L	4	0	4	18	22	18	0	

Act	Dur	ES	EF	LS	LF	TF	FF	Cr
M	5	13	18	31	36	18	18	
N	8	19	27	19	27	0	0	*
O	3	3	6	9	12	6	5	
P	7	5	12	5	12	0	0	*
Q	8	3	11	4	12	1	0	
R	3	7	10	24	27	17	17	
S	5	2	7	19	24	17	0	
T	3	27	30	33	36	6	6	
U	8	5	13	19	27	14	14	
V	6	0	6	3	9	3	0	
W	3	6	9	9	12	3	3	
X	7	12	19	12	19	0	0	*

(4-23)

Node	EET	LET	EW
2	0	0	0
4	3	4	1
6	3	9	6
8	5	5	0
10	6	9	3
12	2	16	14
14	4	22	18

Node	EET	LET	EW
16	4	25	21
18	6	12	6
20	12	12	0
22	5	19	14
24	7	24	17
26	13	32	18

Node	EET	LET	EW
28	19	19	0
30	19	19	0
32	27	27	0
34	27	33	6
36	27	27	0
38	36	36	0

(4-24)

JIMBEAU PROJECT

J1 Perform the CPM calculations for the project using the arrow diagram calculation method and using the durations given in Chap. 2 [see (2-4)].

J2 Use program CPM-A in the Appendix to perform network calculations.

J3 Perform the CPM calculations for the project using the matrix method.

J4 Use program CPM-N in the Appendix to perform network calculations.

J5 List the event times for the project.

SUPPLEMENTARY PROBLEMS

Perform network calculations using both the arrow diagram and matrix methods, and list event times, for the given networks. (*Note:* IPA lists and sequence steps can be easily obtained from the arrow diagram.)

S1 See Fig. 4-S1.

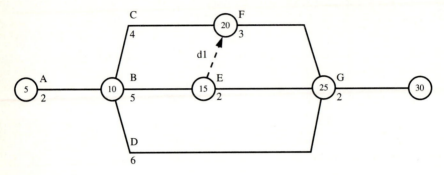

Figure 4-S1

S2 See Fig. 4-S2.

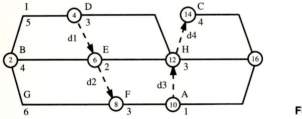

Figure 4-S2

S3 See Fig. 4-S3.

Figure 4-S3

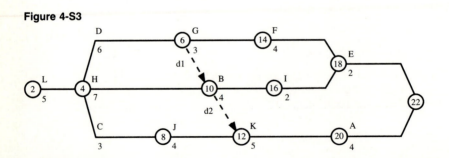

S4 See Fig. 4-S4.

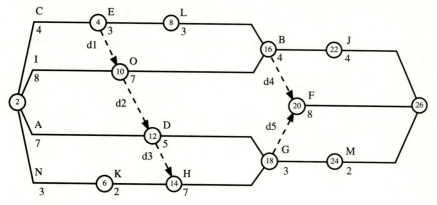

Figure 4-S4

S5 See Fig. 4-S5.

Figure 4-S5

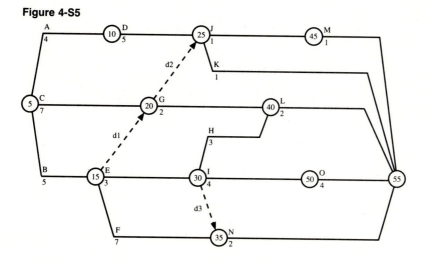

S6 See Fig. 4-S6.

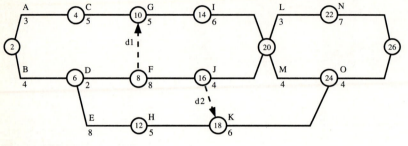

Figure 4-S6

S7 See Fig. 4-S7.

Figure 4-S7

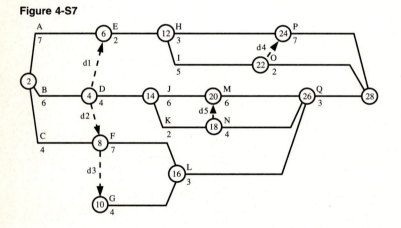

S8 See Fig. 4-S8.

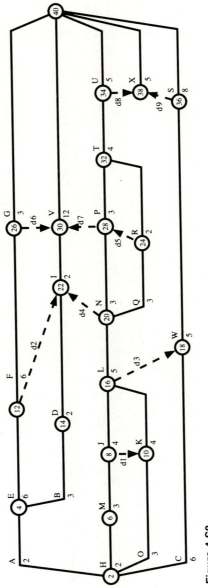

Figure 4-S8

PROJECT CONTROL

NEW WORDS

Project control   To monitor and update the target schedule to reflect actual progress
Target schedule   The project time schedule
Time-phase   To display a schedule against a time scale
Update   To modify the target schedule, based on the latest data, to create a new schedule starting from the time of update

Project control, for scheduling, consists of monitoring and updating, that is, monitoring the actual progress and comparing it to the planned progress, and updating the network schedule to reflect any revised planning for the remainder of the project. In order to effectively monitor the project, it is helpful to have a time-based representation of the project's schedule, such as a time-phased diagram.

WHAT IS A TIME-PHASED DIAGRAM?

A time-phased diagram is simply a diagram that visually associates the durations of activities with periods of time. All the diagrams we've discussed can be time-phased: bar charts, arrow diagrams, and node diagrams.

A bar chart used as a time-phased diagram to represent a CPM schedule is shown in Fig. 5-1. The arrow diagram in the figure is used for the CPM calculations and the bar chart is used to display the schedule. A decision must be made where to show each activity starting. In Fig. 5-1 the early-start schedule was used. If desired, additional information can be displayed on the time-

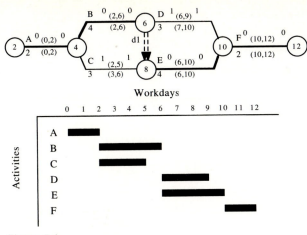

Figure 5-1

phased diagram as shown in the modified bar chart of Fig. 5-2. Notice that not all the calculated values can be easily shown directly, but each can be readily determined from those given. The arrow and node diagrams themselves can be time-phased as shown in Figs. 5-3 and 5-4. *Note:* We cannot show total float because it doesn't belong to any single activity. The hardware and software required to generate these diagrams are relatively expensive, but a simple bar chart produced by a microcomputer, as shown in Fig. 5-5, can be quite effective.

While many managers in construction prefer to show workdays on time-phased diagrams, some prefer to use calendar days. If calendar days are desired, you can simply replace the horizontal time line across the top with dates or actually insert weekend and holiday breaks in the diagram as shown in Fig. 5-6.

Figure 5-2

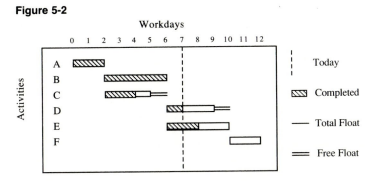

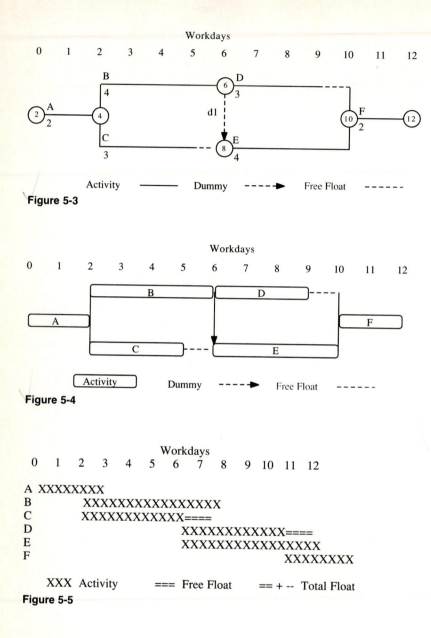

Figure 5-3

Figure 5-4

Figure 5-5

Program TPD, in the Appendix, generates time-phased diagrams such as the one shown in Fig. 5-5. Examples of time-phased diagrams generated by commercial software packages are provided in Chap. 12, Microcomputer Applications.

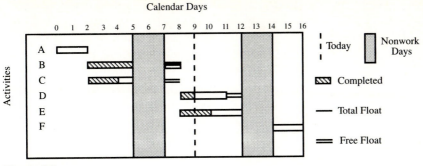

Figure 5-6

WHAT IS A TARGET SCHEDULE?

A target schedule is *the* time schedule we are going to use for the project.

While the network calculations give us start and finish limits for each activity, it is usually better to provide field personnel with a schedule where each activity has only one start and finish time—the target schedule. This practice helps to avoid confusion on the job site and prevents various individuals from deciding where float should be used.

The target schedule is somewhere between the early-start and late-start schedules. A good way to look at this is by using S curves which plot resource expenditure vs. time. Figure 5-7 shows S curves for a typical project using workdays as the *x* axis and worker-days as the *y* axis. We see that if we start every activity as soon as possible (ES schedule), the curve is pushed to the left and, conversely, the LS schedule is pushed to the right.

Figure 5-7

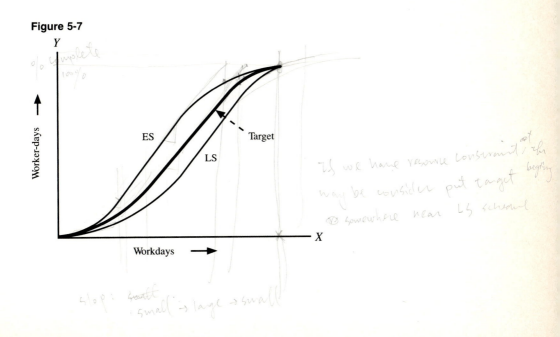

The primary reason the curve is shaped somewhat like the letter S is that at the beginning of most projects a limited number of activities can take place, such as site preparation and foundation work. Then the number of different activities gradually increases until most trades have work under way; and finally at the end, the variety of activities gradually decreases with only the finishing work remaining.

The decision on where to put the target schedule depends on several factors. In general, the advantages of an ES schedule are that it will accomplish work faster, earn larger progress payments early, and allow maximum cushion for unanticipated delays. On the other hand, rushing too many trades onto the job site early often results in supervision problems and other job inefficiencies. For the LS schedule, productivity is usually better because new resources are gradually added on, but there is no cushion for delay. In practice the scheduler must use experience to predict where potential problem areas lie and set the target schedule accordingly. For instance, where there might be a weather problem, start early; where there might be a material delay, start late; where supervision is lean because there are too many activities going on in parallel, spread out the activities. Other considerations are whether the company has follow-up work, in which case you'll want to free your resources as soon as possible. Conversely, if there is not an immediate follow-up job, you will want to spread out the work. It is important to remember that the project will take the same number of days either way, so the target schedule should be set to optimize efficiency, overall profit, or other company goals.

WHY SHOULD WE UPDATE THE NETWORK SCHEDULE?

We update our schedule so, at any point in time, it will reflect our best estimate of future progress.

Updating is a very important step in successful CPM use and is a vital part of project control. Feedback is obtained via monitoring of the project's progress; then the network schedule is revised to reflect that progress and any additional information that has become available since the last update.

In updating, the scheduler notes what has happened prior to the time of update and modifies the schedule accordingly. The new (updated) schedule that is generated then shows the schedule for the future, and in combination with prior versions of the schedule, can show when delays, accelerations, and changes took place. This information is needed for project control, cost accounting, claims defense, etc.

Remember, a CPM schedule is simply a model for a real phenomenon—a plan, not a mandatory sequence of events. Therefore, anything in the schedule is subject to change. Three possible changes are:

1 Change the duration of an activity.
2 Add or cancel an activity.
3 Change the logical relationship among activities.

[handwritten margin notes: update → actual data (happened) → future time estimate (not hap... ...)]

WHAT INFORMATION IS NEEDED TO UPDATE?

To update we need all actual data to date plus the latest time estimates for future activities.

As the project progresses, we will want to see how we are doing with regard to our target schedule. We do this by monitoring our progress and using the feedback derived to update our schedule. Of course, we realize that the network schedule is only a model and fully expect the actual progress to deviate. Therefore, it is important that we understand which deviations are serious and which are relatively insignificant. Often this is done by paying special attention to critical or near-critical activities and allowing noncritical activities to vary somewhat.

The physical recording of actual progress can be done by marking up the target schedule and/or by keeping a tabular record of some sort. To reduce the monitoring effort, exception reporting is used. This means that once the target schedule is set, any activities that take place as planned, within a set tolerance, are not reported, but any activity that is out of tolerance is. Also, any probable changes to future activities that have become known should be added. For instance, we could classify any change in ES, LS, duration, or logic to a critical activity to be an exception, while the duration of a noncritical activity could vary by 10 percent. In the case of monitoring, probably a daily record of deviations to the target schedule is appropriate.

WHEN SHOULD WE UPDATE?

We should update at times which are most cost-effective.

In deciding how often to update our target schedule we seek an optimum somewhere between continuous updating and no updating. The proper frequency depends on a number of factors, but briefly the answer is whatever frequency is most cost-effective or is required by the contract. To update the network schedule daily would be very expensive and of questionable value.

The most common updating frequencies are those based on contract requirements, fixed time intervals, and milestones. Many contracts call for progress payments monthly and require a schedule update as part of the contractor's payment request. When there is no such requirement, a fixed time interval can be set monthly or otherwise. Most projects have a few significant events, called milestones, which provide natural points at which to review the progress and update the target schedule, assuming the milestones are not too far apart and are fairly evenly spread throughout the project.

One of the most important procedures a project manager must establish is a method for field supervisors to record update information. One way this can be done is to address all activities due to be in progress on the update day, plus any changes to the plan. The following example demonstrates this more clearly.

Example

Update the schedule shown in Fig. 5-8 on day 5.

We had planned to maintain an early-start schedule, so any activities that should be in progress or any changes among activities not scheduled to be in progress must be addressed. *Note:* Any activity not mentioned is assumed to remain as planned.

The field notes in (5-1) were recorded.

Day 5

A,C,D completed
B,E started; 2 days left
H started; 1 day left
I's new Dur = 3   (5-1)
K canceled
New activity L: IPA = E,I; Dur = 4

We mark up our initial schedule as shown in Fig. 5-9. Finally, we draw the new network schedule and do the calculations using day 5 as time zero to determine the new critical path(s) and project duration, as shown in Fig. 5-10.

Notice that the project now takes 16 days to complete and that some critical activities have changed. If we are going to finish as originally planned, on day 14, we must take some action. (We'll discuss this more in Chap. 6, Least-Cost Scheduling.) *Note:* We usually can determine the new critical path(s) and new project duration with only a forward pass. If we need more information, we can also do the backward pass.

Figure 5-8

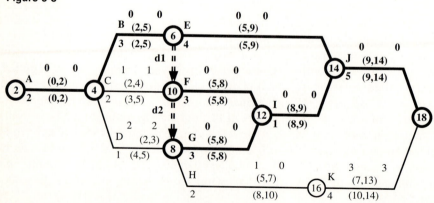

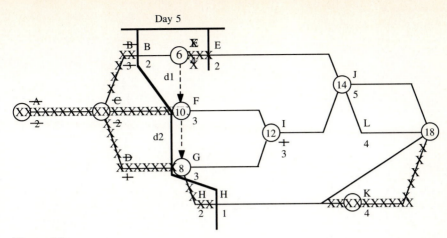

Figure 5-9

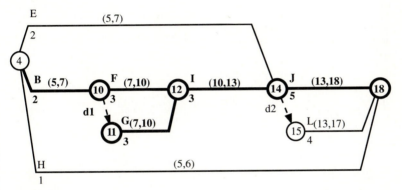

Figure 5-10

Figure 5-11

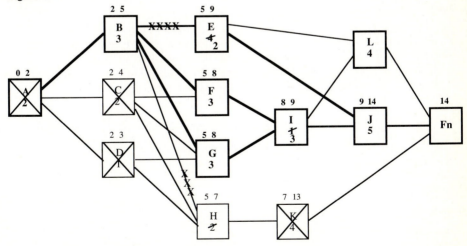

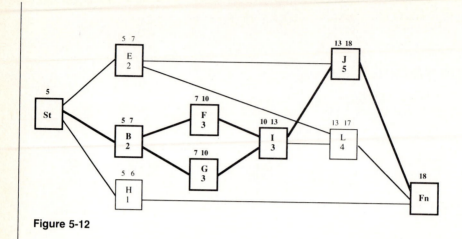

Figure 5-12

If we prefer, we can also use the same field data and mark up the node diagram for updating as shown in Fig. 5-11. The updated node diagram is shown in Fig. 5-12.

PRACTICE PROBLEMS

P1 Draw a bar chart for the network in Prob. 4-P1.
P2 Draw a bar chart for the network in Prob. 4-P5.
P3 Draw a time-phased arrow diagram for the network in Prob. 4-P2.
P4 Draw a time-phased arrow diagram for the network in Prob. 4-P6.
P5 Draw a time-phased node diagram for the network in Prob. 4-P3.
P6 Draw a time-phased node diagram for the network in Prob. 4-P6.
P7 Draw a bar chart using program TPD for the network in Prob. 4-P6.
P8 Draw a bar chart using program TPD for the network in Prob. 4-P7.
    Update the following network schedules according to the notes given, redraw the networks, and determine the new critical path(s) and project completion dates.

P9 See Fig. 5-8 (arrow diagram) and the notes in (5-2).

Day 7
A,B,C,D complete
E,F,G started on day 5
H starts today; K follows H
New Act L: IPA = I,K; Dur = 3

(5-2)

P10 See Fig. 3-Ps5*a*, Prob. 4-P5, and the notes in (5-3).

Day 7

A,B complete
C,D started; 1 day left
E started on day 5   (5-3)
G's new Dur = 4
H canceled

P11 See Fig. 3-Ps6*n*, Prob. 4-P6, and the notes in (5-4).

Day 12

A,B,C,E,F,M complete
I,J,K,L not started
D started; 2 days left
G,O started; 1 day left   (5-4)
I's new IPA = D
New Act P: IPA = H; Dur = 2

P12 See Fig. 3-Ps8*n*, Prob. 4-P8, and the notes in (5-5).

Day 6

F,L,O complete
D,Q started; 2 days left
M started; 6 days left
C,N started; 8 days left   (5-5)
G,H not started
K's new Dur = 6
New Act R: IPA = C,G; Dur = 12
E's new IPA = R

P13 See Fig. 3-Ps9*a*, Prob. 4-P9, and the notes in (5-6).

Day 5

C,P,S,T complete
A,B started; 2 days left
R started; 3 days left   (5-6)
E,O,U not started
Q started; 10 days left
G, L, K canceled
New Act X: IPA = N; Dur = 3
I's new IPA = X

P14 See Fig. 3-Ps10*n*, Prob. 4-P10, and the notes in (5-7).

Day 10

A,C,D,G,H,J,L,O,P,Q,R,S,V,W complete
K,U started; 6 days left
F started; 5 days left
K started; 4 days left   (5-7)
T's new Dur = 6
New Act Y: IPA = M,K; Dur = 5

ANSWERS TO PRACTICE PROBLEMS

P1 See Fig. 5-Ps1.

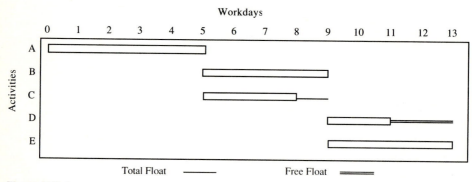

Figure 5-Ps1

P2 See Fig. 5-Ps2.

Figure 5-Ps2

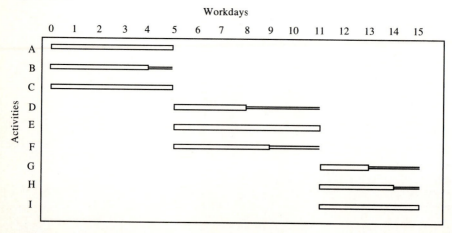

P3 See Fig. 5-Ps3.

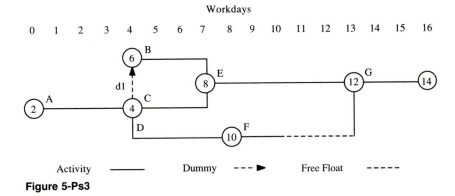

Figure 5-Ps3

P4 See Fig. 5-Ps4.

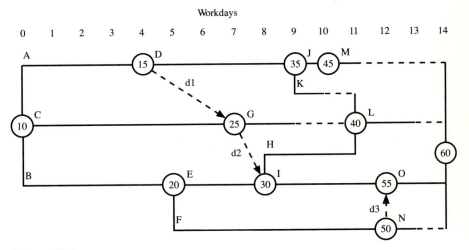

Figure 5-Ps4

P5 See Fig. 5-Ps5.

Figure 5-Ps5

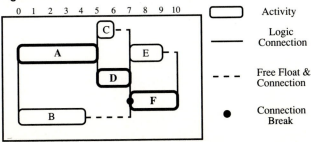

P6 See Fig. 5-Ps6.

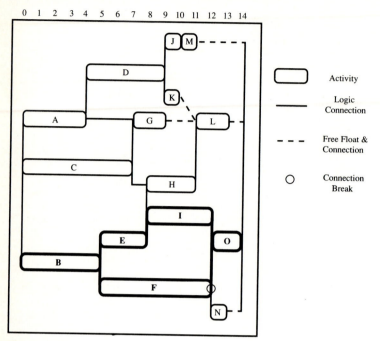

Figure 5-Ps6

P7 See Fig. 5-Ps7.

Figure 5-Ps7

```
                              Workdays
      0   1   2   3   4   5   6   7   8   9   10  11  12  13  14
A XXXXXXXXXXXXXXXXX--------
B XXXXXXXXXXXXXXXXXXXX
C XXXXXXXXXXXXXXXXXXXXXXXXXXXXXX----
D             XXXXXXXXXXXXXXXXXXXXX--------
E             XXXXXXXXXXX
F             XXXXXXXXXXXXXXXXXXXXXXXXXXXXXXX
G                 XXXXXXXX=========----
H                 XXXXXXXXXXXX----
I                 XXXXXXXXXXXXXXXX
J                     XXXX------------
K                     XXXX====----
L                               XXXX====
M                     XXXX============
N                               XXXX====
O                               XXXXXXXX

    XXX Duration      === Free Float      == + --- Total Float
```

P8 See Fig. 5-Ps8.

```
                        Workdays
 0   1   2   3   4   5   6   7   8   9  10  11  12

A XXXX====
B XXXX═══════════════════════
C XXXX═══════════════
D XXXX------------
E XXXX══════════════════════
F XXXX════════════════════----------------
G XXXX═══════════════════════════════════
H XXXX═══════════════
I XXXX═══════════════------------
J XXXX═══════════════════════════------------
K XXXX
L       XXXX
M           XXXXXXX
N               XXXX
O                   XXXXXXX
P                       XXXX
Q                           XXXXXXX
R                               XXXX
S               XXXXXXX════════════════
T                               XXXX
U XXXX------------
V           XXXXXXX════════════
W               XXXXXXX════════════════════
X               XXXXXXX------------
Y                   XXXX════════════
Z                       XXXX════════════
```

        XXX Duration   === Free Float   == + -- Total Float

Figure 5-Ps8

P9 See Fig. 5-Ps9.

Figure 5-Ps9

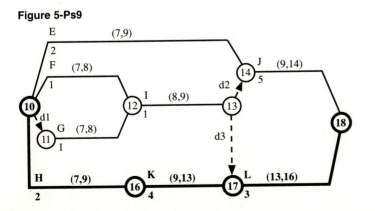

P10 See Fig. 5-Ps10.

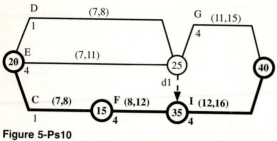

Figure 5-Ps10

P11 See Fig. 5-Ps11.

Figure 5-Ps11

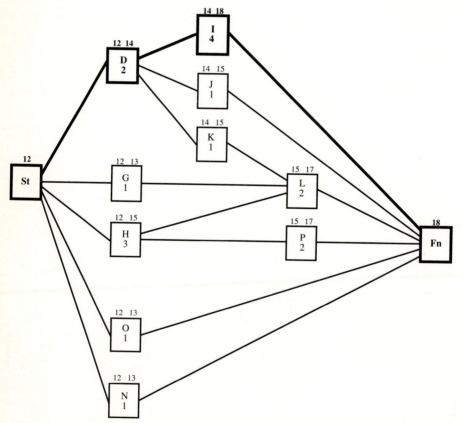

P12 See Fig. 5-Ps12.

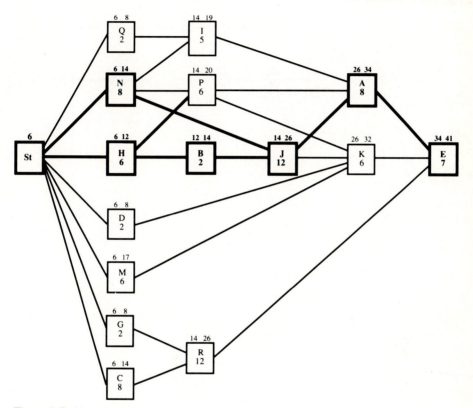

Figure 5-Ps12

P13 See Fig. 5-Ps13.

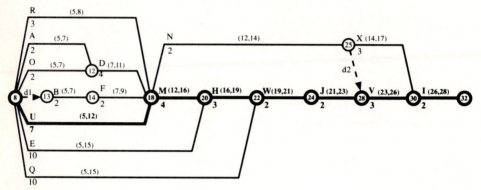

Figure 5-Ps13

P14 See Fig. 5-Ps14.

Figure 5-Ps14

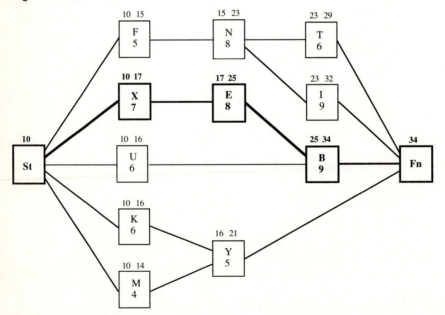

JIMBEAU PROJECT

J1 Draw a time-phased arrow diagram for the JIMBEAU project.

J2 Draw a bar chart using program TPD for the JIMBEAU project.

Update, redraw, and determine the new critical path(s) and project completion dates for the project according to the given notes. The updates are progressive; i.e., the day 15 update depends on the day 10 update which depends on the day 5 update.

J3 See (5-8).

Day 5

A,B,C,D,O,R complete
E starts today
G,H started on ES
U started; 8 days left
K started; 7 days left
M started; 1 day left
Q follows M; new Dur = 7

(5-8)

J4 See (5-9).

Day 10

E,F,G,H,M,X complete
K,U have 1 day left
I started; 2 days left
Q starts today
New Act Z: IPA = W,V; Dur = 5
V's new Dur = 4

(5-9)

J5 See (5-10).

Day 15

I,J,K,N,T,U,V complete
L,Q have 1 day left
Y's new Dur = 3

(5-10)

SUPPLEMENTARY PROBLEMS

S1 Draw a bar chart for the network in Prob. 4-S1.

S2 Draw a bar chart for the network in Prob. 4-S5.

S3 Draw a time-phased arrow diagram for the network in Prob. 4-S2.

S4 Draw a time-phased arrow diagram for the network in Prob. 4-P5.

S5 Draw a time-phased node diagram for the network in Prob. 4-P2.

S6 Draw a time-phased node diagram for the network in Prob. 4-P4.
S7 Draw a bar chart using program TPD for the network in Prob. 4-S2.
S8 Draw a bar chart using program TPD for the network in Prob. 4-S5.

Update the following network schedules according to the notes given, redraw the networks, and determine the new critical path(s) and project completion dates.

S9 See Fig. 3-Ps3*a*, Prob. 4-P3, and the notes in (5-11).

Day 5

A,B complete
A finished today   (5-11)
New Act G: IPA = E; Dur = 4
New Act H: IPA = F,G; Dur = 3

S10 See Fig. 3-Ps5*a*, Prob. 4-P5, and the notes in (5-12).

Day 5

B,C complete
A started; 2 days left   (5-12)
D,E start today
F started; 3 days left
G canceled

S11 See Fig. 5-11 (node diagram) and the notes in (5-13).

Day 10

A,B,C,D,H,I complete
E starts today   (5-13)
F,G started; 1 day left
K follows F,G
J's new Dur = 7

S12 See Fig. 3-Ps7*n*, Prob. 4-P7, and the notes in (5-14).

Day 3

A to L complete
M started; 1 day left   (5-14)
N starts today
R's new Dur = 3
T,W follows X

S13 See Fig.3-Ps8*a*, Prob. 4-P8, and the notes in (5-15).

Day 10

B,D,F,G,H,L,O,Q complete
N started; 7 days left
C started; 8 days left
M started; 9 days left
New Act R: IPA = A; Dur = 7

(5-15)

S14 See Fig. 3-Ps10*n*, Prob. 4-P10, and the notes in (5-16).

Day 12

A,C,G,H,L,O,T,V,W, complete
K,M,P,Q started; 4 days left
B started; 7 days left
S starts today; U follows S
New Act Y: IPA = E,U; Dur = 5
New Act Z: starts today; Dur = 4
I's new IPA = J,N,Z
D's new IPA = K

(5-16)

CHAPTER **6**

LEAST-COST SCHEDULING

NEW WORDS

Complex compression   When direct costs of activities vary nonlinearly with their durations, or the overhead costs vary nonlinearly with time

Crash   Shortening project activities in order to shorten the project length

Crash cost   The cost of an activity at crash duration

Crash duration   The minimum practicable duration for any activity

Direct costs   The costs directly attributable to project work items (e.g., labor and materials). These costs are usually nonlinear; to accelerate or to delay the work costs more

Least cost   The least total cost for a project

Normal cost   The cost of an activity at normal duration

Normal duration   The duration of an activity

Optimum time   The project duration at least cost

Overhead costs   The costs which are spread over the entire project (e.g., office, staff, management, equipment). These costs are usually linear, within a range; i.e., one day saved on a project saves one day's overhead costs, and one day's delay costs the same amount

Simple compression   When direct costs of activities vary linearly with their durations, and the overhead costs vary linearly with time

WHAT IS A LEAST-COST SCHEDULE?

A least-cost schedule is one with an optimum project duration such that to lengthen or shorten it would increase the total cost.

Time and cost are the two most important components of project economy. If time is not important, management can utilize its resources in the most efficient way, even stopping work on one project, moving to another for a while, and then coming back. If money is not important, management can obtain the best of resources and schedule work around the clock. This process is usually inefficient but produces a completed project in a minimum time. Both ways have their uses, but in the normal situation cost-effectiveness calls for a study of the trade-off between time and cost which yields a "least-cost" solution.

There is no absolute, provable least-cost solution to a real problem because the value of variables cannot be known exactly in advance. For instance, we cannot know exactly what working overtime on a particular activity will achieve. Generally, we know that premium pay for overtime will increase our direct cost but will reduce the number of days needed to complete the activity, which in turn, should reduce the time needed to complete the project, thereby saving some overhead. How much time can be saved, and the importance of saving that time, must be analyzed.

HOW DO DIRECT COSTS VARY WITH TIME?

Direct costs, once a target schedule has been developed, increase with either an increase or decrease in time.

To solve the time/cost problem—searching for a least-cost solution—we must make some assumptions. Let us consider an activity AX which normally would require 6 days at a direct cost of $6000. We estimate that by adding more equipment or more labor hours per day (more workers or overtime) we could reduce the time to 3 days at a new direct cost of $9000. We also estimate we could do AX in 5 days for $7000 or in 4 days for $8000. Therefore, the "normal" duration for AX, considering our available resources, is 6 days, and the "crash" duration is 3 days. There is an implicit assumption that to increase the duration beyond 6 days would not result in a direct cost reduction because of underutilization of resources—otherwise the "normal" duration would not have been 6 days. So to recap, we have a choice of 6 days at a cost of $6000, 5 days at $7000, 4 days at $8000, or 3 days at $9000. For simple compression we consider that the direct cost curve for each activity is linear, so these figures result in the time/cost curve shown in Fig. 6-1.

Another scenario would be that 6 days cost $6000, 5 days cost $6500, 4 days cost $7500, and 3 days cost $9000. This is often the case because 1 day can be saved with overtime, while to save 2 days requires new hires and to save 3 days requires more equipment. For complex compression we consider that the direct cost curve for each activity is nonlinear, so these figures result in the curve shown in Fig. 6-2.

Once we know the cost of shortening each activity, we can see the effect on the project schedule. Shortening some activities—those on the critical path—may result in advancing the completion date, while shortening other activities may simply add more float. Sometimes it is advantageous to shorten an activ-

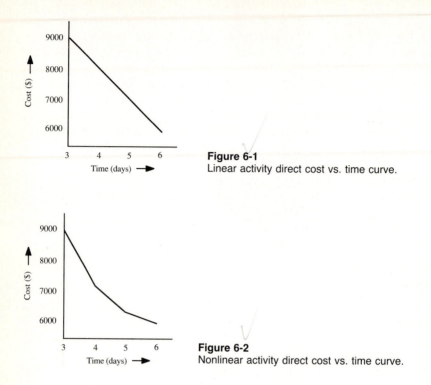

Figure 6-1
Linear activity direct cost vs. time curve.

Figure 6-2
Nonlinear activity direct cost vs. time curve.

ity to free up a resource, but it is almost always beneficial to shorten an activity that would cause the completion date to be advanced, if the cost isn't too great. In our discussion we will only consider taking action to shorten the project duration.

HOW DO OVERHEAD COSTS VARY WITH TIME?

Generally, overhead costs vary directly with time; i.e., increase in time causes an increase in overhead costs, and vice versa.

So far we have only talked about increasing our direct cost while shortening a project's duration, but along with this project shortening there is a cost benefit. For example, if we finish a project 1 week early, we save on security costs at the job site, management costs, equipment rental costs, etc.—these are overhead costs. Like direct costs, overhead costs may be linear (often called periodic costs) or nonlinear. The simplest case, and the one we'll use for this study, is where overhead is a periodic cost of Y per workday, as shown in Fig. 6-3.

The total cost is the sum of direct costs plus overhead and is shown in Fig. 6-4 for the cases mentioned above. For the linear direct and overhead costs (Fig. 6-4a) the optimum time is 6 days with a least cost of $1050, and for the

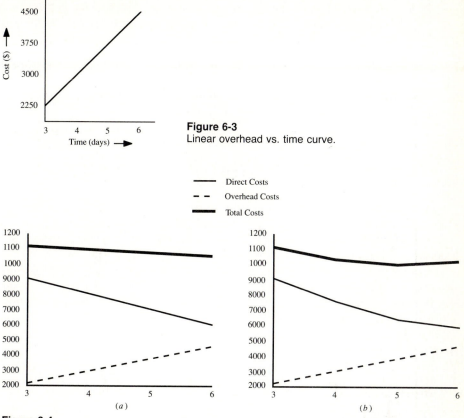

Figure 6-3
Linear overhead vs. time curve.

Figure 6-4
(a) Linear direct and overhead costs; (b) nonlinear direct and linear overhead cost.

nonlinear direct and linear overhead costs the optimum time is 5 days at a least cost of $1025. Now the problem becomes clearer—find the optimum point, called the least-cost solution.

WHAT IS SCHEDULE COMPRESSION?

The systematic process of arriving at the least-cost solution is sometimes called schedule compression. When direct costs of activities and overhead costs vary linearly with time, we have simple compression, while if we have one or more costs which vary nonlinearly, we have complex compression.

Least-cost scheduling is an optimization process whereby project activities are shortened in order to shorten the overall project length. When activities are shortened, their direct costs increase. When the overall project is shortened, its overhead costs decrease. If we can shorten a schedule so that the overhead cost savings are greater than the increased direct costs, let's do it!

First, let's consider only simple compression where both the direct and overhead costs vary linearly with time. The planner must do the following:

1 Assign to each activity a direct cost to complete the activity at the normal duration, which is called "normal cost."

2 Assign a minimum duration (less than or equal to the normal duration) for every activity, which is called "crash duration."

3 Assign to each activity a direct cost (greater than the normal cost) to complete the activity at the minimum duration. This is called "crash cost."

In order to investigate a method of least-cost scheduling, we'll make the following assumptions:

Assumption 1: The planned duration of an activity can be any whole day value between and including the normal and crash durations. For example, if A has a normal duration = 10 days and a crash duration = 7 days, then it has a possible duration = 7, 8, 9, or 10 days.

Assumption 2: The direct cost of an activity is linear between the normal and crash direct costs. For example, if A's cost for a 10-day duration = $1700 and for a 7-day duration = $2000, then A's cost for an 8-day duration = $1900 and for a 9-day duration = $1800.

Assumption 3: The overhead cost is linear during the entire project. It is simply the number of days times the overhead cost per day.

Example

Let's find the least-cost schedule for the network shown in Fig. 6-5a using simple compression.

Figure 6-5a

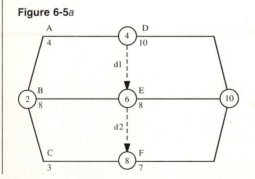

Act.	Duration		Cost, $	
	Normal	Crash	Normal	Crash
A	4	2	400	500
B	8	5	800	980
C	3	2	600	700
D	10	6	500	600
E	8	6	800	950
F	7	4	700	1000

Overhead Costs = $100/day

Step 1: How much are the normal duration and the normal cost?

Normal duration = 16 days

$$
\begin{aligned}
\text{Direct cost} &= (400 + 800 + 600 + 500 + 800 + 700 = 3800 \\
+ \quad \text{overhead cost} &= (16 \times 100) & = 1600 \\
\hline
\text{normal cost} & & = \$5400
\end{aligned}
$$

Step 2: How much can each activity be shortened, and what does it cost per day? See (6-1).

A:	(4−2)	@	(500−400)	= 2 days	@	$50 per day
B:	(8−5)	@	(980−800)	= 3 days	@	$60 per day
C:	(3−2)	@	(700−600)	= 1 day	@	$100 per day
D:	(10−6)	@	(600−500)	= 4 days	@	$25 per day
E:	(8−6)	@	(950−800)	= 2 days	@	$75 per day
F:	(7−4)	@	(1000−700)	= 3 days	@	$100 per day

(6-1)

It is helpful here to use a worksheet such as is shown in Fig. 6-5*b*.

Figure 6-5*b*

Act.	Duration Norm	Duration Crash	Cost, $ Norm	Cost, $ Crash	Δ Cost	Δ Days	Δ Cost Days	Days Shortened						
A	4	2	400	500	100	2	50							
B	8	5	800	980	180	3	60							
C	3	2	600	700	100	1	100							
D	10	6	500	600	100	4	25							
E	8	6	800	950	150	2	75							
F	7	4	700	1000	300	3	100							
			Days Cut		▨									
			Project Duration		16									
			Increased Cost/Day		▨									
			Direct Cost		3800									
			Overhead Cost		1600									
			TOTAL COST		5400									

Cycle 1

Step 3: Which activities would shorten the project? (Which activities are on the critical path?)

B and E

Step 4: Which activity or activities would shorten the project at the least cost?

B @ \$60 per day or E @ \$75 per day;   B

Step 5: Shorten the activity by 1 day.

B (new duration) = 7

Step 6: Calculate the new project duration and cost; then, modify the arrow diagram and worksheet. See Fig. 6-5c.

New duration = 15 days

New cost = old cost + (1 day @ \$60 per day)
$$- (1 \text{ day } @ \$100 \text{ per day}) = \$5360$$

Figure 6-5c

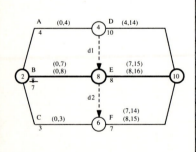

Act.	Δ Days	Δ Cost/Days	Days Shortened				
A	2	50					
B	~~3~~ 2	60	1				
C	1	100					
D	4	25					
E	2	75					
F	3	100					
Days Cut	▨	1					
Proj. Dur	16	15					
Inc. Cost/Day	▨	60					
Dir. Cost	3800	3860					
Ovhd. Cost	1600	1500					
TOTAL COST	5400	5360					

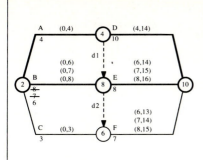

Act.	Δ Days	Δ Cost Days	Days Shortened				
A	2	50					
B	~~2~~ 1	60	1	1			
C	1	100					
D	4	25					
E	2	75					
F	3	100					
Days Cut	▨		1	1			
Proj. Dur	16		15	14			
Inc. Cost/Day	▨		60	60			
Dir. Cost	3800		3860	3920			
Ovhd. Cost	1600		1500	1400			
TOTAL COST	5400		5360	5320			

Figure 6-5d

Cycle 2

Repeat steps 3 to 6. See Fig. 6-5d.

Step 3: B and E
Step 4: B @ $60
Step 5: B (new duration) = 6; modify the arrow diagram
Step 6: New duration = 14 days
New cost = old cost + (1 day @ $60 per day)
− (1 day @ $100 per day) = $5320

Cycle 3

Repeat steps 3 to 6. *Note:* Now there are multiple critical paths to shorten.
See Fig. 6-5e.

Step 3: (B or E) and (A or D)
Step 4: B and D @ (60 + 25) = $85
Step 5: B (new duration) = 5; D (new duration) = 9; modify the diagram.
Step 6: New duration = 13 days
New cost = old cost + (1 day @ $85 per day)
− (1 day @ $100 per day) = $5305

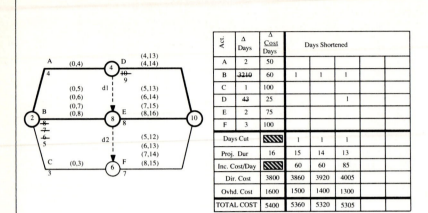

Act.	Δ Days	Δ Cost/Days	Days Shortened				
A	2	50					
B	~~3210~~	60	1	1	1		
C	1	100					
D	~~43~~	25				1	
E	2	75					
F	3	100					
Days Cut	▨	1	1	1			
Proj. Dur	16	15	14	13			
Inc. Cost/Day	▨	60	60	85			
Dir. Cost	3800	3860	3920	4005			
Ovhd. Cost	1600	1500	1400	1300			
TOTAL COST	5400	5360	5320	5305			

Figure 6-5e

Cycle 4

Repeat steps 3 to 6. *Note:* B is now completely crashed. See Fig. 6-5*f*.

Step 3: (E) and (A or D)
Step 4: E and D @ (75 + 25) = $100
Step 5: E (new duration) = 7; D (new duration) = 8; modify the diagram.

Figure 6-5f

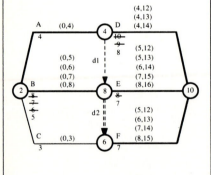

Act.	Δ Days	Δ Cost/Days	Days Shortened				
A	2	50					
B	~~3210~~	60	1	1	1		
C	1	100					
D	~~432~~	25				1	1
E	~~21~~	75					1
F	3	100					
Days Cut	▨	1	1	1	1		
Proj. Dur	16	15	14	13	12		
Inc. Cost/Day	▨	60	60	85	100		
Dir. Cost	3800	3860	3920	4005	4105		
Ovhd. Cost	1600	1500	1400	1300	1200		
TOTAL COST	5400	5360	5320	5305	5305		

Step 6: New duration = 12 days
　　　New cost = old cost + (1 day @ $100 per day)
　　　　　　　　− (1 day @ $100 per day) = $5305

Cycle 5

Repeat steps 3 to 6. *Note:* There is now another critical path. See Fig. 6-5g.

　Step 3: (E) and (A or D) and (F)
　Step 4: E and D and F @ (75 + 25 + 100) = $200
　Step 5: E (new duration) = 6; D (new duration) = 7; modify the diagram.
　Step 6: New duration = 11 days
　　　New cost = old cost + (1 day @ $200 per day)
　　　　　　　　− (1 day @ $100 per day) = $5405

Note: B and E make up a critical path and are now as short as possible; therefore, the project is completely crashed. *Note:* This does not mean all the activities are as short as possible. To shorten the remaining activities would simply add more float and not save overhead costs.

　The graph of time vs. costs in Fig. 6-5h shows that the least cost = $5305 and the optimum time = 12 or 13 days.

A few points should be discussed:

1 Once the increased direct cost to shorten the project 1 day equals or exceeds the decreased overhead cost (such as in Cycle 4), you have found the

Figure 6-5g

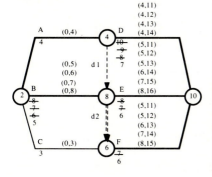

Act.	Δ Days	Δ Cost Days	Days Shortened				
A	2	50					
B	3210	60	1	1	1		
C	1	100					
D	4321	25			1	1	1
E	210	75				1	1
F	32	100					1
Days Cut	▨		1	1	1	1	1
Proj. Dur	16		15	14	13	12	11
Inc. Cost/Day	▨		60	60	85	100	200
Dir. Cost	3800		3860	3920	4005	4105	4305
Ovhd. Cost	1600		1500	1400	1300	1200	1100
TOTAL COST	5400		5360	5320	5305	5305	5405

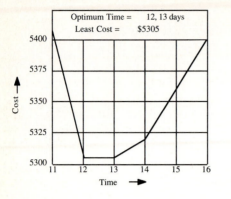

Figure 6-5*h*

least-cost schedule. But don't stop. Now, if the total cost versus project duration is plotted on a graph, not only will the least cost and optimum duration become obvious, but we will also have an indication of the importance of maintaining the planned schedule. If a company has several projects under way and each is scheduled at its least cost, then the slope of the time/cost lines is very important. If one project suffers a delay and its time/cost line adjacent to its optimum time is very steep, then perhaps some of the workforce could be borrowed from a project whose time/cost line is not so steep.

2 The least-cost schedule shows that the optimum duration is either 12 or 13 days. Other factors, not included in the model, might indicate a preference between these two durations, but the model cannot. For instance, a company with future work would probably opt to finish on day 12, while a company looking for future work might choose 13 days.

3 In cycles 1 and 2 we shortened the same activity B. If we had looked ahead and anticipated this, then we could have shortened B by 2 days in cycle 1. However, we must be very careful because for more complex network diagrams the emerging critical paths are often difficult to detect. So, to be safe, it is better to shorten activities 1 day at a time.

4 For complex compression the process is the same, and the need to shorten activities 1 day at a time becomes even more important to avoid mistakes.

A worksheet that could be used for complex compression is shown as Fig. 6-6*a*, with the above example again worked with nonlinear crash costs.

The graph of time vs. costs in Fig. 6-6*b* shows least cost = $5305 and optimum time = 12 or 13 days. *Hint:* The graph of time vs. total cost must always have the slopes of the daily costs decreasing as they near the least-cost point. This is because we shorten the activities which yield maximum savings first and continue with increasing lesser savings. It may be that the least-cost point is a saddle, as in Fig. 6-7*a*, or at normal duration, as shown in Fig. 6-7*b*, or at

Overhead Costs = $100/day

Act.	Δ Days	Δ Cost/Days				Days Shortened					
A	2	30	70								1
B	3	25	70	85		1		1	1		
C	1	100									
D	4	15	20	30	45			1	1		
E	2	65	85				1				1
F	3	40	100	160							1
	Days Cut	▨				1	1	1	1	1	
	Proj. Dur	16				15	14	13	12	11	
	Inc. Cost/Day	▨				25	65	85	105	155	
	Dir. Cost	3800				3825	3890	3975	4080	4235	
	Ovhd. Cost	1600				1500	1400	1300	1200	1100	
	TOTAL COST	5400				5325	5290	5275	5280	5335	

Figure 6-6*a*

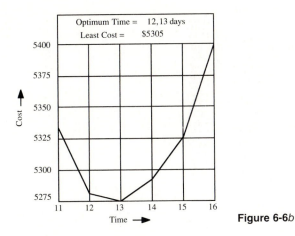

Optimum Time = 12,13 days
Least Cost = $5305

Figure 6-6*b*

crash duration, as shown in Fig. 6-7*c*. If your time vs. total cost graph looks like the incorrect examples of Fig. 6-8, you shortened activities out of proper sequence.

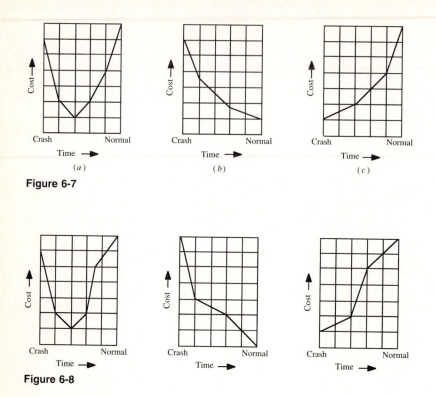

(a)   (b)   (c)

Figure 6-7

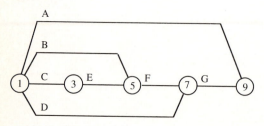

Figure 6-8

PRACTICE PROBLEMS

Completely crash the following network schedules using simple compression, and find the optimum time and least cost.

P1 See Fig. 6-P1.

Figure 6-P1

Act.	Duration		Cost, $	
	Normal	Crash	Normal	Crash
A	6	3	300	360
B	6	4	450	500
C	4	2	360	420
D	6	3	600	675
E	3	2	325	350
F	2	1	250	285
G	2	1	310	350

Overhead Costs = $60/day

P2 See Fig. 6-P2.

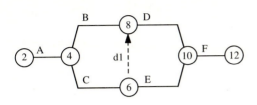

Act.	Duration		Cost, $	
	Normal	Crash	Normal	Crash
A	6	4	600	780
B	10	7	500	875
C	12	8	600	900
D	8	4	800	940
E	6	3	600	795
F	4	2	800	850

Overhead Costs = $100/day

Figure 6-P2

P3 See Fig. 6-P3.

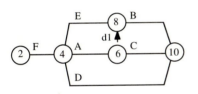

Act.	Duration		Cost, $	
	Normal	Crash	Normal	Crash
A	10	8	1000	1100
B	4	3	500	575
C	10	6	400	800
D	19	14	1000	1100
E	13	9	300	400
F	6	4	120	200

Overhead Costs = $75/day

Figure 6-P3

P4 See Fig. 6-P4.

Figure 6-P4

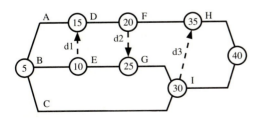

Act.	Duration		Cost, $	
	Normal	Crash	Normal	Crash
A	5	3	400	530
B	3	2	350	410
C	7	4	1020	1095
D	4	3	525	560
E	6	3	825	975
F	4	2	610	750
G	6	3	430	565
H	7	4	1250	1415
I	4	2	390	450

Overhead Costs = $80/day

P5 See Fig. 6-P5.

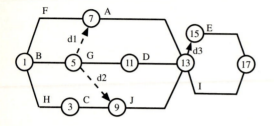

Act.	Duration		Cost, $	
	Normal	Crash	Normal	Crash
A	3	2	400	430
B	4	2	1020	1100
C	2	2	350	350
D	7	5	1250	1300
E	5	3	825	895
F	6	3	610	700
G	4	2	430	490
H	5	2	525	660
I	3	2	390	410
J	6	3	615	765

Overhead Costs = $90/day

Figure 6-P5

Completely crash the following network schedule using complex compression, and find the optimum time and least cost.

P6 Use the network of Prob. 6-P2 above.

Act.	Duration		Cost, $				
	Normal	Crash	Normal	Crash 1	Crash 2	Crash 3	Crash 4
A	6	4	800	890	1010		
B	10	7	1100	1225	1350	1475	
C	12	8	1400	1475	1560	1650	1760
D	8	4	1000	1035	1115	1195	1295
E	6	3	900	965	1040	1130	
F	4	2	800	825	865		

Overhead Costs = $100/day

Figure 6-P6

ANSWERS TO PRACTICE PROBLEMS

P1 See Fig. 6-Ps1.

Overhead Costs = $60/day

Act.	Δ Days	Δ Cost Days		Days Shortened				
A	3	20						
B	2	25					1	1
C	2	30					1	1
D	3	25						1
E	1	25		1				
F	1	35			1			
G	1	40				1		
Days Cut			▨	1	1	1	1	1
Proj. Dur			11	10	9	8	7	6
Inc. Cost/Day			▨	25	35	40	55	80
Dir. Cost			2595	2620	2655	2695	2750	2830
Ovhd. Cost			660	600	540	480	420	360
TOTAL COST			3255	3220	3195	3175	3170	3190

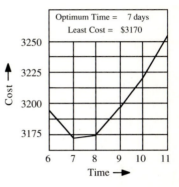

Optimum Time = 7 days
Least Cost = $3170

Figure 6-Ps1

P2 See Fig. 6-Ps2.

Figure 6-Ps2

Overhead Costs = $100/day

Act.	Δ Days	Δ Cost Days		Days Shortened					
A	2	90					2		
B	3	125							2
C	4	75				2			2
D	4	35			2			2	
E	3	65						2	
F	2	25		2					
Days Cut			▨	2	2	2	2	2	2
Proj. Dur			30	28	26	24	22	20	18
Inc. Cost/Day			▨	25	35	75	90	100	200
Dir. Cost			3900	3950	4020	4170	4350	4550	4950
Ovhd. Cost			3000	2800	2600	2400	2200	2000	1800
TOTAL COST			6900	6750	6620	6570	6550	6550	6750

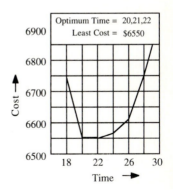

Optimum Time = 20,21,22
Least Cost = $6550

P3 See Fig. 6-Ps3.

Overhead Costs = $75/day

Act.	Δ Days	Δ Cost/Days	Days Shortened					
A	2	50			1	1		
B	1	75						
C	4	100					1	3
D	5	20				1	1	3
E	4	25						3
F	2	40		2				
Days Cut	▨			2	1	1	1	3
Proj. Dur	26			24	23	22	21	18
Inc. Cost/Day	▨			40	50	70	120	145
Dir. Cost	3320			3400	3450	3520	3640	4075
Ovhd. Cost	1950			1800	1725	1650	1575	1350
TOTAL COST	5270			5200	5175	5170	5215	5425

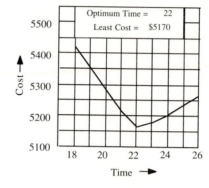

Optimum Time = 22
Least Cost = $5170

Figure 6-Ps3

P4 See Fig. 6-Ps4.

Figure 6-Ps4

Overhead Costs = $80/day

Act.	Δ Days	Δ Cost/Days	Days Shortened					
A	2	65					2	
B	1	60						
C	3	25						
D	1	35				1		
E	3	50					2	1
F	2	70						1
G	3	45		2		1		
H	3	55			3			
I	2	30						
Days Cut	▨			2	3	1	2	1
Proj. Dur	22			20	17	16	14	13
Inc. Cost/Day	▨			45	55	80	115	130
Dir. Cost	5800			5890	6055	6135	6365	6495
Ovhd. Cost	1760			1600	1360	1280	1120	1040
TOTAL COST	7560			7490	7415	7415	7485	7535

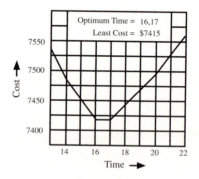

Optimum Time = 16,17
Least Cost = $7415

P5 See Fig. 6-Ps5.

Overhead Costs = $90/day

Act.	Δ Days	Δ Cost Days	Days Shortened				
A	1	30					
B	2	40				1	1
C	0	--					
D	2	25	2				
E	2	35		2			
F	3	30					
G	2	30			2		
H	3	45			2	1	
I	1	20					
J	3	50					1
Days Cut	▨	2	2	2	1	1
Proj. Dur	20	18	16	14	13	12
Inc. Cost/Day	▨	25	35	75	85	90
Dir. Cost	6415	6465	6535	6685	6770	6860
Ovhd. Cost	1800	1620	1440	1260	1170	1080
TOTAL COST	8215	8085	7975	7945	7940	7940

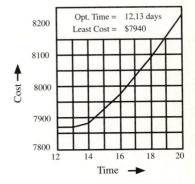

Opt. Time =   12,13 days
Least Cost = $7940

(Cost vs. Time graph)

Figure 6-Ps5

P6 See Fig. 6-Ps6.

Figure 6-Ps6

Overhead Costs = $100/day

Act.	Δ Days	Δ Cost Days				Days Shortened											
A	2	90	120										1	1			
B	3	125	125	125											1	1
C	4	75	85	90	110			1		1						1	1
D	4	35	80	80	100		1			1				1	1		
E	3	65	75	90										1	1		
F	2	25	40			1		1									

	Days Cut	▨	1	1	1	1	1	1	1	1	1	1	1	1
	Proj. Dur	30	29	28	27	26	25	24	23	22	21	20	19	18
	Inc. Cost/Day	▨	25	35	40	75	80	85	90	120	145	175	215	235
	Dir. Cost	6000	6025	6060	6100	6175	6255	6340	6430	6550	6695	6870	7085	7320
	Ovhd. Cost	3000	2900	2800	2700	2600	2500	2400	2300	2200	2100	2000	1900	1800
	TOTAL COST	9000	8925	8860	8800	8775	8755	8740	8730	8750	8795	8870	8985	9120

Optimum Time = 23 Days; Least-Cost = $8730

JIMBEAU PROJECT

J1 *Completely* crash the JIMBEAU network schedule using simple compression and the data given in Fig. 6-J1.

Act.	Duration Normal	Duration Crash	Cost, $ Normal	Cost, $ Crash
A	2	2	100	100
B	2	2	500	500
C	3	2	1000	1065
D	2	2	1000	1000
E	3	2	500	555
F	3	3	300	300
G	10	7	3000	3060
H	7	5	525	665
I	4	1	400	460
J	1	1	50	50
K	8	6	8100	8120
L	6	3	1500	1560
M	6	6	1140	1140

Act.	Duration Normal	Duration Crash	Cost, $ Normal	Cost, $ Crash
N	4	3	1200	1250
O	5	3	2000	2050
P	3	2	1000	1040
Q	5	2	800	890
R	3	2	800	825
S	4	1	800	1100
T	2	2	500	500
U	10	7	1000	1060
V	2	2	200	200
W	5	3	1000	1120
X	4	2	1000	1070
Y	1	1	50	50

Overhead Costs = $80/day

Figure 6-J1

J2 *Completely* crash the JIMBEAU network schedule using complex compression and the data given in Fig. 6-J2.

Figure 6-J2

Act.	Duration Normal	Duration Crash	Cost, $ Normal	Cost, $ Crash		
A	2	2	100	100		
B	2	2	500	500		
C	3	3	1000	1000		
D	2	2	1000	1000		
E	3	2	500	580		
F	3	3	300	300		
G	10	7	3000	3020	3050	3090
H	7	5	1000	1030	1070	
I	4	2	400	430	470	
J	1	1	50	50		
K	8	5	8000	8040	8090	8150
L	6	4	1500	1530	1575	
M	6	4	1100	1175	1250	

Act.	Duration Normal	Duration Crash	Cost, $ Normal	Cost, $ Crash		
N	4	3	1200	1250		
O	5	3	2000	2025	2060	
P	3	2	1000	1040		
Q	5	2	800	830	860	920
R	3	2	800	825		
S	4	3	800	840		
T	2	2	500	500		
U	10	7	1000	1020	1050	1080
V	2	2	200	200		
W	5	3	1000	1060	1130	
X	4	3	1000	1035		
Y	1	1	50	50		

Overhead Costs = $75/day

SUPPLEMENTAL PROBLEMS

Completely crash the following network schedules using simple compression, and find the optimum time and least cost.

S1 Use the network of Prob. 6-P1 above.

Act.	Duration		Cost, $	
	Normal	Crash	Normal	Crash
A	8	4	300	420
B	6	4	450	520
C	2	1	360	430
D	6	3	600	690
E	3	2	325	365
F	2	1	250	330
G	3	1	310	360

Overhead Costs = $75/day

Figure 6-S1

S2 Use the network of Prob. 6-P2 above.

Act.	Duration		Cost, $	
	Normal	Crash	Normal	Crash
A	6	4	600	670
B	12	8	500	660
C	10	6	600	760
D	8	5	800	890
E	6	4	600	690
F	4	2	800	900

Overhead Costs = $30/day

Figure 6-S2

S3 Use the network of Prob. 6-P3 above.

Figure 6-S3

Act.	Duration		Cost, $	
	Normal	Crash	Normal	Crash
A	10	8	1000	1120
B	5	3	500	630
C	6	3	400	505
D	19	12	1000	1210
E	12	8	300	480
F	6	4	120	200

Overhead Costs = $50/day

S4 Use the network of Prob. 6-P4 above.

Act.	Duration		Cost, $	
	Normal	Crash	Normal	Crash
A	4	2	400	570
B	5	2	350	455
C	11	6	1020	1145
D	4	2	525	575
E	6	4	825	935
F	6	5	610	650
G	6	4	430	570
H	3	2	1250	1325
I	5	3	390	450

Overhead Costs = $50/day   **Figure 6-S4**

S5 Use the network of Prob. 6-P5 above.

Act.	Duration		Cost, $	
	Normal	Crash	Normal	Crash
A	3	2	400	425
B	8	4	1020	1140
C	2	2	350	350
D	3	2	1250	1315
E	3	2	825	850
F	6	3	610	700
G	4	2	430	550
H	5	3	525	625
I	4	2	390	480
J	8	5	615	675

Overhead Costs = $80/day   **Figure 6-S5**

Completely crash the following network schedule using complex compression, and find the optimum time and least cost.

S6 Use the network of Prob. 6-P2 above.

Figure 6-S6

Act.	Duration		Cost, $				
	Normal	Crash	Normal	Crash 1	Crash 2	Crash 3	Crash 4
A	6	4	800	865	940		
B	12	8	1100	1170	1255	1350	1455
C	10	6	1400	1475	1565	1665	1785
D	8	5	1000	1035	1115	1215	
E	6	4	900	985	1125		
F	4	3	800	840			

Overhead Costs = $30/day

CHAPTER 7

RESOURCE LEVELING

NEW WORDS

Labor allocation The assigning of workers to a project in order to stabilize the work force

WHAT IS RESOURCE LEVELING?

Resource leveling is an attempt to assign resources to project activities in a manner that will improve productivity and efficiency. In this section we will deal with labor, called the work force, but the same approach can be used for allocating other resources such as equipment and money.

WHY SHOULD WE LEVEL THE WORK FORCE?

not alway

Leveling the daily labor allocation may be desirable for several reasons. Some of these are:

1 *Fixed crew size:* Obviously, if the schedule demands more workers per day than are available or if we have workers standing around without jobs, we have a problem.

2 *Learning curve:* When a new hire is trained, there is a loss of productivity. So, if we can keep the trained people and reduce the number of new hires, we should be better off.

3 *Start-up problems:* Every project suffers from start-up problems of some sort. At this time the supervisors are very busy trying to get everybody working in a productive manner. Therefore, if we can start with a small crew and increase its size gradually, we will eliminate some of the start-up problems.

123

4 *Completion congestion:* Most projects suffer from congestion around project completion time because of reduced work areas. Thus, if we can gradually reduce the crew size as we approach project completion, we can improve productivity by reducing congestion.

The hierarchy of importance of these reasons is somewhat arbitrary, but the one we'll use is:

1 Allocate within the crew size available.
2 Try for a level midproject crew size.
3 Try for a gradual buildup of crew size at the start of the project.
4 Try for a gradual drop-off of crew size at the end of the project.

In order to take advantage of labor allocation techniques, the planner must assign a minimum crew size to each activity (less than or equal to the normal crew size). This minimum crew size represents the least number of workers per day that are needed to complete the activity within the planned worker-days (workers times days).

WHAT ASSUMPTIONS SHOULD WE MAKE?

The following assumptions are made:

1 Any worker can do any activity. While this isn't usually the case for a complete project, the allocation techniques are still useful. They can be applied to activities of a certain trade where the assumption is probably true.
2 The number of worker-days needed to complete an activity is fixed. If a planner assigns a normal duration of 5 days and a normal crew size of 4, then the activity will take 20 worker-days. If the planner also assigns a minimum crew size of 3, then the activity could be completed by 4 workers in 5 days, or by 3 workers in 5 days plus 5 workers for 1 day, etc., as long as the crew size was 3, 4, or 5 and the crew's combined efforts totaled 20 worker-days.
3 An activity once started will continue. While this is not a necessary constraint on a real project, it is usually the most efficient way to proceed. Also, this assumption makes the discussion of the allocation techniques somewhat easier.

There are several methods used for resource leveling of the work force, *none of which is much use manually;* however, we will look at a trial-and-error method to get a feel for the tasks involved. We will also look at an algorithm that can be used to assist us in resource leveling.

HOW CAN WE USE TRIAL AND ERROR TO LEVEL THE WORK FORCE?

The following example will help to demonstrate a trial-and-error resource leveling technique for the work force.

Example

Allocate the daily work force for the network schedule shown in Fig. 7-1*a* for a maximum crew size of 13 workers per day. Let's now level the labor requirements, following the rules given:

Rule 1: The CPM logic must be maintained. This means that a preceding activity must be finished, not just in progress, before a succeeding activity can start.

Rule 2: Activities on the critical path(s) must use a normal crew size. This is necessary so that the project will be completed on time.

Rule 3: The planned crew size must be between, and including, the minimum and normal crew sizes.

A histogram created by the early-start and late-start schedules (i.e., all activities start on their early-start or late-start dates) is helpful in visualizing the leveling task to be accomplished. The early-start and late-start histograms for the example problem are shown in Fig. 7-1*b*.

Step 1: Fill in the worksheet of Fig. 7-1*c*, putting brackets around the time frame in which each activity can take place (ES to LF), and fill in the daily allocation for critical activities.

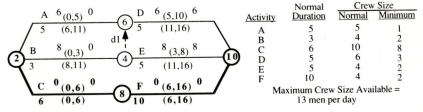

Figure 7-1a
Trial-and-error resource leveling example.

Figure 7-1b
Early-start and late-start histograms.

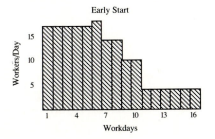
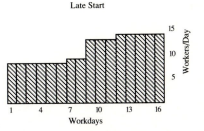

Act.	Norm Dur.	Required Worker-days	Norm	Min.	1	2	3	4	5	6	7	8	9	10	11	12	13	14	15	16
			Crew Size											Workdays						
A	5	25	5	1																
B	3	12	4	2																
C	6	48	8	8	8	8	8	8	8	8										
D	5	30	6	3																
E	5	20	4	2																
F	10	40	4	4							4	4	4	4	4	4	4	4	4	4
	Total = 175		Daily =																	

Figure 7-1c
Trial-and-error resource leveling—critical activities.

Step 2: Try different combinations of labor allocation to find the best fit for the hierarchy of importance and rules given above. Figure 7-1d shows *one possible solution.*

Step 3: Check that (*a*) all daily allocations are within the minimum and maximum crew sizes, (*b*) the network logic is maintained, and (*c*) the sum of the daily allocations equals the total project labor requirement.

The solution shown in Fig. 7-1d fits our maximum crew size of 13 workers per day, but perhaps we can do even better (i.e., require a smaller maxi-

Figure 7-1d
Trial-and-error resource leveling—13 workers per day.

Act.	Norm Dur.	Required Worker-days	Norm	Min.	1	2	3	4	5	6	7	8	9	10	11	12	13	14	15	16
			Crew Size											Workdays						
A	5	25	5	1		3	3	3	3	3	5	5								
B	3	12	4	2			2	2	2	2	4									
C	6	48	8	8	8	8	8	8	8	8										
D	5	30	6	3									5	5	5	5	5	5		
E	5	20	4	2								4	4	4	4	4				
F	10	40	4	4							4	4	4	4	4	4	4	4	4	4
	Total = 175		Daily =		8	11	13	13	13	13	13	13	13	13	13	13	9	9	4	4

Check = 175 Worker-days

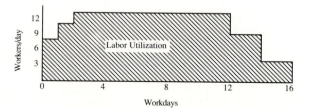

mum crew size). First, let's determine the "theoretical" maximum crew size that would be required if the allocation could be perfectly spread out over the project duration.

$$\text{Maximum crew size} = \frac{175 \text{ worker-days}}{16 \text{ days}} = 10.9 \approx 11 \text{ workers per day}$$

This simply means that it *might* be possible to accomplish the work with no more than 11 workers per day. If the theoretical maximum crew size were 13, no further reduction in the daily allocation would be possible. We can now try steps 2 and 3 again to see if we can reduce the daily requirement. Figure 7-1e shows an allocation requiring a maximum of 12 workers per day. Figure 7-1f shows an allocation requiring only 11 workers per day—the theoretical maximum. No further reduction is possible.

Note: Rarely can a real project approach the theoretical maximum crew size because of work sequencing and the completion congestion mentioned earlier.

HOW CAN WE USE AN ALGORITHM TO LEVEL RESOURCES?

We can also use an algorithm to level resources and use heuristics to eliminate steps that obviously won't lead to a satisfactory solution. Even though this method is sometimes called the histogram method, histograms really have

Figure 7-1e
Trial-and-error resource leveling—12 workers per day.

Act.	Norm Dur.	Required Worker-days	Crew Size Norm	Crew Size Min.	1	2	3	4	5	6	7	8	9	10	11	12	13	14	15	16
A	5	25	5	1		2	2	2	2	2	5	5	5							
B	3	12	4	2				2	2	2	3	3								
C	6	48	8	8	8	8	8	8	8	8										
D	5	30	6	3										5	5	4	4	4	4	4
E	5	20	4	2									3	3	3	3	3	3	2	
F	10	40	4	4							4	4	4	4	4	4	4	4	4	4
Total = 175			Daily =		8	10	10	12	12	12	12	12	12	12	12	11	11	11	10	8

Check = 175 Worker-days

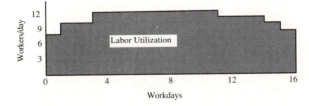

Act.	Norm Dur.	Required Worker-days	Crew Size Norm	Crew Size Min.	Workdays 1	2	3	4	5	6	7	8	9	10	11	12	13	14	15	16
A	5	25	5	1	1	1	1	1	1	1	5	5	5	5						
B	3	12	4	2	2	2	2	2	2	2										
C	6	48	8	8	8	8	8	8	8	8										
D	5	30	6	3											5	5	5	5	5	5
E	5	20	4	2							2	2	2	2	2	2	2	2	2	2
F	10	40	4	4							4	4	4	4	4	4	4	4	4	4
	Total = 175		Daily =		10	11	11	11	11	11	11	11	11	11	11	11	11	11	11	11

Check = 175 Worker-days

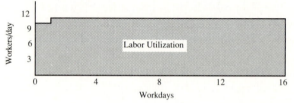

Figure 7-1f
Trial-and-error resource leveling—11 workers per day.

nothing to do with the solution but rather are a convenient way to show the leveling tasks involved. We'll again use the project of Fig. 7-1a as an example to demonstrate this algorithm.

Example

Let us assume that we have 13 workers per day available for the project, and we must try to level our requirements. We will start with a worksheet similar to the one used for the trial-and-error method, filled in with the early-start resource requirements and using a normal crew size, as shown in the upper part of Fig. 7-2.

To start the algorithm we must reduce the resource level for day 1 by at least 4 worker-days (WD). We can only do this by shifting resources from activities A or B because activity C is critical. Keeping in mind that we cannot shift resources from critical activities and that we must maintain the network logic, let's proceed. The lower part of the worksheet of Fig. 7-2 shows our progress.

Day 1: We must move at least 4 WD. Let's choose B and move 4 WD from day 1 to day 4.
Day 2: We must move at least 4 WD. Move 4 WD from B to day 5.
Day 3: We must move at least 4 WD. Move 4 WD from B to day 6.
Day 4: We must move at least 8 WD. Since E can't start until B finishes,

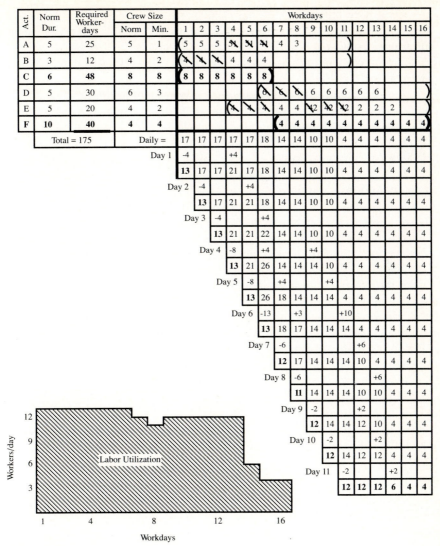

Figure 7-2
Resource leveling algorithm example.

let's move 4 WD from E to day 9. The minimum level for A is 1, so we can move 4 WD from A to day 6.

Day 5: We must move at least 8 WD. Move 4 WD from A to day 7 and 4 WD from A to day 8.

Day 6: We must move at least 13 WD. Since we still must delay E (E follows A), we move 4 WD from E to day 11, 6 WD from D to day 11, and 3 WD from A to day 8.

Day 7: We must move at least 5 WD. Since we must move D (D follows A), we'll move 6 WD to day 12 (we cannot move only 5 WD because the minimum crew size is 3).

Day 8: We must move at least 4 WD. Again we'll move 6 WD from D to day 13.

Day 9: We must move at least 1 WD. We can either move 2 from E (minimum crew size is 2) or 3 from D (minimum crew size is 32). Let's choose E and move 3 WD to day 12.

Day 10: We must move at least 1 WD. Move 3 WD from E to day 13.

Day 11: We must move at least 1 WD. Move 3 WD from E to day 14.

Days 12 to 16: All are equal to or less than 13 workers per day—no further reduction is required.

If we want to go further in reducing the daily labor requirement, we can redo the algorithm from the 13 worker per day schedule or use the 12 or 11 workers per day from our original schedule.

Even though the algorithm is more straightforward than the trial-and-error method, there is no guarantee that it will yield solutions that are as good or better. One major reason for this is that when you move part of the worker-days for an activity, you have to keep in mind the minimum crew size, which restricts how many worker-days you can move. For instance, in the example for 11 workers per day, shown in Fig. 7-1f, we changed activity D from 5 days at 6 workers per day to 6 days at 5 workers per day, but using the algorithm we would never have moved 1 day leaving 5 or moved 5 days leaving 1 because the minimum crew size is 3. This is why manual methods are not very successful for resource leveling. Computers can run the algorithm many times, trying different solutions, until it finds an allocation that levels the resources in accordance with all the rules.

PRACTICE PROBLEMS

P1 Level the daily labor requirement to no more than 9 workers per day, and draw the histogram for your solution. See Fig. 7-P1 and (7-1).

Figure 7-P1

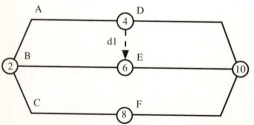

Activity	Normal duration	Crew size	
		Normal	Minimum
A	3	5	3
B	6	4	4
C	4	4	1
D	3	3	1
E	6	4	4
F	2	6	4

(7-1)

P2 Level the daily labor requirement to no more than 10 workers per day, and draw the histogram for your solution. See Fig. 7-P2 and (7-2).

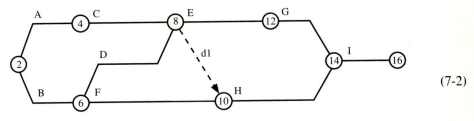

(7-2)

Figure 7-P2

Activity	Normal duration	Crew size	
		Normal	Minimum
A	3	2	1
B	4	2	2
C	6	5	3
D	7	4	2
E	4	3	2
F	10	3	3
G	2	2	1
H	6	3	3
I	2	3	3

P3 Level the daily labor requirement to no more than 8 workers per day, and draw the histogram for your solution. See Fig. 7-P3 and (7-3).

Figure 7-P3

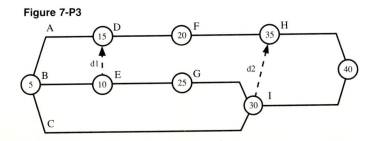

| | Normal | Crew size | |
Activity	duration	Normal	Minimum
A	3	4	2
B	5	4	2
C	6	5	3
D	5	3	1
E	3	2	1
F	5	4	2
G	3	3	2
H	2	3	3
I	3	3	2

(7-3)

P4 Level the daily labor requirement to no more than 10 workers per day, and draw the histogram for your solution. See Fig. 7-P4 and (7-4).

| | Normal | Crew size | |
Activity	duration	Normal	Minimum
A	2	4	2
B	2	5	2
C	5	4	3
D	4	4	2
E	4	3	1
F	4	4	2
G	3	3	1
H	2	3	2
I	3	4	1
J	2	4	2
K	4	3	2
L	3	6	2
M	4	1	1

(7-4)

Figure 7-P4

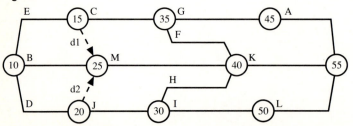

ANSWERS TO PRACTICE PROBLEMS

P1 See Fig. 7-Ps1.

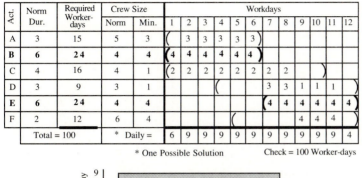

Act.	Norm Dur.	Required Worker-days	Crew Size Norm	Min.	1	2	3	4	5	6	7	8	9	10	11	12
A	3	15	5	3		3	3	3	3	3						
B	6	24	4	4	4	4	4	4	4	4						
C	4	16	4	1	2	2	2	2	2	2	2	2				
D	3	9	3	1							3	3	1	1	1	
E	6	24	4	4							4	4	4	4	4	4
F	2	12	6	4									4	4	4	
	Total = 100		* Daily =		6	9	9	9	9	9	9	9	9	9	9	4

* One Possible Solution   Check = 100 Worker-days

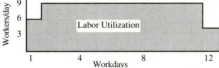

Figure 7-Ps1

P2 See Fig. 7-Ps2.

Figure 7-Ps2

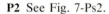

Act.	Norm Dur.	Required Worker-days	Crew Size Norm	Min.	1	2	3	4	5	6	7	8	9	10	11	12	13	14	15	16	17	18	19	20	21	22
A	3	6	2	1	2	2	2																			
B	4	8	2	2	2	2	2	2																		
C	6	30	5	3				3	5	5	5	3	3	3	3											
D	7	28	4	2								4	4	4	4	4	4	4								
E	4	12	3	2															3	3	3	3				
F	10	30	3	3					3	3	3	3	3	3	3	3	3	3								
G	2	4	2	1																			2	2		
H	6	18	3	3															3	3	3	3	3	3		
I	2	6	3	3																					3	3
	Total = 142		* Daily =		4	4	4	5	8	8	8	10	10	10	10	7	7	7	6	6	6	6	5	5	3	3

* One Possible Solution   Check = 142 Worker-days

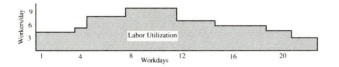

P3 See Fig. 7-Ps3.

P4 See Fig. 7-Ps4.

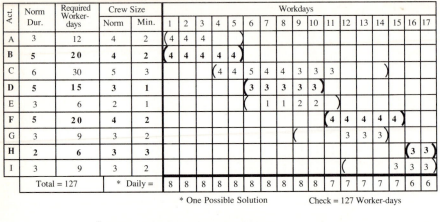

Act.	Norm Dur.	Required Worker-days	Crew Size Norm	Crew Size Min.	1	2	3	4	5	6	7	8	9	10	11	12	13	14	15	16	17
A	3	12	4	2	4	4	4														
B	5	20	4	2	4	4	4	4	4												
C	6	30	5	3				4	4	5	4	4	3	3	3						
D	5	15	3	1						3	3	3	3	3							
E	3	6	2	1							1	1	2	2							
F	5	20	4	2											4	4	4	4	4		
G	3	9	3	2												3	3	3			
H	2	6	3	3																3	3
I	3	9	3	2															3	3	3
	Total = 127		* Daily =		8	8	8	8	8	8	8	8	8	8	7	7	7	7	7	6	6

* One Possible Solution Check = 127 Worker-days

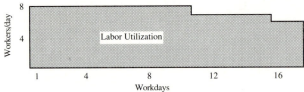

Figure 7-Ps3

Labor Utilization

Figure 7-Ps4

Act.	Norm Dur.	Required Worker-days	Crew Size Norm	Crew Size Min.	1	2	3	4	5	6	7	8	9	10	11	12	13	14	15	16	17
A	2	8	4	2													3	3	2		
B	2	10	5	2	2	2	3	3													
C	5	20	4	3					4	4	4	4	4								
D	4	16	4	2	4	4	4	4													
E	4	12	3	1	3	3	3	3													
F	4	16	4	2										4	4	4	4				
G	3	9	3	1										3	3	3					
H	2	6	3	2							2	2	2								
I	3	12	4	1							4	4	4								
J	2	8	4	2					4	4											
K	4	12	3	2														3	3	3	3
L	3	18	6	2										3	3	3	3	3	3		
M	4	4	1	1					2	2											
	Total = 151		* Daily =		9	9	10	10	10	10	10	10	10	10	10	10	10	9	8	3	3

* One Possible Solution Check = 151 Worker-days

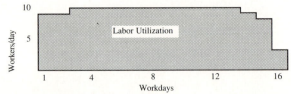

Labor Utilization

JIMBEAU PROJECT

J1 Show the labor allocation worksheet for the ES schedule.
J2 Show the labor allocation worksheet for the LS schedule.
J3 Level the daily labor requirement to no more than 11 workers per day, and draw the resource histogram for your solution.

SUPPLEMENTARY PROBLEMS

S1 Level the daily labor requirement for the schedule of Prob. 3-P3 to no more than 6 workers per day, and draw the histogram for your solution. See (7-5).

Activity	Normal duration	Crew size Normal	Crew size Minimum	Activity	Normal duration	Crew size Normal	Crew size Minimum	(7-5)
A	4	4	2	D	4	3	1	
B	4	3	1	E	4	2	1	
C	2	3	2	F	3	4	2	

S2 Level the daily labor requirement for the schedule of Prob. 3-P4 to no more than 7 workers per day, and draw the histogram for your solution. See (7-6).

Activity	Normal duration	Crew size Normal	Crew size Minimum	Activity	Normal duration	Crew size Normal	Crew size Minimum	(7-6)
A	4	3	2	F	3	3	2	
B	2	3	2	G	4	4	3	
C	5	3	1	H	2	4	2	
D	5	4	2	I	4	3	2	
E	2	6	3					

S3 Level the daily labor requirement for the schedule of Prob. 3-P5 to no more than 9 workers per day, and draw the histogram for your solution. See (7-7).

Activity	Normal duration	Crew size Normal	Crew size Minimum	Activity	Normal duration	Crew size Normal	Crew size Minimum	(7-7)
A	3	5	3	F	2	8	2	
B	5	3	3	G	3	6	3	
C	4	3	1	H	5	3	2	
D	3	3	2	I	3	3	1	
E	5	4	3					

S4 Level the daily labor requirement for the schedule of Prob. 3-P6 to no more than 13 workers per day, and draw the histogram for your solution. See (7-8).

Activity	Normal duration	Crew size Normal	Crew size Minimum	Activity	Normal duration	Crew size Normal	Crew size Minimum	
A	3	2	1	I	4	3	3	
B	2	2	2	J	4	3	2	(7-8)
C	5	3	2	K	2	4	3	
D	3	4	2	L	5	4	2	
E	4	4	3	M	2	4	3	
F	5	2	2	N	3	6	2	
G	5	4	3	O	5	2	2	
H	1	5	1					

PRECEDENCE DIAGRAMING

NEW WORDS

Lead-lag factor   A factor expressing the amount of time one activity must lead or lag another

In an actual construction project many activities have relationships that are not easily expressed with traditional CPM logic. The traditional logic is called finish-start because one activity must finish before the following one can start. In precedence diagraming we use some additional relationships which allow for a better model of the construction process. These relationships allow activities to overlap by letting more than one relationship exist between them.

HOW CAN WE OVERLAP ACTIVITIES?

The relationships allowed in precedence diagraming are shown in Fig. 8-1.

1 *Start-start:* (*a*) This relationship says that after activity A starts, activity B can start.

2 *Finish-finish:* (*b*) This relationship says that after A finishes, B finishes.

3 *Start-finish:* (*c*) This relationship says that after A starts, B can finish. (Activities requiring this relationship are rarely found in construction schedules.)

4 *Finish-start:* (*d*) This relationship says that after A finishes, B can start. (This is the familiar relationship used in traditional CPM.)

In addition to using different relationships, precedence diagraming also uses lead-lag factors which indicate the amount of time that must expire before the action expressed by the relationship can transpire. For instance, in the tradi-

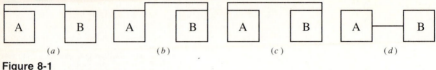

Figure 8-1
Precedence relationships.

tional CPM relationship an activity could start immediately when its predecessor finished—this is a lead-lag factor of 0 because zero time was required after the first activity finished before the latter activity started. In precedence diagraming we can assign a lead-lag factor of any real number (even a percentage can be used). A factor of 2 means that after the first activity finishes, we must wait 2 workdays before starting the latter activity. For example, we have the following sequence of activities:

    A: Place concrete (1 day)
    B: Cure concrete (2 days)
    C: Strip forms (1 day)

    Using traditional CPM relationships, our node diagram would look like the CPM diagram in Fig. 8-2 and with precedence diagraming like the PD diagram in Fig. 8-2. The number 2 is the lead-lag factor. This says C can start 2 days after A finishes. This relationship is useful where a lapse of time between activities is necessary.

    Another common relationship that can be handled well in precedence diagraming is where we have parallel activities but where one must start before the other. For instance, we must pump a pit for 1 day before starting a concrete pour and keep pumping while we pour. The diagrams for this relationship are shown in Fig. 8-3.

    A1: Pump before pour
    A2: Pump during pour
    B: Pour

    This says we can start our pour after pumping for one day, and we keep pumping while we pour.

    The biggest advantage of precedence diagraming is not in the various single

Figure 8-2
Finish-start lead-lag.

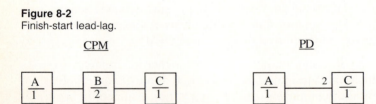

CPM   PD

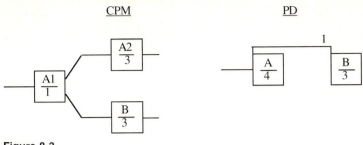

Figure 8-3
Start-start lead-lag.

relationships but in being able to assign multiple relationships between activities. Let us now compare some common construction activities using precedence diagraming relationships with those of CPM.

Start-Start and Finish-Finish: A—clear and grub (4 days); B—lay out site (4 days). We want to start laying out 1 day after we start clearing, but we cannot finish until 1 day after clearing finishes.

CPM: A = A1 (1 day) + A2 (1 day) + A3 (1 day) + A4 (1 day)
        B = B1 (1 day) + B2 (1 day) + B3 (1 day) + B4 (1 day)

Figure 8-4 shows that B can start 1 day after A starts and can finish 1 day after A finishes.

Obviously, this is a better model (i.e., more closely represents what actually happens) for a construction project. In reality, we start our excavation; then as soon as it is safe, we can start our pipe laying. Our pipe laying can follow the excavation until excavation is complete, and then the pipe laying can be completed. In this model we avoid having to break activities into smaller activities and assigning real durations to those small activities, as we must do in the traditional CPM model.

Let's look at the simple example of (8-1).

Figure 8-4
Start-start—finish-finish relationship.

CPM   PD

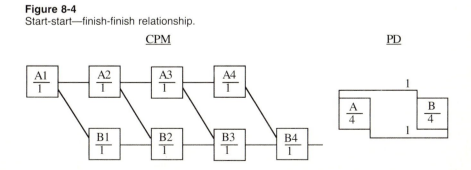

Activity	Duration (days)
A: Clear and grub	2
B: Excavate for foundation	2 (starts 1 day after A starts)
C: Form foundation	2
D: Place rebar	1
E: Place concrete	1
F: Cure concrete	3
G: Strip forms	2
H: Backfill excavation	1

$$(8\text{-}1)$$

Figure 8-5 is a little more complex than the traditional node diagram, but it requires fewer activities. In the traditional node diagram, for start-start—finish-finish relationships, we would have to divide each activity into smaller activities and assign small durations to each. If we wanted to use only whole workdays, our CPM model would indicate a much longer project duration than is necessary. Also, we see that activity F wasn't needed; it was a "wait" activity and was replaced by a lead-lag factor.

Also, it should be noted that this model isn't entirely realistic either. For example, we could not possibly excavate, form, and place rebar in the same place at the same time, but also we don't have to complete one before the next starts. In practice we would start excavating; then as soon as the excavating machine moved a safe distance away, we would start erecting forms; and then after the forms were in place, we would start placing our rebar. By the same token, we would finish erecting forms shortly after excavation was completed, followed by finishing rebar placement.

We can do network calculations for precedence diagrams, but it is not quite as simple as for the traditional CPM network. Let's do the calculations for the previous example to see how it's done. Figure 8-6 shows the calculations.

Forward Pass

A starts on day 0 and finishes on day 2 (0 + duration).

B starts on day 1 (1 day after A starts) and finishes on day 3 (1 + duration).

C starts on day 1 (0 days after B starts) and finishes on day 3 (1 + duration) or (0 days after B finishes), whichever is later.

D starts on day 1 (0 days after C starts) and finishes on day 3 (1 + duration) or (0 days after C finishes), whichever is later.

Figure 8-5
Example—precedence diagraming.

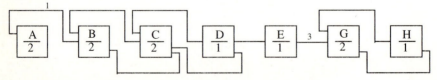

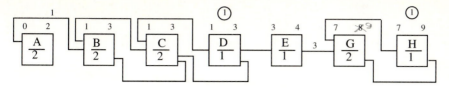

Figure 8-6
Network calculations.

E starts on day 3 (0 days after D finishes) and finishes on day 4 (3 + duration).

G starts on day 7 (3 days after E finishes) and finishes on day 9 (7 + duration).

H starts on day 7 (0 days after G starts) and finishes on day 9 (7 + duration) or (0 days after G finishes), whichever is later.

Float

We can determine the float by subtracting the duration from the difference between EF and ES. See (8-2).

A: $(2-0) - 2 = 0$
B: $(3-1) - 2 = 0$
C: $(3-1) - 2 = 0$
D: $(3-1) - 1 = 1$ (8-2)
E: $(4-3) - 1 = 0$
G: $(9-7) - 2 = 0$
H: $(9-7) - 1 = 1$

The float here is an indication of the slack time an activity will have and does not indicate a discretionary start time as in traditional CPM. For instance, activity D (place rebar) has 1 day float which could be used up by not starting to place rebar until 1 day after starting to erect the forms, or it could be used up by taking work breaks to allow the forming crew to stay ahead, but it could not be used up by completing rebar placement 1 day before form erection was completed.

The previous example is extremely simple. More complex examples require both forward and backward passes, and the critical path is never quite as clear as in traditional CPM. Although it is possible to do precedence diagram calculations manually, it is better left to computers. Actually, many commercial CPM software packages have the capability to perform precedence diagram calculations.

In summary, precedence diagraming, while not a perfect model, is much more realistic for construction operations than traditional CPM or PERT. Because of its complexity, it has not been used much in the past; however, due to the recent availability of network-scheduling software which is capable of precedence networking, its use is growing rapidly in the construction industry.

CHAPTER **9**

PERT

NEW WORDS

Central limit theorem A mathematical theorem that allows us to combine PERT activities with continuous probability distributions to determine the probability distribution of a critical path

PERT Program evaluation and review technique

PERT was developed in the late 1950s for the U.S. Navy's Polaris missile program. While it is similar to CPM and many of the rules for network manipulation are the same, the techniques were developed independently. Basically, the only difference between the two methods is that CPM uses a fixed duration for each activity, while PERT uses a probability distribution.

WHAT ASSUMPTIONS MUST BE MADE?

The following assumptions are made when using PERT:

    1 Each activity's duration can be represented by a continuous probability distribution whose mean (t_e), standard deviation (σ_{te}) and variance (v) can be calculated.

    2 The distribution of the critical path's duration can be found from the t_e's and v's of the activities on the critical path.

    Since PERT is very similar to CPM, only the differences between the two need to be discussed. Briefly, the sequence of events for PERT is as follows:

    1 Plan activities and logic as in CPM, but instead of assigning a fixed duration, assign three duration estimates: optimistic, pessimistic, and most likely.

2 Translate the three estimates into a continuous distribution; then find its mean (t_e), standard deviation (σ_{te}), and variance (v).

3 Use each activity's t_e as its duration, and find the critical path just as we did in CPM.

4 Combine the activities on the critical path to get a probability distribution for the critical path.

5 Using the critical path's distribution, make inferences about the likelihood of the project being completed on or after any given day.

Now let's look at some of the things we just glossed over. First, how do we get the three estimates: optimistic, pessimistic, and most likely? Well, we can find the three estimates just as we found the one estimate in CPM. If we have a history on an activity, perhaps the optimistic estimate would be our best time ever, the pessimistic our worst time ever, and the most likely an average of all previous times. Perhaps we would ask the workers something like, "If all goes well, how long should it take?" If we guess, just guess 3 times.

Second, how do we describe an activity's continuous probability distribution from our three estimates? Well, we describe it by its t_e, σ_{te}, and v which are calculated as follows:

$$t_e = \frac{a + 4m + b}{6}$$

$$\sigma_{te} = \frac{b - a}{6}$$

$$v = \sigma_{te}^2$$

where a = optimistic
m = most likely
b = pessimistic

Then we find the critical path by using the t_e of each activity as its duration.

Third, how do we combine the distributions of the critical path activities to find the distribution of the critical path? The mean of the critical path T_E is the sum of the means t_e of the activities on the critical path, and the variance of the critical path V is the sum of the variances of the same activities. Therefore, the standard deviation of the critical path $\sigma_{TE} = \sqrt{V}$.

Fourth, how do we make inferences about the total project's duration once we have described the distribution of the critical path. This is a tough problem; however, with one little assumption the calculations become rather simple. That assumption is: The critical path does not change. (The importance of this assumption will be discussed later.)

For those who have studied statistics, the critical path has a normal distribution (by using the central limit theorem); thus, the probability of completing an activity by any specific time T_s can be determined by using the Z table (9-1). For those who are strangers to statistics—not to worry!

$$Z = \frac{T_s - T_E}{\sigma_{TE}}$$

where Z = number of standard deviations from mean
$\quad T_E$ = critical path (project) mean
$\quad \sigma_{TE}$ = critical path (project) standard deviation
$\quad T_s$ = any date you choose

Figure 9-1 shows the normal distribution curve.

Z TABLE

Z	P, probability of completing by T_s	Z	P, probability of completing by T_s	
− 3.0	0	+0.1	.54	
−2.5	.01	+0.2	.58	
−2.0	.02	+0.3	.62	
−1.5	.07	+0.4	.66	
−1.4	.08	+0.5	.69	
−1.3	.10	+0.6	.73	
−1.2	.12	+0.7	.76	(9-1)
−1.1	.14	+0.8	.79	
−1.0	.16	+0.9	.82	
−0.9	.18	+1.0	.84	
−0.8	.21	+1.1	.86	
−0.7	.24	+1.2	.88	
−0.6	.27	+1.3	.90	
−0.5	.31	+1.4	.92	
−0.4	.34	+1.5	.93	
−0.3	.38	+2.0	.98	
−0.2	.42	+2.5	.99	
−0.1	.46	+3.0	1.00	
0.0	.50			

For instance, suppose the critical path had a T_E = 20 and a σ_{TE} = 2; then the probability of finishing *by the end* of day 20 is

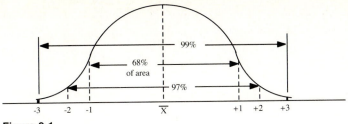

Figure 9-1

$$Z = \frac{20 - 20}{2} = 0$$

From the Z table, $Z = 0$; therefore $P = 50$ percent.

The probability of finishing *by the end* of day 18 is:

$$Z = \frac{18 - 20}{2} = -1$$

From the Z table, $Z = -1$; therefore $P = 16$ percent. *Note:* For any day T_s, the Z table gives the probability of finishing *on or before the end* of that day, *not only on* that day.

WHAT ERRORS MUST BE ACCEPTED?

As with any mathematical model representing a real phenomenon, PERT used on any project is likely to contain errors. Some sources of these errors can be overcome by better mathematical models, while others are uncontrollable. Some questions to ponder are:

1 "The activity's distribution can be described by t_e, σ_{te}, and v where

$$t_e = \frac{a + 4m + b}{6} \qquad \sigma_{te} = \frac{b - a}{6} \qquad \text{and} \qquad v = \sigma_{te}^2$$

How can this be true for every continuous distribution? "Continuous" describes many different distributions as is shown in Fig. 9-2.

Figure 9-2

2 How accurate are a, m, and b?

3 What happens when another path is close to the critical path in duration? What if the critical path(s) changes?

4 What if there are two critical paths, each with the same T_E but different σ_{TE}'s?

5 "Every activity can be described by a continuous probability distribution." This statement may not always be true. Consider the activity "obtain windows." Windows are delivered once a week. What would the activity's distribution look like?

Questions 1 and 2 are uncontrollable by mathematical models because they involve the judgment or estimating ability of a planner. In computer talk this is called garbage-in–garbage-out (GIGO) which means the usefulness of the information derived from the schedule is no better than the information put into its preparation. Questions 3 and 4 can be addressed by PERT but require joint probabilities (i.e., the probability of completing the activity by a certain time depends on the probability of path 1 completing times the probability of path 2 completing, etc.). For question 5, if a planner can somehow describe the probability distributions of all the activities (whether continuous or not), then this question, along with questions 3 and 4, can be answered by simulation (discussed in Chap. 10).

One last question is, "What happens to the PERT model if each activity has a $\sigma_{te} = 0$?" Right! It becomes the CPM model.

HOW DO WE DO PERT NETWORK CALCULATIONS?

Let's look at the example shown in (9-2), but first let's define our terms and subscripts. When we say "by the end of a day," we mean any time from the past up until the end of the day and we use a subscript of -30; if we are concerned only with "on a day" itself, we use 30; and if we refer to "after the end of a day," we use $30 - $.

Example

Assume we perform the CPM calculations with durations $= t_e$ and we find the critical activities given in (9-2).

Crit. act.	a	m	b	σ_{te}	σ_{te}	v
A	4	6	8	6.0		
B	1	7	13	7.0		
C	5	6	7	6.0		
D	5	5	11	6.0		
E	2	4	8	4.3		
F	1	5	7	4.7		
G	7	7	7	7.0		

(9-2)

First, fill out the table of (9-2). See (9-3).

Crit. act.	a	m	b	t_e	σ_{te}	v
A	4	6	8	6.0	.67	.45
B	1	7	13	7.0	2.00	4.00
D	5	5	11	6.0	1.00	1.00
F	1	5	7	4.7	1.00	1.00
G	7	7	7	7.0	.00	.00
				30.7		6.45

(9-3)

Find the following:

1 $T_E = (\sigma_{te}$ rounded to whole day$) = 31$

2 $\sigma_{TE} = \sqrt{\Sigma v} = \sqrt{6.45} = 2.54$

Find the probability that the project will finish:

3 *by the end of* day 31.

$$Z_{-31} = \frac{T_s - T_E}{\sigma_{TE}} = \frac{31 - 31}{2.54} = 0 \qquad P_{-31} = 50\%$$

4 *before the start of* day 37 = *by the end of* day 36.

$$Z_{-36} = \frac{36 - 31}{2.54} = 1.97 \qquad P_{-36} = 98\%$$

5 *during* day 34 = (*by the end of* day 34) − (*by the end of* day 33).

$$Z_{-34} = \frac{34 - 31}{2.54} = 1.18 \qquad P_{-34} = 88\%$$

$$Z_{-33} = \frac{33 - 31}{2.54} = 0.79 \qquad P_{-33} = 79\%$$

$$P_{34} = P_{-34} - P_{-33} = 88 - 79 = 9\%$$

6 *on* days 34, 35, or 36 = (*by the end of* day 36) − (*by the end of* day 33).

$$P_{34,35,36} = P_{-36} - P_{-33} = 98\% \text{ (from step 4)} - 79\%$$

$$\text{(from step 5)} = 19\%$$

7 Find the date of completion with *at least* 93 percent confidence.

$$\text{For } P > 93 \text{ percent, } Z > 1.5 = \frac{T_s - 31}{2.54} \qquad X = 34.81$$

Therefore, the completion date = end of day 35 with *at least* 93 percent confidence.

In the preceding example we assumed that there was only one path that could ever be critical. If there is more than one possible critical path, we must use joint probabilities. Let's look at a network with three possible critical paths.

Path A: $T_e = 31 \qquad \sigma_{TE} = 2.5$
Path B: $T_e = 30 \qquad \sigma_{TE} = 3.0$
Path C: $T_e = 31 \qquad \sigma_{TE} = 2.0$

What is the probability of completing the project by the end of day 30?

$A: Z_{-30} = (30 - 31)/2.5 = -0.40; P_{-30} = 34\%$
$B: Z_{-30} = (30 - 30)/3.0 = 0.50; P_{-30} = 50\%$
$C: Z_{-30} = (30 - 31)/2.0 = -0.50; P_{-30} = 31\%$

$$P_{-30} = (.34) \times (.5) \times (.31) = .053 \approx 5\%$$

PRACTICE PROBLEMS

Fill in the given tables and answer the questions. *Note:* Round t_e, σ_{te}, v, and σ_{TE} to two decimal places, and round T_E to the nearest whole day.

P1 See (9-4).

Crit. act.	a	m	b	t_e	σ_{te}	v
A	6	6	6			
D	2	5	8			
E	2	3	7			
F	6	8	10			
I	2	2	5			

(9-4)

1 $T_E =$
2 $\sigma_{TE} =$

Find the probability that the project will finish:

3 by the end of day 26.
4 before the start of day 25.
5 during day 24.
6 Find the date of completion with *at least* 93 percent confidence.

P2 See (9-5).

Crit. act.	a	m	b	t_e	σt_e	v
A	1	3	5			
C	1	1	4			
E	2	4	6			
F	2	3	7			
H	3	3	9			

(9-5)

1 $T_E =$
2 $\sigma_{TE} =$

Find the probability that the project will finish:

3 at least 2 days early.
4 no more than 1 day early.
5 on T_E.
6 on day 13, 14, *or* 15.
7 by the end of day 17.
8 before the start of day 18.
9 Find the date of completion with at least 83 percent confidence.

P3 See (9-6).

Crit. act.	a	m	b	t_e	σ_{te}	v
B	8	10	12			
D	11	11	15			
F	4	9	11			
G	5	5	7			
I	8	8	8			
K	7	9	11			
L	5	8	8			
M	7	8	9			

(9-6)

1 $T_E =$
2 $\sigma_{TE} =$

Find the probability that the project will finish:

3 by the end of day 69.
4 on day 66.
5 before the start of day 67.
6 Find the date of completion with at least 98 percent confidence.

P4 Here you are given two paths. See (9-7) for path 1 and (9-8) for path 2.

Crit. act.	a	m	b	t_e	σ_{te}	v	
A	6	6	6				
D	3	4	5				(9-7)
G	5	5	8				
J	5	7	9				
M	5	8	8				

Crit. act.	a	m	b	t_e	σ_{te}	v	
B	1	5	6				
C	2	6	10				
E	1	8	9				(9-8)
F	1	4	7				
H	5	7	12				

1 T_E and σ_{TE} (for both paths) =

Find the probability that the project will finish:

2 by the end of day 30.
3 before the start of day 32.
4 after the end of day 31.
5 Find the date of completion with at least 93 percent confidence.

P5 Here you are given three paths. See (9-9).

Path	T_E	σ_{TE}	
1	50	1.00	
2	48	3.00	(9-9)
3	45	5.00	

Find the probability that the project will finish:

1 by the end of day 50.
2 before the start of day 50.

3 after the end of day 52.

4 Find the date of completion with at least 90 percent confidence.

ANSWERS TO PRACTICE PROBLEMS

P1 See (9-10).

Crit. act.	a	m	b	t_e	σ_{te}	v
A	6	6	6	6.0	0	0
D	2	5	8	5.0	1.0	1.0
E	2	3	7	3.5	.83	.69
F	6	8	10	8.0	.67	.45
I	2	2	5	2.5	.50	.25

(9-10)

1 $T_E = 25$

2 $\sigma_{TE} = 1.55$

3 $Z_{-26} = (26 - 25)/1.55 = 0.65; P_{-26} = 75\%$

4 $Z_{-24} = (24 - 25)/1.55 = -0.65; P_{-24} = 26\%$

5 $Z_{-23} = (23 - 25)/1.55 = -1.29; P_{-23} = 10\%; P_{24} = P_{-24} - P_{-23} = 26\% - 10\% = 16\%$

6 For $P > 93\%$, $Z > 1.5 = (X - 25)/1.55; X = 27.325$. Therefore, the completion date = end of day 28 for at least 93 percent confidence.

P2 See (9-11).

Crit. act.	a	m	b	t_e	σ_{te}	v
A	1	3	5	3.0	.67	.45
C	1	1	4	1.5	.50	.25
E	2	4	6	4.0	.67	.45
F	2	3	7	3.5	.83	.69
H	3	3	9	4.0	1.0	1.0

(9-11)

1 $T_E = 16$

2 $\sigma_{TE} = 1.69$

3 $T_E - 2 = 14; Z_{-14} = (14 - 16)/1.69 = -1.18; P_{-14} = 12\%$

4 $T_E - 1 = 15; Z_{-15} = (15 - 16)/1.69 = -0.59; P_{-15} = 27\%$, so $P_{15-} = 100 - 27 = 73\%$

5 $P_{-16} = 50\%; P_{-15} = 27\%; P_{16} = 50 - 17 = 23\%$

6 $P_{-15} = 27\%; Z_{-12} = (12 - 16)/1.69 = -2.37; P_{-12} = 1\%; P_{13,14,15} = 27 - 1 = 26\%$

7 $Z_{-17} = (17 - 16)/1.69 = 0.59; P_{-17} = 73\%$

8 Same as part 7. $P_{-17} = 73\%$

9 For $P > 83\%$, then $Z > 0.95 = (X - 16)/1.69; X = 17.6$

P3 See (9-12).

Crit. act.	a	m	b	t_e	σ_{te}	v
B	8	10	12	10.00	.67	.45
D	11	11	15	11.67	.67	.45
F	4	9	11	8.50	1.17	1.37
G	5	5	7	5.33	.33	.11
I	8	8	8	8.00	.00	.00
K	7	9	11	9.00	.67	.45
L	5	8	8	7.50	.50	.25
M	7	8	9	8.00	.33	.11

$$(9\text{-}12)$$

1 $T_E = 68$

2 $\sigma_{TE} = 1.79$

3 $Z_{-69} = (69 - 68)/1.79 = 0.56; P_{-69} = 71\%$

4 $Z_{-69} = (66 - 68)/1.79 = -1.12; P_{-69} = 14\%$

$Z_{-69} = (65 - 68)/1.79 = -1.68; P_{-69} = 5\%;$

$P_{-69} = 14 - 5 = 9\%$

5 Before the start of day 67 is the same as by the end of day 66, so from part 4, $P_{-66} = 14\%$

6 $P = 98\%$, so $Z = 2.00 = (T_s - 68)/1.79$; Then $T_s = 68.59$ or day 69.

P4 See (9-13) for path 1 and (9-14) for path 2.

Crit. act.	a	m	b	t_e	σ_{te}	v
A	6	6	6	6.0	.00	.00
D	3	4	5	4.0	.33	.11
G	5	5	8	5.5	.50	.25
J	5	7	9	7.0	.67	.45
M	5	8	8	7.5	.50	.25

$$(9\text{-}13)$$

Crit. act.	a	m	b	t_e	σ_{te}	v
B	1	5	6	4.5	.83	.69
C	2	6	10	6.0	1.17	1.37
E	1	8	9	7.0	1.33	1.77
F	1	4	7	4.0	1.00	1.00
H	5	7	12	7.5	1.17	1.37

$$(9\text{-}14)$$

1 For path 1: $T_E = 30$; $\sigma_{TE} = 1.03$
  For path 2: $T_E = 29$; $\sigma_{TE} = 2.57$
2 For path 1: $Z_{-30} = (30 - 30)/1.03 = 0.00$; $P_{-30} = 50\%$
  For path 2: $Z_{-30} = (29 - 30)/2.57 = -0.39$; $P_{-30} = 34\%$
  $\qquad P_{-30} = (0.50) \times (0.34) = 17\%$
3 Before the start of day 32 = before the end of day 31.
  For path 1: $Z_{-31} \qquad = (31 - 30)/1.03 = 0.97$; $P_{-31} = 84\%$
  For path 2: $Z_{-31} \qquad = (31 - 29)/2.57 = 0.78$; $P_{-31} = 78\%$
  $\qquad P_{-31} \qquad = (0.84) \times (0.78) = 66\%$
4 After the end of day 31 = 1 − (before the end of day 31). So from part 3,
$P_{31-} = 1 - 66\% = 34\%$
5 Use trial and error: Try day 33.
  For path 1: $Z_{-33} = (33 - 30)/1.03 = 2.91$; $P_{-33} = 100\%$
  For path 2: $Z_{-33} = (33 - 29)/2.57 = 1.56$; $P_{-33} = 96\%$
  $\qquad P_{-33} = (0.96) \times (1.00) = 96\%$

P5

1 For path 1: $Z_{-50} = (50 - 50)/1.00 = 0.00$; $P_{-50} = 50\%$
  For path 2: $Z_{-50} = (50 - 48)/3.00 = 0.67$; $P_{-50} = 75\%$
  For path 3: $Z_{-50} = (50 - 45)/5.00 = 1.00$; $P_{-50} = 84\%$
  $\qquad P_{-50} = (0.50) \times (0.75) \times (0.84) = 32\%$
2 Before the start of day 50 = by the end of day 49.
  For path 1: $Z_{-49} = (49 - 50)/1.00 = -1.00$; $P_{-49} = 16\%$
  For path 2: $Z_{-49} = (49 - 48)/3.00 = 0.33$; $P_{-49} = 63\%$
  For path 3: $Z_{-49} = (49 - 45)/5.00 = 0.80$; $P_{-49} = 79\%$
  $\qquad P_{-49} = (0.16) \times (0.63) \times (0.79) = 8\%$
3 After the end of day 52 = 1 − (before the end of day 52).
  For path 1: $Z_{-52} = (52 - 50)/1.00 = 2.00$; $P_{-52} = 98\%$
  For path 2: $Z_{-52} = (52 - 48)/3.00 = 1.33$; $P_{-52} = 91\%$
  For path 3: $Z_{-52} = (52 - 45)/5.00 = 1.40$; $P_{-52} = 92\%$
  $\qquad P_{52-} = 1 - [(0.98) \times (0.91) \times (0.92)] = 18\%$
4 Looking at part 3, for before the end of day 52, $P_{-52} = 82\%$.
Try day 53.
  For path 1: $Z_{-53} = (53 - 50)/1.00 = 3.00$; $P_{-53} = 100\%$
  For path 2: $Z_{-53} = (53 - 48)/3.00 = 1.40$; $P_{-53} = 92\%$
  For path 3: $Z_{-53} = (53 - 45)/5.00 = 1.60$; $P_{-53} = 94\%$
  $\qquad P_{-53} = (1.00) \times (0.92) \times (0.94) = 86\%$
This is too low; try day 54:

$$P_{-54} = (1.00) \times (0.94) \times (0.96) = 90\%$$

JIMBEAU PROJECT

J1 Answer the following questions with the data given in (9-15). (*Hint:* There is only 1 critical path.)

Act	a	m	b	Act	a	m	b	Act	a	m	b
A	2	2	2	J	1	1	1	R	3	3	3
B	1	2	3	K	6	8	10	S	3	4	5
C	2	3	4	L	3	6	6	T	2	2	5
D	2	2	2	M	4	6	8	U	6	10	14
E	3	3	6	N	3	4	5	V	2	2	2
F	2	3	4	O	2	5	5	W	2	5	5
G	8	10	12	P	2	3	4	X	3	4	5
H	6	7	8	Q	7	10	13	Y	1	1	1
I	1	1	1								

(9-15)

1 Find T_E and σ_{TE}.

Find the probability that the project will finish:
  2 at least 1 day early.
  3 on day 47.
  4 more than 2 days late.
  5 Find the completion date with at least 80 percent confidence.

J2 Use program PERT, in the Appendix, to perform the PERT calculations for Prob. J1.

SUPPLEMENTAL PROBLEMS

Fill in the given tables and answer the questions.

S1 See (9-16).

Crit. act.	a	m	b	t_e	σ_{te}	v
B	6	8	10			
C	7	7	7			
G	5	5	8			
H	3	6	9			
J	3	6	6			

(9-16)

  1 $T_E =$
  2 $\sigma_{TE} =$

Find the probability that the project will finish:
  3 by the end of day 33.
  4 before the start of day 32.
  5 during day 31.
  6 Find the date of completion with at least 80 percent confidence.

S2 See (9-17).

Crit. act.	a	m	b	t_e	σ_{te}	v
B	3	6	9			
D	2	3	7			
F	3	3	9			
H	6	8	10			
J	1	3	8			

(9-17)

1 $T_E =$
2 $\sigma_{TE} =$

Find the probability that the project will finish:

3 at least 2 days early.
4 no more than 1 day early.
5 on T_E.
6 on days 23, 24, or 25.
7 Find the date of completion with at least 93 percent confidence.

S3

Crit. act.	a	m	b	t_e	σ_{te}	v
A	5	6	7			
B	3	5	7			
E	8	9	13			
F	1	4	4			
I	6	6	6			
J	5	7	9			
M	9	10	14			
N	8	8	11			

(9-18)

1 $T_E =$
2 $\sigma_{TE} =$

Find the probability that the project will finish:

3 by the end of day 58.
4 on day 55.
5 before the start of day 56.
6 Find the date of completion with at least 98 percent confidence.

S4 Here you are given two paths. See (9-19) for path 1 and (9-20) for path 2.

Crit. act.	a	m	b	t_e	σ_{te}	v
B	5	5	5			
D	6	6	9			
F	3	6	6			
H	5	7	9			
J	7	8	9			

(9-19)

Crit. act.	a	m	b	t_e	σ_{te}	v
A	5	5	8			
C	3	6	9			
E	2	6	10			
G	3	6	6			
I	5	7	9			

(9-20)

1 T_E and σ_{TE} (for both paths) =

Find the probability that the project will finish:
2 by the end of day 32.
3 before the start of day 32.
4 after the end of day 31.
5 Find the date of completion with at least 98 percent confidence.

S5 Here you are given three paths. See (9-21).

Path	T_E	σ_{TE}
1	40	1.00
2	37	3.00
3	38	2.00

(9-21)

Find the probability that the project will finish:
1 by the end of day 40.
2 before the start of day 39.
3 after the end of day 41.
4 Find the date of completion with at least 90 percent confidence.

CHAPTER 10

SIMULATION

NEW WORDS

Monte Carlo technique   A technique using random numbers to determine possible activity durations

Random number   A number, in a set of numbers, that has the same chance of being selected as any other number in the set

HOW CAN WE OVERCOME PERT LIMITATIONS?

Some PERT limitations can be overcome by simulation.

Simulation is a relatively new approach in construction network scheduling, made possible by high-speed computers, that can resolve the shortcomings of the PERT model, i.e., handling noncontinuous distributions and multiple critical (or near-critical) paths. It does this by using the Monte Carlo technique—associating random numbers with values in a probability distribution. Let's look at three different cases.

Case 1

Activity E (pour driveway) takes 1 day; no more, no less. Its distribution is shown in Fig. 10-1. So, the probability of finishing in 1 day (P_1) is 100 percent.

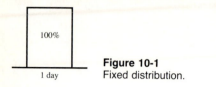

100%

1 day

Figure 10-1
Fixed distribution.

Case 2

Activity N (obtain windows) is expected to take 35 workdays (7 weeks). Since windows are delivered only once a week, it is possible we may get them in 30 days (6 weeks) or in 40 days (8 weeks), etc. We assess the probability of receiving the delivery on time (35 days) as 80 percent, 1 week early (30 days) as 5 percent, 1 week late (40 days) as 15 percent, and less than 30 days or greater than 40 days essentially 0 percent. The noncontinuous distribution is shown in Fig. 10-2. If we choose a random number, such that $0 \leq \# < 1$, and let $0 \leq \# < 0.05 = 30$ days, $0.05 \leq \# < 0.85 = 35$ days, and $0.85 \leq \# < 1 = 40$ days, then $P_{30} = 5$ percent, $P_{35} = 80$ percent, and $P_{40} = 15$ percent.

Case 3

Activity M (framing building) is expected to take 20 days. The probability of being a certain number of days late is considered to be about the same as being the same number of days early. So, we estimate that the distribution is normal with a mean $\bar{X}$ of 20 days and a standard deviation σ of, say, 1 day. The distribution would look like that in Fig. 10-3. From PERT:

$$Z = f(T_s, T_e, \sigma_{TE}) = f(\#) \qquad \text{where } 0 \leq \# < 1$$

Then any random number #, such that $0 \leq \# < 1$, can be equated to a probability which can be associated to Z (by the Z table), and a value of T_s can be calculated. Then T_s will be used as the duration for activity M. For instance, day 20 has Z values of -0.5 to -1.5, day 17 has Z values less than or equal to -2.5, etc. Probabilities are shown in (10-1).

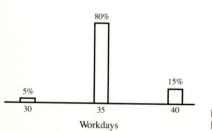

80%

15%

5%

30   35   40

Workdays

Figure 10-2
Noncontinuous distribution.

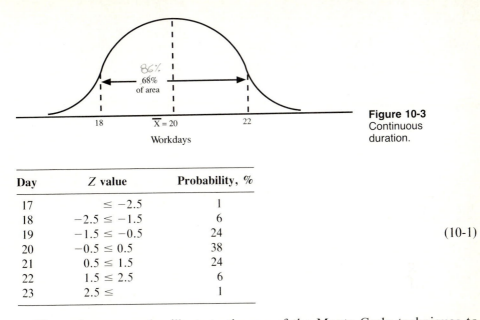

Figure 10-3
Continuous
duration.

Day	Z value	Probability, %
17	≤ -2.5	1
18	$-2.5 \leq -1.5$	6
19	$-1.5 \leq -0.5$	24
20	$-0.5 \leq 0.5$	38
21	$0.5 \leq 1.5$	24
22	$1.5 \leq 2.5$	6
23	$2.5 \leq$	1

(10-1)

These three examples illustrate the use of the Monte Carlo techniques to assign durations to the activities. These assignments correspond to the activities' probability distributions. After the activities in a network are assigned durations by the Monte Carlo technique, the CPM algorithm can be used for network calculations and the project length can be determined. This length represents a possible project length—one iteration in the simulation process. If this process of assigning durations and then solving the CPM calculations is repeated many times, the density of resultant project lengths will describe the probability distribution of the project. Let's look at a simple example.

Example

For the project activities shown in Fig. 10-4, we have historical data recorded from like activities in past projects, as given in (10-2).

Act	Durations	Act	Durations	Act	Durations	
A	6,6,7,7,7	F	7,6	K	(4, 6, 8)	
B	6,5,6,8,8	G	(3, 6)	L	3,3,3,3,3,3	(10-2)
C	(8)	H	($\bar{X} = 4$; $\sigma = 1$)	M	4,5,3,3,6	
D	4,5,6,6,7	I	6,6,6,6,8	N	2,1,2,2,3	
E	5,5,5,7,7,7,	J	5,5,5,6	O	4,1,6,2,4	

For new activities C, G, H, and K we estimate the following: C will take 8 days; G will take either 3 or 6 days with equal probability; K will take either 4, 6, or 8 days with equal probability; and H is normal with a mean and standard deviation as shown above.

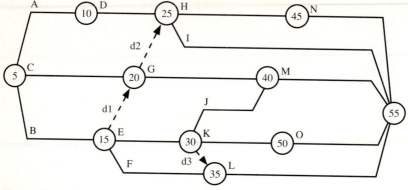

Figure 10-4
Example—arrow diagram.

Step 1: Assign random number ranges to the activities as given in (10-3).

A: 0.00−0.39 = 6; 0.40−0.99 = 7
B: 0.00−0.19 = 5; 0.20−0.59 = 6; 0.60−0.99 = 8
C: 0.00−0.99 = 8
D: 0.00−0.19 = 4; 0.20−0.39 = 5; 0.40−0.79 = 6; 0.80−0.99 = 7
E: 0.00−0.49 = 5; 0.50−0.99 = 7
F: 0.00−0.49 = 6; 0.50−0.99 = 7
G: 0.00−0.49 = 3; 0.50−0.99 = 6
H: 0.00   = 1; 0.01−0.06 = 2; 0.07−0.30 = 3; 0.31−0.68 = 4;
   0.69−0.92 = 5; 0.92−0.98 = 6; 0.99 = 7
I: 0.00−0.79 = 6; 0.80−0.99 = 8   (10-3)
J: 0.00−0.74 = 5; 0.75−0.99 = 6
K: 0.00−0.32 = 4; 0.33−0.66 = 6; 0.67−0.99 = 8
L: 0.00−0.99 = 3
M: 0.00−0.39 = 3; 0.40−0.59 = 4; 0.60−0.79 = 5; 0.80−0.99 = 6
N: 0.00−0.19 = 1; 0.20−0.79 = 2; 0.80−0.99 = 3
O: 0.00−0.19 = 1; 0.20−0.39 = 2; 0.40−0.79 = 4; 0.80−0.99 = 6

Note: Ranges for H are derived from $Z = (T_S - T_E)/\sigma_{TE}$.

Step 2: A random number, $0 \le \# < 1$, is generated for each activity, and then a duration is assigned in accordance with the assignment scheme of step 1. Let's assume on the first passes that the random numbers and the assignments are as given in (10-4).

A:	0.09−6	F:	0.34−6	K:	0.73−6	
B:	0.18−5	G:	0.62−5	L:	0.94−3	
C:	0.81−10	H:	0.44−5	M:	0.65−5	(10-4)
D:	0.39−5	I:	0.38−6	N:	0.17−1	
E:	0.71−6	J:	0.01−1	O:	0.59−4	

Step 3: Perform a forward pass as in CPM to determine the early finish of the project for this iteration, which in this case is as follows:

$$\text{Project length} = \text{ET(55)} = 24 \text{ days}$$

Step 4: Repeat steps 2 and 3 twenty times and record ET(55) for each simulation iteration. Program SIM, in the appendix, gave the results shown in (10-5).

#	ET(55)	#	ET(55)	#	ET(55)	#	ET(55)	
1	27	6	22	11	23	16	25	
2	25	7	23	12	21	17	29	
3	23	8	26	13	22	18	21	(10-5)
4	25	9	22	14	22	19	24	
5	22	10	25	15	24	20	23	

Step 5: Plot the project durations to determine the probability curve for project completion, as shown in Fig. 10-5.

The above example was abbreviated, but for best results from simulation you should perform many iterations, hundreds or thousands. Also, the usefulness is enhanced when you use standard activities for which you have a history and on projects where many critical paths are possible. Figure 10-6 shows how the project length distribution takes shape with increased iterations. Figure 10-6*a* shows 100 iterations, and Fig. 10-6*b* shows 1000 iterations.

In summary, the advantage of this method is that it eliminates the need for

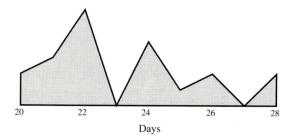

Days

Figure 10-5
Example—project completion distribution.

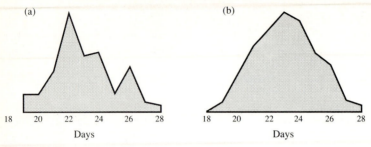

Figure 10-6
Example—project completion distribution.

activities to be described by continuous distributions and the need to keep track of changing critical paths. The disadvantages include the loss of information about the critical path(s) and float; however, modifications to the technique can allow for critical path and float information to be recorded for each simulation iteration and a summary of most likely critical activities and float values to be displayed.

PRACTICE PROBLEMS

P1 For the following project describe a process for using five balls numbered 1 to 5 to perform simulation using the Monte Carlo technique. Past activity times are shown below the activity name. See Fig. 10-P1.

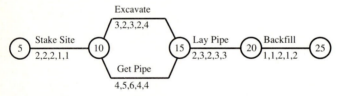

Figure 10-P1

P2 Using random numbers 0 to 99 make an assignment for the schedule of Prob. 3-P6 (5-P6) using past activity durations or estimates given in (10-6).

Act	Past Dur	Estimate	Act	Past Dur	Estimate
A	4,4,5,4,6		I	4,4,4,5	
B	4,5,6		J		1 @ 75%; 2 @ 25%
C		Normal $(\bar{X} = 7; \sigma = 1)$	K		1 @ 100%
			L	2,2,4,2,3	
D	3,3,6,7,5		M	1,1,1,2	
E	3,3,3,3		N	1,1,1,2,1	
F		Normal $(\bar{X} = 6; \sigma = .5)$	O		1 @ 60%; 3 @ 40%
G	1,2,2,3,1				
H	3,5,2				

(10-6)

P3 Use program SIM, in the appendix, to simulate 10 iterations (random number seed = − 1111) for the schedule of Prob. 10-P2.

P4 Use program SIM, in the appendix, to simulate 100 iterations (random number seed = 100) for the schedule of Prob. 3-P9 with the data given in (10-7).

Act	Past Dur	Estimate	Act	Past Dur	Estimate	
A	5,5,6,7,4		M	4,4,4,5		
B	3,3,3		N	2,2,2		
C	2,4,2,2		O	2,2,1,3		
D		$(\bar{X} = 4; \sigma = 1)$	P		2 @ 40%; 4 @ 60%	
E	6,8,11,9		Q	10,17,13		(10-7)
F	2,2,2,3		R	4,5,6,4		
G	6,6,4,5		S		1 @ 100%	
H		3 @ 100%	T	1,1,1,1,2		
I	3,1,2,2		U	7,5,8		
J	3,3,1		V	2,3,3,5,2		
K		1 @ 100%	W	2,3,2		
L	1,3					

ANSWERS TO PRACTICE PROBLEMS

P1 Put the balls in a box and let them represent random numbers.
Step 1: Assign specific balls to past durations.
Step 2: Draw a ball for one activity to determine the duration for one iteration.
Step 3: Do a forward pass to find the simulated project length.

For each activity, let ball numbers represent duration [see (10-8)].

Activity	Ball #'s	Dur, days	
Stake site	1,2	1	
	3,4,5	2	
Excavate	1,2	2	
	3,4	3	
	5	4	
Get pipe	1,2,3	4	(10-8)
	4	5	
	5	6	
Lay pipe	1,2	2	
	3,4,5	3	
Backfill	1,2,3	1	
	4,5	2	

Assume that for each activity the ball number we draw yields the duration [see (10-9)].

Activity	Ball #	Dur, days
Stake site	2	1
Excavate	3	3
Get pipe	1	4
Lay pipe	5	3
Backfill	3	1

(10-9)

Then the project length for one iteration equals 9 days.

P2 One possible assignment scheme is given in (10-10).

A: $0-59 = 4$; $60-79 = 5$; $80-99 = 6$
B: $0-32 = 4$; $33-66 = 5$; $67-99 = 6$
C: $0=4$; $1-6 = 5$; $7-30 = 6$; $31-68 = 7$; $69-92 = 8$; $93-98 = 9$; $99 = 10$
D: $0-39 = 3$; $40-59 = 5$; $60-79 = 6$; $80-99 = 7$
E: $0-99 = 3$
F: $0-32 = 4$; $33-66 = 6$; $67-99 = 8$
G: $0-39 = 1$; $40-79 = 2$; $80-99 = 3$
H: $0-32 = 2$; $33-66 = 3$; $67-99 = 5$
I: $0-74 = 4$; $75-99 = 5$
J: $0-74 = 1$; $75-99 = 2$
K: $0-99 = 1$
L: $0-59 = 2$; $60-79 = 3$; $80-99 = 4$
M: $0-74 = 1$; $75-99 = 2$
N: $0-79 = 1$; $80-99 = 2$
O: $0-59 = 1$; $60-99 = 3$

(10-10)

P3 The output shown in Fig. 10-Ps3a resulted from 10 iterations and a random number seed = -1111. *Note:* You must add activities St $(0 - 99 = 0)$ and Fn $(0 - 99 = 0)$. The DATA statements shown in Fig. 10-Ps3b were used.

P4 The output shown in Fig. 10-Ps4a resulted from 100 iterations and a random number seed = 100. *Note:* You must add activities St $(0 - 99 = 0)$. The DATA statements shown in Fig. 10-Ps4b were used.

JIMBEAU PROJECT

J1 Use program SIM, in the appendix, to simulate 100 iterations (random number seed = 12345) with the data given in (10-11).

Figure 10-Ps3a

TABLE

```
Days-Freq    Days-Freq                      X
  13   2       14   1                        X
  15   4       16   2              X       X  X
  17   1                           X  X  X  X  X
                                  13 14 15 16 17
                         Iterations = 10    Scale Factor = 1
```

The DATA statements shown in Figure 10-Ps3b were used:

```
1320 REM =============== DATA STATEMENTS ===================
1330 DATA 17,4,10,12,-1111
1340 DATA ST,0,1,0,100, A,1,ST,3,4,60,5,20,6,20
1350 DATA B,1,ST,3,4,33,5,34,6,33,
1360 DATA C,1,ST,7,4,1,5,6,6,24,7,38,8,24,9,6,10,1
1370 DATA D,1,A,4,3,40,5,20,6,20,7,20, E,1,B,1,3,100
1380 DATA F,1,B,3,4,33,5,34,6,33
1390 DATA G,2,A,C,3,1,40,2,40,3,20, H,3,A,E,C,3,2,33,3,34,5,33
1400 DATA I,3,A,E,C,2,4,75,5,25, J,1,D,2,1,75,2,25, K,1,D,1,1,100
1410 DATA L,3,G,H,K,3,2,60,3,20,4,20, M,1,J,2,1,75,2,25
1420 DATA N,1,F,2,1,80,2,20, O,2,F,I,2,1,60,3,40
1430 DATA FN,4,L,M,N,O,1,0,100
```

Figure 10-Ps3*b*

TABLE

Days-Freq		Days-Freq	
23	2	24	14
25	17	26	24
27	21	28	15
29	6	31	1

```
                                        X
                                        X
                                        X   X
                                        X   X
                                        X   X
                                        X   X
                                    X   X   X
                                    X   X   X
                                X   X   X   X   X
                                X   X   X   X   X
                                X   X   X   X   X
                                X   X   X   X   X
                                X   X   X   X   X
                                X   X   X   X   X
                                X   X   X   X   X
                                X   X   X   X   X   X
                                X   X   X   X   X   X
                                X   X   X   X   X   X
                            X   X   X   X   X   X   X
                            X   X   X   X   X   X   X   X
                            23 24 25 26 27 28 29 30
                  Iterations = 100    Scale Factor = 1.2
```

Figure 10-Ps4*a*

Figure 10-Ps4*b*

The DATA statements shown in 10-Ps3b were used:

```
1320 REM =============== DATA STATEMENTS ===================
1330 DATA 24,4,100,7,100
1340 DATA ST,0,1,0,100, A,1,ST,4,4,20,5,40,6,20,7,20
1350 DATA B,1,S,1,3,100, C,1,S,2,2,75,4,25
1360 DATA D,2,A,O,7,1,1,2,6,3,24,4,38,5,24,6,6,7,1
1370 DATA E,1,ST,4,6,25,8,25,9,25,11,25, F,2,B,C,2,2,75,3,25
1380 DATA G,4,D,F,R,T,3,4,25,5,25,6,50, H,2,E,M,1,3,100
1390 DATA I,1,V,3,1,25,2,50,3,25, J,1,W,2,1,33,3,67, K,1,W,1,1,100
1400 DATA L,2,H,Q,2,1,50,3,50, M,2,G,U,2,4,75,5,25
1410 DATA N,2,G,U,1,2,100, O,1,S,3,1,25,2,50,3,75
1420 DATA P,1,ST,2,2,40,4,60, Q,1,ST,3,10,33,13,34,17,33
1430 DATA R,1,ST,3,4,50,5,25,6,25, S,1,P,1,1,100
1440 DATA T,1,ST,2,1,80,2,20, U,1,ST,3,5,33,7,34,8,33
1450 DATA V,4,J,K,L,N,3,2,40,3,40,5,20, W,2,H,Q,2,2,67,3,33
```

Act	Durations	Act	Durations	Act	Durations
A	2,2,2	J	4,5,6	R	3,3,3
B	1,2,2,1,3	K	8,8,9,7	S	3,3,2,4,5
C	($\bar{X} = 4$; $\sigma = 1$)	L	4,8,6,7	T	9,11,12,8
D	6,6,7,7	M	4,6,6,8	U	($\bar{X} = 9$; $\sigma = .5$) (10-11)
E	3,4,3,6	N	($\bar{X} = 13$; $\sigma = 1$)	V	2,2,2,3
F	2,3,3,4	O	20,23	W	17,18,15
G	22,17	P	10,11,12	X	3,4,5,3,3
H	($\bar{X} = 22$; $\sigma = .5$)	Q	7,10,13	Y	1,1,1
I	5,5,5,5				

SUPPLEMENTARY PROBLEMS

Use program SIM, in the appendix, to find the project length distribution for the data given in each problem.

S1 Using the schedule of Prob. 5-S3 and the data in (10-12), run program SIM using a random number seed = − 100. Run the program 4 times with iterations = 10, 25, 50, and 500. How does the shape of the curve change with an increase in the number of iterations?

Act	Durations	Act	Durations	Act	Durations
A	5,5,6,6	E	5,6,6,6	I	5,5,5,5
B	7,7,8,6	F	6,8,9,7	J	3,3,2,2 (10-12)
C	4,7,5,5	G	4,5,6,4	K	9,7,8,8
D	6,6,5,5	H	4,6,6,8	L	5,5,6,5

S2 Using the schedule of Prob. 5-S4 and the data in (10-13), run program SIM for 50 iterations. Run the program 3 times, with random number seeds = 32100, 0, −32100. How does the shape of the curve change with an increase in the number of iterations?

Act	Durations	Act	Durations	Act	Durations
A	5,5,5,5	F	8,9	K	3,3,3
B	6,4,4,7,6	G	5	L	3,3,2,4,5 (10-13)
C	5,6,5,6	H	4,3,6,4	M	2,6,4
D	($\bar{X} = 7$; $\sigma = 1$)	I	6,6,8,4	N	($\bar{X} = 4$; $\sigma = .5$)
E	8,8,9,6	J	3,4,4,4,4	O	5,7,4,4,5

OTHER USES FOR NETWORK SCHEDULES

NEW WORDS

Cash flow   The inflow and outflow of cash during a project due to paying for resources (outflow) and receiving progress payments (inflow)

Claims   A legal question, where one party says the other owes something

Cost control   Accounting for the resources expended on the project activities, comparing these to the estimated or budgeted costs, noting variances, and taking action

Progress payment   A periodic payment to the contractor by the owner for work accomplished to date

Sensitivity analysis   An analysis to see how a change in durations of a category of activities affects the project completion date

Trend analysis   An analysis to see if certain categories of activities are habitually early or late

Network schedules were developed, and are primarily used, for scheduling project activities and events against time. However, when a network schedule has been developed for this purpose, you may use it for other important functions.

HOW CAN WE USE CPM IN CLAIMS?

During a project, many unanticipated things happen that cause activities not to be executed as planned. If a contractor gets behind schedule because of an action of the owner which is not in accordance with the contract, he or she will invariably make a claim against the owner for more money and/or more time in which to finish the project. Likewise, if the contractor is not proceeding close to the planned schedule, the owner may claim that the contractor is not living up to contractual obligations and order the contractor to apply more resources to the job. In either case a well-developed and often-updated CPM schedule is very valuable to the claim resolution process.

In order to make use of a CPM schedule to defend, justify, and/or avoid a claim, you should have a detailed schedule approved by both the owner and contractor prior to project commencement. This schedule is then periodically updated and all deviations annotated to explain the rationale for the change. Many of these changes are merely a reflection of the inability of the CPM model to accurately represent a real construction project, but others are caused by actions or inactions by one party which are not in accordance with the contract. These schedules (original, updates, and as-constructed) then add significantly to the project history and help to address claims that pertain to delay.

HOW CAN WE USE CPM IN COST CONTROL?

Assigning estimated costs to activities and summing actual costs for completed activities can help a contractor to keep track of the performance on the current project and help to establish an activity cost history which can be used for estimating future projects.

HOW CAN WE USE CPM IN CASH-FLOW ANALYSIS?

By estimating the direct cost for each activity, the overhead cost for each progress payment period, and the value of work-in-place when each progress payment is due, the contractor can use the CPM network schedule to generate a cash-flow table. Let's look at a simple example.

Example

First, the direct-cost outflow can be determined for both the early-start and late-start schedules.

Direct Cost (× $100)   See (11-1).

Act	Dur	ES	EF	LS	LF	Cost		Act	Dur	ES	EF	LS	LF	Cost	
A	4	0	4	2	6	40		I	4	4	12	8	12	40	
B	5	0	5	0	5	50		J	1	1	10	12	13	10	
C	7	0	7	1	8	70		K	1	1	10	11	12	10	(11-1)
D	5	4	9	6	11	50		L	2	2	13	12	14	20	
E	3	5	8	5	8	30		M	1	1	11	13	14	10	
F	7	5	12	5	12	70		N	1	1	13	13	14	10	
G	2	7	9	10	12	20		O	2	2	14	12	14	30	20
H	3	8	11	9	12	30		P	1	1	15	14	15	10	

Assuming a linear expenditure for the duration of an activity, the direct-cost daily outflow is given in (11-2).

	Day														
	1	2	3	4	5	6	7	8	9	10	11	12	13	14	15
ES	30	30	30	30	30	40	40	40	50	50	40	30	30	10	10
LS	10	20	30	30	30	40	40	40	30	40	50	50	30	40	10

(11-2)

The cumulative direct-cost outflow is given in (11-3).

	Day														
	1	2	3	4	5	6	7	8	9	10	11	12	13	14	15
ES	30	60	90	120	150	190	230	270	320	370	410	440	470	480	490
LS	10	30	60	90	120	160	200	240	270	310	360	410	440	480	490

(11-3)

A graph of the cumulative direct-cost outflow is shown as Fig. 11-1.

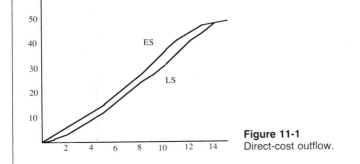

Figure 11-1
Direct-cost outflow.

   In the example suppose the contractor bid $60,000 for the job and is to get paid at the end of each week (5 days) in accordance with how much work-in-place has been accomplished. If the contractor anticipates an early-start schedule with work-in-place equal to 25 percent at the end of week 1, 60 percent at the end of week 2, 100 percent at the end of week 3, and an overhead cost of $2000 per week, cash flow would look as shown in Fig. 11-2. Cash-flow information is very important to the contractor, especially in the case of borrowing working capital to pay for resources—the overdraft is the amount that must be borrowed.

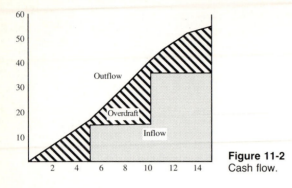

Figure 11-2
Cash flow.

HOW CAN WE USE CPM TO DETERMINE PROGRESS PAYMENTS?

Progress payments, which are paid periodically to the contractor during the construction of a project, are based on the amount of work accomplished to date. Usually this involves the contractor submitting an estimate of the value of work-in-place to the owner and the owner verifying and agreeing to this estimate and then making payments. In addition to the time expended to make and verify the estimate, time is often expended arguing over its accuracy. To reduce this time expenditure and the possibility of conflict over in-progress estimates, the activities in a network schedule can be assigned a value as a percentage of total project price. For instance, an activity such as "placing slab" may be assigned a value of 0.01. It is very easy to determine if this activity is completed, and if it is, the contractor has earned 1 percent of the contract price. At progress payment time, determination of the value of work-in-place requires only an estimate of in-progress activities (percent complete times activity value) plus summing up the activities completed since the last progress payment. To make the process even easier, the contract can call for payment only of completed activities and eliminate the need for estimating the percent complete of in-progress activities. This process requires a somewhat subjective, and never accurate, assignment of values to each project activity, but the savings in overhead by not having to spend time estimating the value of work-in-place and getting involved with the inevitable haggling between contractor and owner make it a worthwhile procedure for many projects, especially where the activities are well-defined and well-understood by both parties.

HOW CAN WE USE CPM IN TREND ANALYSIS?

Sometimes a trend develops where durations of certain categories of activities are habitually more or less than estimated. This can happen for a variety of reasons such as the scheduler for a certain category being overly optimistic or pessimistic or a certain trade performing consistently above or below expectations. A rather simple modification to the standard CPM updating routine can provide information that will help us detect trends and see what effect they will have if allowed to continue.

In order to implement this option, an additional input called "category" is provided for each activity—actually several categories can be added, but for now we'll only address the case of one category. This category is based on the attributes of the activity and identifies those activities that have like attributes for studying their behavior as a group. Some possible categories are listed in (11-4).

GC	General contractor		WE	Welding	
SA	(S)ubcontractor A		EM	Earth moving	
SB	(S)ubcontractor B		WS	Weather sensitive	
CA	Carpenters		PA	Permits and approval	(11-4)
IW	Iron workers		SM	Special material	
LE	Lifting equipment		RT	Radiological testing	

Initially, the CPM schedule which meets the contractual time requirement is agreed upon as the "contract schedule." Following this, periodic updates to the schedule are performed, incorporating the actual performance to date. The differences between planned durations and the actual durations for completed activities are calculated, and an activity performance factor (APF) is generated. To increase the actual performance data available early in the project, we may use both completed activities and in-progress activities, based on the assumption that if an activity has started, its time to completion can be estimated accurately. If we feel that this assumption cannot be made for a certain activity, such as for a long activity, then that activity shouldn't be included in the "actual durations" figure. The APF is a ratio of planned performance to actual performance and is calculated as follows:

$$APF = \frac{actual\ duration}{planned\ duration}$$

An analysis is then run on the completed activities of various categories to determine an overall performance factor for the category. The category performance factor is calculated as follows:

$$CPF = \frac{\Sigma APF\ for\ the\ category}{number\ of\ activities\ for\ the\ category}$$

Also, a check is made on the variance of the APFs within the categories to determine which ones are fairly consistent and which ones are random. Those categories whose APFs are fairly consistent may represent a trend. The more updates, i.e., the more actual data available, the better indicator the APF is.

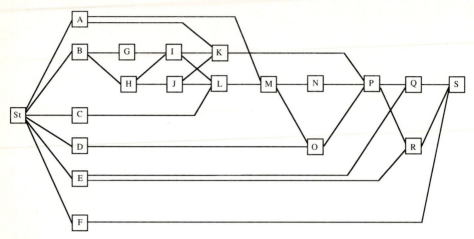

Figure 11-3
Trend and sensitivity analysis.

We will then use these performance factors to draw certain conclusions. If the variance of the APFs within a given category is fairly consistent—either plus *or* minus—then we might deduce either that the scheduler is consistently overoptimistic or underoptimistic with the estimate of activity durations or that there is some problem that is causing activities of that category to be early or late very often. If the variance seems to be random—plus *and* minus—we might deduce that there is no trend and maybe no problem, especially if the variance is small. On the other hand, if the variance is large, it might indicate poor estimating or poor supervision of activities in that category. The following example illustrates the procedure.

Example

Figure 11-3 shows a typical CPM schedule which is the contract schedule agreed upon by the owner and contractor. The project is going to be constructed by the general contractor (GC), subcontractor A (SA), and subcontractor B (SB). The categories are in (11-5).

Activity	Category	Activity	Category	Activity	Category
A	SA	H	SB	N	SA
B	GC	I	SB	O	SA
C	GC	J	GC	P	GC	(11-5)
D	GC	K	SB	Q	GC
E	SA	L	GC	R	SB
F	SA	M	GC	S	SB
G	SB				

The contract schedule is calculated giving the results in (11-6).

Act	Dur	ES	EF	LS	LF	TF	FF	Cat	Cr
A	2	0	2	11	13	11	10	SA	
B	5	0	5	0	5	0	0	GC	*
C	3	0	3	9	12	9	9	GC	
D	4	0	4	13	17	13	13	GC	
E	10	0	10	12	22	12	12	SA	
F	2	0	2	35	37	35	35	SA	
G	3	5	8	7	10	2	2	SB	
H	5	5	10	5	10	0	0	SB	*
I	2	10	12	10	12	0	0	SB	*
J	2	10	12	10	12	0	0	GC	*
K	2	12	14	17	19	5	5	SB	
L	1	12	13	12	13	0	0	GC	*
M	4	13	17	13	17	0	0	GC	*
N	2	17	19	17	19	0	0	SA	*
O	2	17	19	17	19	0	0	SA	*
P	3	19	22	19	22	0	0	GC	*
Q	15	22	37	22	37	0	0	GC	*
R	5	22	27	32	37	10	10	SB	
S	1	37	38	37	38	0	0	SB	*

(11-6)

Ten days after project start the schedule is updated and the status in (11-7) is obtained.

Activity	Status	Category	Days used	Days remaining	APF
A	Complete	SA	3	0	1.50
B	Complete	GC	5	0	1.00
C	Complete	GC	4	0	1.33
D	Complete	GC	4	0	1.00
E	In-progress	SA	10	2	1.20
F	Complete	SA	3	0	1.50
G	In-progress	SB	2	1	1.00
H	In-progress	SB	3	1	0.80
I–J	Not started				

(11-7)

Using the updated data, the scheduler can derive the category performance factors (CPFs), number of activities involved, number of activities over or under the estimated time, and high and low APF [see (11-8)].

Category	CPF	# Act	# over	# under	High APF	Low APF	
SA	1.40	3	3	0	1.50	1.20	(11-8)
SB	0.90	2	0	1	1.00	0.80	
GC	1.11	3	1	0	1.33	1.00	

We can now decide which of the activities appears to indicate a trend that can be factored into the remaining schedule, which indicates poor estimating and bears a close watch, and which shows the expected normal variation.

For those categories that seem to indicate a trend, we can simulate the remaining schedule to see what the results would be if the trend continues. This is done by applying the CPFs to the remaining activities to get new durations and then solving the CPM calculations. New durations are calculated as follows:

$$\text{New duration} = \text{old duration} \times \text{CPF}$$

With the new durations the "what if" schedule can be calculated. If we decide that categories GC and SA will likely continue their performance (i.e., a trend exists) while SB will likely vary about its current estimates, the simulated results are as in (11-9).

Act	Dur	ES	EF	LS	LF	TF	FF	Cat	Cr	
E	2	10	12	22	24	12	12	SA		
G	1	10	11	10	11	0	0	SB	*	
H	1	10	11	10	11	0	0	SB	*	
I	2	11	13	11	13	0	0	SB	*	
J	2	11	13	11	13	0	0	GC	*	
K	2	13	15	19	21	6	6	SB		
L	1	13	14	13	14	0	0	GC	*	(11-9)
M	4	14	18	14	18	0	0	GC	*	
N	3	18	21	18	21	0	0	SA	*	
O	3	18	21	18	21	0	0	SA	*	
P	3	21	22	21	24	0	0	GC	*	
Q	17	24	41	24	41	0	0	GC	*	
R	5	24	29	36	41	12	12	SB		
S	1	41	42	41	42	0	0	SB	*	

Note that project completion has been delayed to day 42, activity K delayed to day 14, etc.

While this example only addresses the case where each activity has only one category, the logic could be applied to multiple categories. For instance, activity A could be categorized as general contractor (GC), carpenters (CA),..., and weather sensitive (WS). If the CE feels that all of these categories exhibit trends, then the new duration is

$$\text{New duration} = \text{old duration} \times \text{CPF}a \times \text{CPF}b \times \cdots \times \text{CPF}n$$

HOW CAN WE USE CPM IN SENSITIVITY ANALYSIS?

Often a contractor must depend on subcontractors to provide a large amount of activity information for a project. This information is then integrated with the contractor's own data to develop the network schedule. It is helpful for the contractor to know which subcontractors have the greatest potential to upset the project schedule and also those which have ample float in their activities. One easy method to gain this information is to perform a sensitivity analysis by varying each subcontractor's activity durations by a percentage and seeing the effect it has on the project completion date. The sensitivity analysis for category SA, with all other categories held constant, gives the results in (11-10).

CPF	Length	CPF	Length	CPF	Length	CPF	Length	
0.5	37	0.9	38	1.3	39	1.7	39	
0.6	37	1.0	38	1.4	39	1.8	40	(11-10)
0.7	37	1.1	38	1.5	39	1.9	40	
0.8	38	1.2	38	1.6	39	2.0	40	

Decisions made from the information derived from the trend and sensitivity analysis procedures cannot be justified by statistics alone for several reasons, among them the small number of samples (activities completed or in progress) and the assumption that activities are independent (i.e., their durations aren't affected by what is happening with other activities). However, the lack of mathematical justification does not negate the usefulness of the additional feedback derived from the procedures. The habitualness of an estimator's time of completion for a category of activities can often be detected and addressed. Also, just the indication of a trend and the results of the sensitivity analysis give a project manager a powerful tool to use to secure schedule adherence. A subcontractor who is showing a trend of poor performance by not completing activities on time, and who, a sensitivity analysis shows, has a great influence on timely completion of the project, can hardly refuse to increase efforts. The excuse that someone else caused the delay can be more easily refuted when it can be shown that the subcontractor's performance is fairly consistent through periodic updates.

MICROCOMPUTER APPLICATIONS

NEW WORDS

Database A computer file containing data on some subject that can be automatically searched and from which desired data can be retrieved

Hardware The physical parts of a computer that you can touch

Software The instructions and data the computer uses

This section discusses some of the many ways computers are used in conjunction with network scheduling.

WHAT TYPES OF COMPUTERS ARE USED?

Computers come in various shapes and sizes, and most can be used for network scheduling. Mainframe computers are large multiuser machines used primarily by institutions and large businesses; minicomputers are midsized machines shared by several users in offices and small businesses; and microcomputers are small, personal computers used by one person at a time. These definitions will serve our purpose here, but be aware that there are many other definitions of computers based on size, speed, number of users, etc.

A computer is made up of hardware and software, the hardware being the physical things and the software being the information. To be more specific, all components are hardware, while programs are software—a disk is hardware, but the information stored on it is software. In this section we will limit our discussion to microcomputers and their commercially available software.

HOW DO WE GET ACCESS TO A COMPUTER?

Like other equipment used in construction, computers and associated peripherals can be purchased, leased, or obtained through a subcontractor. Some advantages and disadvantages for each of these acquisition methods are:

Purchasing: The advantages of purchasing computer equipment are that you can do what you want with it and, theoretically, the cost will be less over the long run than the cost of the other two methods. The principal disadvantage is that computer technology is changing so fast that the owned equipment might suffer obsolescence very quickly.

Leasing: The advantages of leasing are that you have access to modern equipment and and an interested agency to assist in maintenance. The main disadvantages are that leasing is more expensive than owning and there is no guarantee the machine you want will be available.

Subcontracting: The advantage of subcontracting for computer services is that you not only get the advantage of leasing but you also eliminate the worry of maintenance. High cost and the inconvenience of not having the equipment at hand when needed are the principal disadvantages.

WHAT CAN A COMPUTER DO IN NETWORK SCHEDULING?

A computer can do many things, but for us the most important ones involve calculations, which include solving mathematical formulas and making comparisons between numeric or character values. In network scheduling we primarily use the computer to add speed to our network calculations.

All the manual tasks involved in network scheduling can be done by computers, such as changing a PA list to an IPA list, doing forward and backward passes, or finding the least-cost solution. Tasks that involve reasoning, such as selecting activities and describing the interrelationships, cannot really be done by computers. It is possible for the computer to select activities and describe the interrelationships if a similar project has been done before and this data is in a database which the computer can retrieve and duplicate. However, the computer is not making the decisions but only copying what a human has stored previously.

In this chapter we will discuss, and show, the capabilities of several relatively inexpensive software packages that are readily available in the marketplace. We will limit our discussion of hardware to IBM PC and compatible machines that run MS-DOS and Apple Macintosh microcomputers, because the vast majority of available software is designed to run on one of these machines. For the IBM PC and compatible machines, the following three packages will be shown: (*a*) INSTAPLAN by InstaPlan, Inc., (*b*) TIMELINE by Breakthrough, Inc., and (*c*) MICROSOFT PROJECT by Microsoft, Inc., and for the Macintosh, MACPROJECT by SoloSoft, Inc., will be shown.

These programs are representative of those available in the marketplace, and no attempt is made here to evaluate them or to make recommendations.

Various features of the programs will be presented and sample output will be shown for the JIMBEAU project using the data in (12-1).

Act	IPA	Dur	Fixed cost, $	D	E	C	P	L	Unit costs,	$/h
A	*	2	1,000						Driver	23.00
B	A	2		1				2	Electrician	25.00
C	A	3	1,000						Carpenter	22.00
D	A	2	1,500						Painter	18.00
E	B,C	3				2		1	Laborer	12.00
F	D,E	3						2		
G	A	10	500							
H	A	7	3,500							
I	G,H,M	4				2		1		
J	I	1	50							
K	A	8	12,500							
L	F,K	6				2		1		
M	L	6				2		1		(12-1)
N	L	4				1		1		
O	A	5	2,000							
P	L	3				2		1		
Q	M	5				2		1		
R	J,O,P,Q	3				1		1		
S	R	4				1		1		
T	J,O	2				2		1		
U	A	10	1,500							
V	T,X	2				1		1		
W	N,P,U	4					2	1		
X	N,S,U	5					2	1		
Y	V,W	1	150							

All the above-mentioned MS-DOS types of programs accept input data in node diagram format and produce a bar chart which can be printed on a dot-matrix printer. The program outputs shown are only representative samples from the different programs. Each program is easy to use and is capable of generating many more reports and charts. *Note:* Some outputs shown have been cut to fit the text page.

Figure 12-1a to 12-1c shows sample output from INSTAPLAN. Figure 12-1a shows a combined tabular listing with a bar chart, Fig. 12-1b shows a cost report for total costs by calendar week, and Fig. 12-1c shows a graph of total cost vs. time.

Figure 12-2a to 12-2c shows sample output from TIMELINE. Figure 12-2a shows a bar chart, Fig. 12-2b shows a cost report for resources by calendar

```
                Jimbeau                                          Jimbeau
                                    Mar 1989                   Apr                    May
NAME   ESTIMATE  START    END     COST  SLACK 1     8    15   22   29    5   12   19   26    3
--------------------------------------------- +++++++++++++++++++++++++++++++++++++++++++++++++

+ JIMBEAU PLAN
  - JO    43d   03-01-89  04-28-89  $4300   0d   ===================================================
  - A      2d   03-01-89  03-02-89  $1000   0d   ==
  - B      2d   03-03-89  03-06-89   $752   1d     ....
  - C      3d   03-03-89  03-07-89  $1000   0d    =====
  - D      2d   03-03-89  03-06-89  $1500   4d     ......
  - E      3d   03-08-89  03-10-89  $1344   0d        ===
  - F      3d   03-13-89  03-15-89   $576   0d          ===
  - G     10d   03-03-89  03-16-89   $500  15d    ....................
  - H      7d   03-01-89  03-09-89  $3500  22d   .......................
  - I      4d   04-03-89  04-06-89  $1984   0d                       ====
  - J      1d   04-07-89  04-07-89    $50   0d                         =
  - K      8d   03-03-89  03-14-89 $12500   1d    ..............
  - L      6d   03-16-89  03-23-89  $2688   0d             ========
  - M      6d   03-24-89  03-31-89  $2688   0d                  ========
  - N      4d   03-24-89  03-29-89  $1088  20d                  .........
  - O      5d   03-03-89  03-09-89  $2000  29d    .........
  - P      3d   03-24-89  03-28-89  $1344  10d                  ...........
  - Q      5d   04-03-89  04-07-89  $2240   0d                       =====
  - R      3d   04-10-89  04-12-89   $816   0d                            ===
  - S      4d   04-13-89  04-18-89  $1088   0d                             ======
  - T      2d   04-10-89  04-11-89   $896  14d                            ..............
  - U     10d   03-03-89  03-16-89  $1500  33d    ....................
  - V      2d   04-26-89  04-27-89   $544   0d                                        ==
  - W      4d   03-30-89  04-04-89  $1536  23d                 ........................
  - X      5d   04-19-89  04-25-89  $1920   0d                                   =======
  - Y      1d   04-28-89  04-28-89   $150   0d                                          =

                                            Scale :  1 Day  = 1 character(s)
a : Actual date                    m  : MileStone   === : Critical    --- : Normal
                                   ### : Actual bar  >>> : Resource Delay  ... : Slack
```

Figure 12-1*a*
INSTAPLAN schedule report: Gantt chart.

Figure 12-1*b*
INSTAPLAN resource report: cash flow.

```
                              Jimbeau
 1-25-89                                                        1
----------------------------------------------------------------------
 Name                          Capacity    Unit Cost    Accrual
 + Total                       Rollup      na           na

 Allocation by period     Period :  Weeks

 Start Date              Hours  Current Cost   Reference   Variance

   2-27-89                 48      $24176
   3-06-89                136       $2220
   3-13-89                136       $1972
   3-20-89                200       $3460
   3-27-89                304       $5220
   4-03-89                304       $5542
   4-10-89                168       $2756
   4-17-89                144       $2196
   4-24-89                120       $1962

   Total resource cost  $49504
```

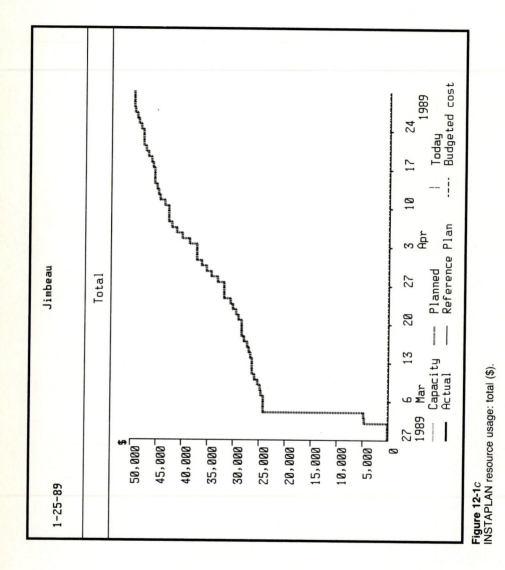

Figure 12-1c
INSTAPLAN resource usage: total ($).

```
Schedule Name:
Project Manager:
As of date:  23-Jan-89     2:15pm    Schedule File: E:JIMBEAU

                  89
                  Mar                    Apr                    May
                  6     13    20    27   3     10    17    24   1     8
A           C ==  .     .     .     .    .     .     .     .    .     .
JO  JO      C ================================================.    .
B   D,L         ==-     .     .     .    .     .     .     .    .     .
D               ==----. .     .     .    .     .     .     .    .     .
C           C   ===     .     .     .    .     .     .     .    .     .
O               =====-----------------.  .     .     .     .    .     .
H               =======---------------.  .     .     .     .    .     .
K               ========-.    .     .    .     .     .     .    .     .
G               ==========--------.   .  .     .     .     .    .     .
U               ==========-------- .   . .     .     .     .    .     .
E   C,L     C   E ===.   .     .     .   .     .     .     .    .     .
F   L       C   . F ===  .     .     .   .     .     .     .    .     .
L   C,L     C   .   .L ======  .     .   .     .     .     .    .     .
P   C,L         .   .     . P ===-    .  .     .     .     .    .     .
N   C,L         .   .     . N ====   .   .     .     .     .    .     .
M   C,L     C   .   .     . M ======. .  .     .     .     .    .     .
W   P,L         .   .     .   .W ====----------------- .   .    .     .
I   E,L     C   .   .     .   . I ==== . .     .     .     .    .     .
Q   C,L     C   .   .     .   . Q =====. .     .     .     .    .     .
J           C   .   .     .   .   . J =. .     .     .     .    .     .
T   C,L         .   .     .   .   . T ==----------- .  .   .    .     .
R   C,L     C   .   .     .   .   . R === .    .     .     .    .     .
S   C,L     C   .   .     .   .   . .S ==== .  .     .     .    .     .
X   P,L     C   .   .     .   .   . . X ===== .      .     .    .     .
V   C,L     C   .   .     .   .   . .     . V == .   .     .    .     .
Y           C   .   .     .   .   . .     . . Y =.   .     .    .     .

------------------------------------------------------------------------
D Done                   === Task           - Slack time (==---), or
C Critical               +++ Started task     Resource delay (---==)
R Resource conflict      M Milestone        > Conflict
r Rescheduled to avoid resource conflict    p Partial dependency
Scale: Each character equals 1 day
------------------------------------------------------------------------
```

Figure 12-2a
TIMELINE Gantt chart report.

week, and Fig. 12-2c shows a histogram depicting the daily requirement for laborers.

Figure 12-3a to 12-3c shows sample output from MICROSOFT PROJECT. Figure 12-3a shows a bar chart, Fig. 12-3b shows a graph of early- and late-start costs vs. time, and Fig. 12-3c shows a cost vs. time report on a workweek basis.

MACPROJECT also uses a node diagram format, but you actually draw the node diagram on the computer screen and the program does the calculations. Figure 12-4a to 12-4c shows sample output from MACPROJECT. Figure 12-4a shows a node diagram drawn by the user, Fig. 12-4b shows a bar chart, and Fig. 12-4c shows a cash-flow table by calendar week.

```
Schedule Name:
Project Manager:
As of date:  23-Jan-89    2:05pm    Schedule File: E:JIMBEAU
```

RESOURCE	27-Feb-89 3-Mar-89	6-Mar-89 10-Mar-89	13-Mar-89 17-Mar-89	20-Mar-89 24-Mar-89	27-Mar-89 31-Mar-89	3-Apr-89 7-Apr-89	10-Apr-89 14-Apr-89	17-Apr-89 21-Apr-89	24-Apr-89 28-Apr-89	TOTAL
C		1,056.00	704.00	2,288.00	2,992.00	1,760.00	1,584.00	352.00	352.00	11,088.00
D	184.00	184.00								368.00
E						1,600.00				1,600.00
JO	300.00	500.00	500.00	500.00	500.00	500.00	500.00	500.00	500.00	4,300.00
L	192.00	480.00	768.00	672.00	1,152.00	1,056.00	672.00	480.00	384.00	5,856.00
M	23,500.00				50.00				1500.00	23,700.00
P					576.00	576.00		864.00	576.00	2,592.00
TOTALS	24,176.00	2,2220.00	1,972.00	3,460.00	5,220.00	5,542.00	2,756.00	2,196.00	1,962.00	49,504.00

Figure 12-2*b*
TIMELINE cost report by period vs. resource.

```
Schedule Name:
Project Manager:
As of date:  23-Jan-89     2:25pm    Schedule File: E:JIMBEAU

          89
          Mar                    Apr                  May
Amount    6    13   20   27     3    10   17   24     1    8
4.00  ...........................................................
3.50  .    .    .    .     .                 .    .    .    .
3.00  .    .    .    .    ###   ##    .    .    .    .
2.50  .    .    .    .    ###   ##    .    .    .    .
2.00  ..##....###......##########.##.....................
1.50  . ##   ###      ##########  ##    .    .    .
1.00  . ## ###################################### .    .
0.50  . ## ###################################### .    .
0.00  -----------------------------------------------------------
```

Figure 12-2*c*
TIMELINE histogram chart report: laborer.

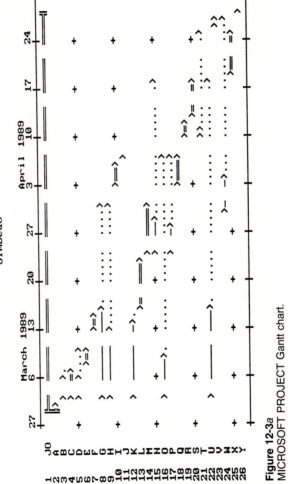

Figure 12-3a
MICROSOFT PROJECT Gantt chart.

183

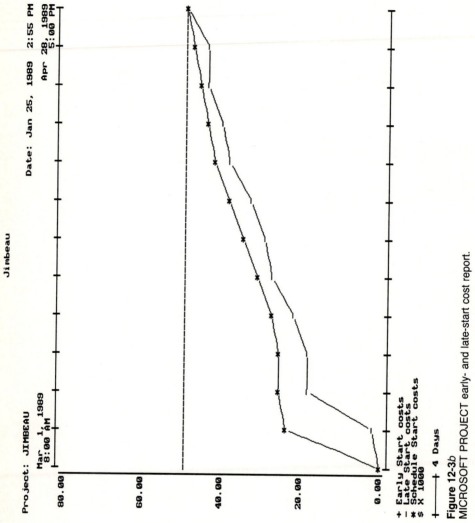

Figure 12-3b
MICROSOFT PROJECT early- and late-start cost report.

Jimbeau

Project: Jimbeau
Time scale: Week

Date: Jan 23, 1898   3:10 PM

Period ending	Mar 8,1989	Mar 15,1989	Mar 22,1989	Mar 29,1989	Apr 5,1989	Apr 12,1989	Apr 19,1989	Apr 26,1989	May 3,1989
1 Driver	$368.00	$0.00	$0.00	$0.00	$0.00	$0.00	$0.00	$0.00	$0.00
2 Elect	$0.00	$0.00	$0.00	$0.00	$800.00	$800.00	$0.00	$0.00	$0.00
3 Carp	$0.00	$1056.00	$1408.00	$3344.00	$1936.00	$2112.00	$880.00	$0.00	$352.00
4 Paint	$0.00	$0.00	$0.00	$0.00	$1152.00	$0.00	$0.00	$1440.00	$0.00
5 Material	$23500.00	$0.00	$0.00	$0.00	$0.00	$50.00	$0.00	$0.00	$150.00
6 Overhead	$500.00	$500.00	$500.00	$500.00	$500.00	$500.00	$500.00	$500.00	$300.00
7 Laborer	$384.00	$672.00	$576.00	$1056.00	$1152.00	$864.00	$480.00	$480.00	$192.00
Total:	$24752.00	$2228.00	$2484.00	$4900.00	$5540.00	$4326.00	$1860.00	$2420.00	$994.00

Figure 12-3c
MICROSOFT PROJECT cash flow.

185

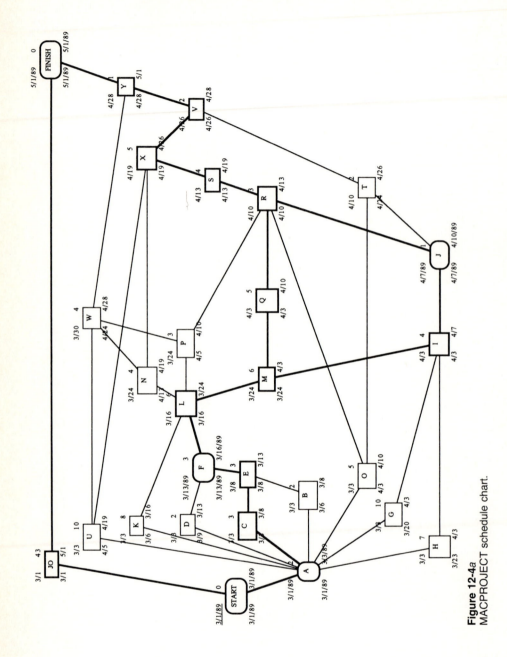

Figure 12-4a
MACPROJECT schedule chart.

186

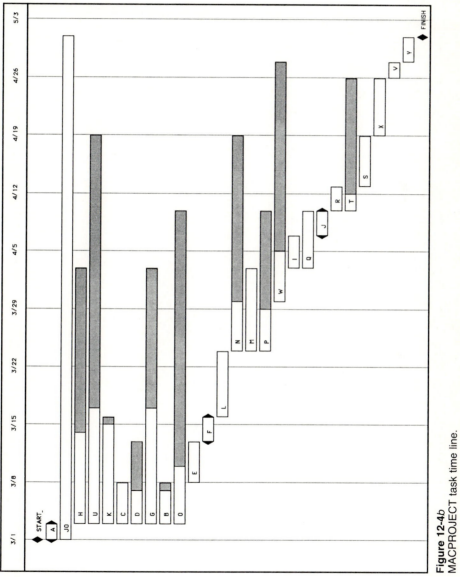

Figure 12-4b
MACPROJECT task time line.

187

Starting	Costs	Income	Ending	Cumulative
3/1/89	24752.00	1000.00	3/8/89	-23752.00
3/8/89	2228.00	20000.00	3/15/89	-5980.00
3/15/89	2484.00	0.00	3/22/89	-8464.00
3/22/89	4900.00	0.00	3/29/89	-13364.00
3/29/89	5540.00	0.00	4/5/89	-18904.00
4/5/89	4326.00	18000.00	4/12/89	-5230.00
4/12/89	1860.00	0.00	4/19/89	-7090.00
4/19/89	2420.00	0.00	4/26/89	-9510.00
4/26/89	994.00	15000.00	5/3/89	4496.00

Figure 12-4c
MACPROJECT cash-flow table.

GLOSSARY

The glossary lists words commonly associated with project scheduling. Most of these words appear in this text, but some do not, and all are included here for easy reference. The definitions given for the words are as they are used in this book, in construction and/or in networks scheduling, not the general meaning of the words as would be given in a dictionary.

Activity   An amount of work that can be identified so that we know what it involves and can recognize when it starts and finishes
Arrow diagram   A method of drawing network schedules using arrows to represent activities; sometimes called an activity-on-arrow diagram
Backward pass   A process to find latest start times and latest finish times for all activities
Bar chart   A nonnetwork scheduling technique (also called a Gantt chart)
Calendar   A normal calendar indicating workdays and nonworkdays for a project
Cash flow   The inflow and outflow of cash during a project due to paying for resources (outflow) and receiving progress payments (inflow)
Central limit theorem   A mathematical theorem that allows us to combine PERT activities with continuous probability distributions to determine the probability distribution of a critical path
Claims   A legal question, where one party says the other owes something
Complex compression   Compression when direct costs of activities vary nonlinearly with their durations or the overhead costs vary nonlinearly with time
Compression   Shortening a project schedule (see Simple and Complex Compression)
Cost control   Accounting for the resources expended on the project activities, comparing them to the estimated or budgeted costs, noting variances, and taking action

CPM A deterministic network-scheduling technique; each activity has a fixed duration

Crash Shortening project activities in order to shorten the project length

Crash cost The cost of an activity at crash duration

Crash duration The minimum practicable duration for any activity

Critical path The longest path or paths from project start to finish

Critical path method See CPM

Database A computer file containing data on some subject that can be automatically searched and from which desired data can be retrieved

Deterministic process Finding a total project duration based on the sum of known activity durations

Direct costs The costs directly attributable to project work items (e.g., labor and materials). These costs are usually nonlinear; to accelerate or to delay the work costs more

Dummy An activity with zero time duration used to express logic, to provide a unique numbering for each activity, and to start or finish a network schedule

Duration The time it takes for an activity to be completed

Early-event time The earliest an event can occur

Early finish The earliest an activity can finish

Early start The earliest an activity can start

Event A connection between two or more activities and at the start and/or finish of a diagram, a node on an arrow diagram, or a link on a node diagram. Events have no duration

Expected time The expected duration of an activity in PERT

Float Flexibility in the starting and/or finishing time of any activity

Forward pass A process to find earliest start and earliest finish times for all activities

Free float The maximum time an activity can be delayed without delaying the start of any succeeding activity

Gantt chart See Bar chart

Hardware The physical parts of a computer that you can touch

Immediate preceding activity See IPA

Independent float Float that can neither interfere with a succeeding activity nor be interfered with by a preceding activity

Interfering float Float that can interfere with succeeding activities but will not delay the project

IPA An activity or activities immediately preceding a given activity

Labor allocation The assigning of workers to a project in order to stabilize the work force

Late-event time The latest an event can occur if the project is to finish on time

Late finish The latest an activity can finish without delaying project completion

Late start The latest an activity can start without delaying project completion

Lead-lag factor A factor expressing the amount of time one activity leads or lags another

Least cost The least total cost for a project

Link A line connecting two activities on a node diagram

Logic relationship The relationship between two activities, such as which, if either, must precede the other

Loop A logic relationship which is circular, such as A before B before C before A. Not allowed in CPM or PERT

Matrix method   A tabular method of solving CPM calculations

Milestone   An event that has some special significance

Monitor   To compare actual project timing with that shown on the target schedule

Monte Carlo technique   A technique using random numbers to simulate possible activity durations for use in simulation

Most-likely time   One of the three activity durations used in PERT (see formulas at the end of the glossary); the one which is most likely to occur

Network   A series of interconnected links with fixed logical relationships

Network schedule   A schedule made up of activities and events that show the interrelationship of these items

Node diagram   A method of drawing network schedules using circles or squares, called nodes, to represent activities; sometimes called an activity-on-node or precedence diagram

Normal cost   The cost of an activity at normal duration

Normal duration   The duration of an activity

Optimistic time   One of the three activity durations used in PERT (see formulas at the end of the glossary); the shortest one which is likely to occur

Optimum time   The project duration at least cost

Overhead costs   The costs which are spread over the entire project (e.g., office, staff, management, equipment). These costs are usually linear, within a range; i.e., one day saved on a project saves one day's overhead costs, and one day's delay costs the same amount

Overlapping activities   Activities that are interdependent but can proceed simultaneously during some period

PA   An activity preceding a given activity

PERT   A stochastic network-scheduling technique; activity durations are described by a probability distribution

Pessimistic time   One of the three activity durations used in PERT (see formulas at the end of the glossary); the longest one which is likely to occur

Planning   Developing a model for the project: identifying activities, assigning durations, and defining relationships

Precedence diagraming   A network scheduling method, similar to CPM, which allows overlapping activities

Preceding activity   See PA

Probability   The chance a project will complete by a specified date in PERT

Program evaluation and review technique   See PERT

Progress payments   The periodic payments to the contractor by the owner for work accomplished to date

Project   An amount of construction work with a well-defined scope

Project control   To monitor and update the target schedule to reflect actual progress

Random number   A number, in a set of numbers, that has the same chance of being selected as any other number in the set

Resource   Something used to construct a project: workers, material, equipment, money, and time

Resource leveling   Allocating resources to a project so as to obtain a desirable daily level

Schedule   A time-based arrangement of project activities; a model showing the sequence and timing of events required for a construction project

Sensitivity analysis   An analysis to see how a change in durations of a category of activities affects the project completion date

Sequence steps   A method to simplify drawing node diagrams

Simple compression   Compression when direct costs of activities vary linearly with their durations, and the overhead costs vary linearly with time

Slack   Same as float, used in PERT; see Float

Software   The information the computer uses; computer programs

Standard deviation   A measure of the expected variation of an activity or a project's duration in PERT

Stochastic process   Finding a probable total project duration based on the sum of probable activity durations

Subnets   Small networks that expand an activity or group of activities used on a network schedule

Target schedule   The project time schedule

Time-phased diagram   A schedule displayed against a time scale

Time zero   The one time of day when work is considered to start and finish

Total float   Maximum time an activity can be delayed without delaying completion of the project

Trend analysis   An analysis to see if certain categories of activities are habitually early or late

Update   To modify the target schedule, based on the latest data, to create a new schedule starting from the time of update

Variance   The square of standard deviation; see Standard deviation

Workday   One day of work on a project

Worker-day   A measure of 1 person working 1 day, used for cost and/or productivity

Worker-hour   A measure of 1 person working 1 hour, used for cost and/or productivity

LIST OF SYMBOLS

a	Optimistic duration for a PERT activity
b	Pessimistic duration for a PERT activity
EET	Earliest an event can occur
EF	Early-finish time for an activity
ER	Early-release time of an event
ES	Early-start time for an activity
FF	Free float of an activity
i	Activity start event
j	Activity finish event
LET	Latest an event can occur
LF	Late-finish time for an activity
LR	Late-release time of an event
LS	Late-start time for an activity
m	Most-likely duration for a PERT activity
t_e	Expected activity duration in PERT
T_E	Expected project duration in PERT
T_s	Scheduled project duration in PERT
v	Activity variance in PERT
V	Critical path or project variance in PERT
σ_{TE}	Critical path or project standard deviation in PERT
σ_{te}	Activity standard deviation in PERT
Z	Number of standard deviations away from the mean for project duration in PERT

FORMULAS

$$t_e = \frac{a + 4m + b}{6}$$

$$\sigma_{t_e} = \frac{b - a}{6}$$

$$v = \sigma_{te}^{\,2}$$

$$V = \Sigma v$$

$$\sigma_{TE} = \sqrt{V}$$

BIBLIOGRAPHY

AGC: *The Use of CPM In Construction*, Associated General Contractors, Washington, D.C., 1976.

Ahuja, Hira N.: *Project Management: Techniques in Planning and Controlling Construction Projects*, John Wiley & Sons, New York, 1984.

Ahuja, Hira N.: *Construction Performance Control by Networks*, John Wiley & Sons, New York, 1976.

Antill, J., and R. Woodhead: *Critical Path Methods in Construction Practice*, 2d ed., John Wiley & Sons, New York, 1982.

Barrie, E., and B. Paulson: *Professional Construction Management*, 2d ed., McGraw-Hill Book Co., New York, 1984.

Benson, B.: *Critical Path Methods in Building Construction*, Prentice-Hall, Englewood Cliffs, N.J., 1970.

Clough, R. H. and G. A. Sears: *Construction Project Management*, 2d ed., John Wiley & Sons, New York, 1979.

Fondahl, J.: *A Non-Computer Approach to the Critical Path Method for the Construction Industry*, Technical Report #9 (revised) 2d ed., Stanford University, The Construction Institute, Department of Civil Engineering, 1962.

Fondahl, J.: *Methods for Extending the Range of Non-Computer Critical Path Applications*, Technical Report #47, Stanford University, The Construction Institute, Department of Civil Engineering, 1964.

Halpin, D. W., and R. W. Woodhead: *Construction Management*, John Wiley & Sons, New York, 1980.

Harris, R.: *Precedence and Arrow Networking Techniques for Construction*, John Wiley & Sons, New York, 1978.

Iannone, A. L., and A. M. Civitello, Jr.: *Construction Scheduling Simplified*, Prentice-Hall, Englewood Cliffs, N.J., 1985.

Moder, J. J. and Phillips, C. R.: *Project Management with CPM and PERT*, 3d ed., McGraw-Hill Book Co., New York, 1983.

O'Brien, James J.: *CPM in Construction Management*, 3d ed., McGraw-Hill Book Co., New York, 1984.

O'Brien, James J.: *Scheduling Handbook*, McGraw-Hill Book Co., New York, 1969.

Paulson, B. C.: *Man-Computer Concepts for Project Management*, The Construction Institute, Technical Report #148, Stanford University, August 1971.

Priluck, Herbert M. and Peter M. Hourihan: *Practical CPM for Construction*, Robert Snow Means Co., Inc., Duxbury, Mass., 1968.

Sears, G. A.: "CPM/Cost: An Integrated Approach," *J. Construction Division*, ASCE, Vol. 107, No. CO2, June 1981, pp. 227–238.

Shaffer, L. R., J. B. Ritter, and W. L. Meyer: *The Critical Path Method*, McGraw-Hill Book Co., New York, 1965.

Stevens, J. D.: *A Study of the Relationship Between Perturbations in Construction Time Schedules and Potential Construction Claims*, Ph.D. Dissertation, Department of Civil Engineering, University of Washington, 1981.

Wiest, J., and F. Levy: *A Management Guide to PERT/CPM*, 2d ed., Prentice-Hall, Englewood Cliffs, N.J., 1977.

COMPUTER PROGRAMS

The following programs are referenced throughout the text. The listings are given in BASIC and can be run on IBM PC (or compatible machines), Apple Macintosh, and other brands.

The BASIC programs listed in the appendix, with enhancements such as color and printing capabilities, plus additional programs which allow data input in both the arrow and node formats are available on 3.5-in or 5.25-in disks in IBM PC format and on 3.5-in disks in Apple Macintosh format. These disks sell for $10.00 each and may be ordered from

> JIMBEAU Construction Management
> P.O. Box 356
> Dawson Springs, KY 42408

The programs are very simple to use "as is" and/or to modify. In an effort to keep the programs simple and their execution times short, many internal checks were forgone. This means that you must be very careful to enter only what is asked for and in the proper format.

All the programs accept input either from the keyboard or from DATA statements. Because of the high probability of making an error when typing in a lengthy set of data from the keyboard, the use of DATA statements is recommended. For those unfamiliar with BASIC programing, detailed instructions for adding your own DATA statements are included at the end of this appendix. *Note:* The DATA statements shown in each listing are those for the example problem in the corresponding section of the text and must be replaced by the appropriate data for the problem you want to solve.

All programs display the output on the screen. The output contains the input data so you can check if the correct data were entered. Some of the programs are given for only node diagram formatted inputs. Programs accepting either arrow or node formatted inputs are available on the disks mentioned above.

PROGRAM PA

This is a simple program that allows the user to input a list of activities and to be queried about which activities must precede others. The output is a preceding activity (PA) list. See (A-1).

Input	Output	
Number of activities	PA list	(A-1)
Activities		

```
10  CLS:PRINT " ========== PA =========="
20  PRINT:INPUT " Type K for Keyboard or D for DATA statement";IM$
30    IF IM$ = "k" THEN IM$ = "K"
40    IF IM$ = "d" THEN IM$ = "D"
50    IF IM$ = "K" THEN PRINT:GOTO 80
60    IF IM$ = "D" THEN READ N:GOTO 90
70  CLS:GOTO 20
80  INPUT "  # OF ACTIVITIES ";N:PRINT
90  DIM A$(N),PA$(N,N),NPA(N)
100 IF IM$ = "D" GOTO 160
110 REM ================ KEYBOARD INPUT =================
120 FOR X = 1 TO N
130  PRINT "Activity #";X;:INPUT A$(X)
140 NEXT X
150 GOTO 200
160 REM =============== DATA STATEMENT INPUT =============
170 FOR X = 1 TO N
180  READ A$(X)
190 NEXT X
200 REM ----------------- CREATE PA LIST ---------------
210 FOR X = 1 TO N
220  CLS:C=1:PRINT:PRINT " MUST PRECEDE  ";A$(X);TAB(40);"TYPE OR N"
230   PRINT "         ========================="
240  FOR Y = 1 TO N
250   IF A$(Y) = A$(X) GOTO 290
260   PRINT A$(Y);:INPUT YN$:IF YN$ = "N" GOTO 290
270    IF YN$ = "n" THEN YN$ = "N":GOTO 290
280     PA$(X,C) = A$(Y):C=C+1:NPA(X)=NPA(X)+1
290  NEXT Y
300 NEXT X
310 GOTO 320
320 REM ================= PA LIST TO SCREEN =============
330 CLS:PRINT " ACT";TAB(33) "PAs":PRINT " ---";TAB(32) "---"
340 FOR X = 1 TO N
350   PRINT A$(X);"  - ";
360  FOR Y = 1 TO NPA(X)
370   PRINT TAB(30) PA$(X,Y)
380    CT=CT+1:IF CT>20 THEN CT=0:INPUT "Hit RETURN To Continue";IM$:CLS
390  NEXT Y
400   CT=CT+1:PRINT
410 NEXT X
420 END
430 REM ================= DATA STATEMENTS ====================
440 DATA 14, "Clear & Grub","Excavate Footing","Rebar Footing"
450 DATA "Place Footing","Install Wall 1","Install Wall 2"
460 DATA "Install Wall 3","Install Wall 4","Install Door 1"
470 DATA "Install Door 3","Install Windows 2&4","Install Roof"
480 DATA "Install Lights","Paint Walls"
```

PROGRAM IPA

This program accepts a PA list and produces an immediately preceding activity (IPA) list. See (A-2).

Input	Output
Number of activities	IPA list
Activities	
Number of PAs	
PAs	

(A-2)

```
10  CLS:PRINT "   ========== IPA =========="
20  PRINT:INPUT " Type K for Keyboard or D for DATA statement ";IM$
30    IF IM$ = "k" THEN IM$ = "K"
40    IF IM$ = "d" THEN IM$ = "D"
50    IF IM$ = "K" THEN PRINT:GOTO 80
60    IF IM$ = "D" THEN READ N:GOTO 90
70  CLS:GOTO 20
80 INPUT "  # OF ACTIVITIES ";N
90  DIM A$(N),PA$(N,N),PA(N,N),IPA(N,N),NPA(N)
100 IF IM$ = "D" THEN GOTO 210
110 REM ---------------- KEYBOARD INPUT -----------------
120 FOR X = 1 TO N
130   CLS:PRINT" ENTER ACTIVITY #";X;:INPUT A$(X)
140    PRINT " # OF PAs FOR " TAB(16) A$(X);:INPUT NPA(X)
150     PRINT "  ENTER PAs FOR " TAB(18) A$(X)
160    FOR Y = 1 TO NPA(X)
170     INPUT "     ";PA$(X,Y)
180    NEXT Y
190  NEXT X
200 GOTO 290
210 REM --------------- DATA STATEMENT INPUT -----------------
220 FOR X = 1 TO N
230   READ A$(X)
240    READ NPA(X)
250    FOR Y = 1 TO NPA(X)
260     READ PA$(X,Y)
270    NEXT Y
280  NEXT X
290 REM ------------- PA REDUCTION TO IPA -------------
300 PRINT:PRINT "   ============ PROCESSING ============"
310 FOR X = 1 TO N
320   FOR Y = 1 TO N
330    FOR Z = 1 TO N
340     IF PA$(X,Y) = A$(Z) THEN PA(X,Y) = Z
350      IPA(X,Y) = PA(X,Y)
360    NEXT Z
370   NEXT Y
380  NEXT X
390 REM ------------------- CREATE IPA LIST -------
400 FOR X = 1 TO N
410   FOR Y = 1 TO NPA(X)
420    FOR Z = 1 TO NPA(X)
430     FOR W = 1 TO NPA(PA(X,Z))
440      IF PA(X,Y) = PA(PA(X,Z),W) THEN IPA(X,Y) = 0
450     NEXT W
460    NEXT Z
470   NEXT Y
480  NEXT X
490 REM ----------------- IPA LIST TO SCREEN -------------
500   CLS:PRINT "ACT - IPAs"
```

```
510  FOR X = 1 TO N
520    PRINT A$(X);"  - ";
530    FOR Y = 1 TO NPA(X)
540      IF IPA(X,Y) = 0 GOTO 560
550        PRINT A$(IPA(X,Y));", ";
560      NEXT Y
570    CT=CT+1:IF CT<18 THEN PRINT:GOTO 600
580    CT=0:PRINT:INPUT "Hit RETURN to see more output ";IM$
590    CLS:PRINT "ACT - IPAs"
600  NEXT X
610 END
620 REM ================ DATA statements ==================
630 DATA 14, A,0, B,1,A, C,2,A,B, D,3,A,B,C, E,4,A,B,C,D, F,4,A,B,C,D
640 DATA G,4,A,B,C,D, H,4,A,B,C,D, I,5,A,B,C,D,E, J,5,A,B,C,D,E
650 DATA K,6,A,B,C,D,F,H, L,8,A,B,C,D,E,F,G,H, M,9,A,B,C,D,E,F,G,H,L
660 DATA N,8,A,B,C,D,E,F,G,H
```

PROGRAM SS

This program accepts an IPA list and produces a sequence-step list. See (A-3).

Input	Output	
Number of activities	SS list	
Activities		(A-3)
Number of IPAs		
IPAs		

```
10 CLS:PRINT "    ============ SS ============":PRINT
20 INPUT " Type K for Keyboard or D for DATA statement ";IM$
30 IF IM$ = "k" THEN IM$ = "K"
40 IF IM$ = "d" THEN IM$ = "D"
50 IF IM$ = "K" THEN PRINT:GOTO 80
60 IF IM$ = "D" THEN READ N:GOTO 90
70 CLS:GOTO 20
80 PRINT:INPUT "  # OF ACTIVITIES ";N
90 M=N+7:DIM A$(M),SS(M),ST(M),NIPA(M),IPA$(M,M),SSC(M,M),FI$(M)
100 IF IM$ = "D" THEN GOTO 200
110 REM --------------- KEYBOARD INPUT ---------------
120 FOR X = 1 TO N
130   CLS:PRINT " Enter Activity #";X;:INPUT A$(X)
140     INPUT " Enter # of IPAs ";NIPA(X)
150     FOR Y = 1 TO NIPA(X)
160     INPUT "  Enter next IPA ";IPA$(X,Y)
170     NEXT Y
180   NEXT X
190 GOTO 280
200 REM -------------- DATA STATEMENT INPUT ---------------
210 FOR X = 1 TO N
220   READ A$(X)
230   READ NIPA(X)
240   FOR Y = 1 TO NIPA(X)
250   READ IPA$(X,Y)
260   NEXT Y
270 NEXT X
280 PRINT:PRINT "  ============ PROCESSING ===========":PRINT
290 REM --------------- CHECK FOR St --------------
300 FOR X = 1 TO N
310   IF NIPA(X) = 0 THEN CS = CS + 1
320   IF CS < 2 GOTO 340
```

```
330  AST = 1:GOTO 350
340  NEXT X
350  REM ---------------- CHECK FOR Fn --------------
360  FOR X = 1 TO N
370  FOR Y = 1 TO N
380   FOR Z = 1 TO N
390    IF A$(X) = IPA$(Y,Z) GOTO 430
400    NEXT Z
410   NEXT Y
420   CF=CF+1:FI$(CF)=A$(X)
430  NEXT X
440  REM ---------------- ADD St ----------------
450  IF AST <> 1 GOTO 550
460  N = N + 1
470  FOR X = N TO 2 STEP -1
480   A$(X) = A$(X-1):NIPA(X) = NIPA(X-1)
490   FOR Y = 1 TO NIPA(X)
500    IPA$(X,Y) = IPA$(X-1,Y)
510   NEXT Y
520   IF NIPA(X)=0 THEN NIPA(X)=1:IPA$(X,1)="St"
530  NEXT X
540  A$(1) = "St":NIPA(1) = 0
550  REM ---------------- ADD Fn ----------------
560   IF CF < 2 GOTO 610
570   N=N+1:A$(N) = "Fn":NIPA(N) = CF
580   FOR X = 1 TO CF
590    IPA$(N,X) = FI$(X)
600   NEXT X
610  REM ----------------- FIND SS -----------------
620   X=1:SS(X)=1
630  FOR U = 2 TO N
640   FOR V = 1 TO NIPA(U)
650    IF IPA$(U,V) = A$(X) THEN SSC(U,V) = SS(X)
660   NEXT V
670  NEXT U
680  FOR X = 2 TO N
690   IF SS(X) > 0 GOTO 750
700   FOR Y = 1 TO NIPA(X)
710    IF SSC(X,Y) = 0 GOTO 750
720    IF SSC(X,Y) > ST(X) THEN ST(X) = SSC(X,Y)
730   NEXT Y
740   SS(X)=ST(X)+1:GOTO 630
750  NEXT X
760  REM -------------------- PRINT SS -----------------------
770  PRINT "ACT-SS   ACT-SS   ACT-SS   ACT-SS   ACT-SS   ACT-SS   ACT-SS"
780  PRINT "----------  ----------  ----------  ----------  ----------  ----------  ----------"
790  FOR X = 1 TO N STEP 7
800   PRINT TAB(2) A$(X);TAB(5) SS(X);:IF X = N GOTO 880
810   PRINT TAB(12) A$(X+1);TAB(15) SS(X+1);:IF X+1 = N GOTO 880
820   PRINT TAB(22) A$(X+2);TAB(25) SS(X+2);:IF X+2 = N GOTO 880
830   PRINT TAB(32) A$(X+3);TAB(35) SS(X+3);:IF X+3 = N GOTO 880
840   PRINT TAB(42) ADATA STATEMENTS --$(X+4);TAB(45) SS(X+4);:IF X+4 = N GOTO 880
850   PRINT TAB(52) A$(X+5);TAB(55) SS(X+5);:IF X+5 = N GOTO 880
860   PRINT TAB(62) A$(X+6);TAB(65) SS(X+6)
870  NEXT X
880  END
890  REM ================= DATA statements ==================
900  DATA 9, A,0, B,0, C,0, D,1,A, E,3,A,B,C, F,3,A,B,C
910  DATA G,2,E,F, H,2,D,G, I,2,D,G
```

PROGRAM CPM-A

This program accepts CPM network data in the arrow diagram format and performs the network calculations. See (A-4).

Input	Output	
Number of activities	Inputs	
Activities	ES, EF, LS, LF, FF, and TF	(A-4)
i and j nodes	Critical activities	
Durations		

```
10 CLS:PRINT " ========== CPM-A ==========":PRINT
20 INPUT " Hit K for Keyboard or D for DATA file ";IM$
30 IF IM$ = "d" THEN IM$ = "D"
40 IF IM$ = "k" THEN IM$ = "K"
50 IF IM$ = "D" THEN READ N:GOTO 100
60 IF IM$ = "K" THEN PRINT:GOTO 90
70 CLS:GOTO 20
80 REM ----------- INPUT -----------
90 PRINT:INPUT " Enter # of activities";N
100 M=N+1:CT=1
110 DIM A$(M),I(M),J(M),D(M),ES(M),EF(M),LS(M),LF(M),FF(M),TF(M)
120 DIM TI(M),TJ(M),TN(M+1),ND(M),ET(M),LT(M)
130 IF IM$ = "D" GOTO 220
140 REM ---------------- KEYBOARD INPUT --------------------
150 FOR X = 1 TO N
160   PRINT:PRINT "Activity #";X;:INPUT A$(X)
170   INPUT "      i,j nodes ";I(X),J(X)
180   INPUT "        Duration";D(X)
190   CT=CT+1:IF CT > 3 THEN CLS:CT=0
200 NEXT X
210 GOTO 260
220 REM ---------------- DATA STATEMENT INPUT -----------------
230 FOR X = 1 TO N
240   READ A$(X),I(X),J(X),D(X)
250 NEXT X
260 PRINT:PRINT " ============== PROCESSING =============="
270 REM ----------- REARRANGE IN TECHNOLOGICAL ORDER ---------
280 FOR X = 1 TO N
290   FOR Y = X+1 TO N
300   IF I(X) < I(Y) THEN GOTO 360
310   IF I(X) = I(Y) THEN GOTO 340
320    SWAP A$(X),A$(Y):SWAP I(X),I(Y):SWAP J(X),J(Y):SWAP D(X),D(Y)
330    GOTO 360
340   IF J(X) < J(Y) THEN GOTO 360
350    SWAP A$(X),A$(Y):SWAP I(X),I(Y):SWAP J(X),J(Y):SWAP D(X),D(Y)
360   NEXT Y
370 NEXT X
380 REM ------------ SAVE ORIGINAL NODE NUMBERS ----------------
390 FOR X = 1 TO N
400   TI(X)=I(X):TJ(X)=J(X)
410 NEXT X
420 REM --------- REDUCE I,J ---------
430 LOI = 9999: HIJ = 0
440 FOR X = 1 TO N
450   IF I(X) < LOI THEN LOI = I(X)
460   IF J(X) > HIJ THEN HIJ = J(X)
470 NEXT X
480 REM ----- FIND # OF NODES -----
```

```
490  FOR X = 1 TO N
500    TN(X) = I(X)
510  NEXT X
520    NN = 1: ND(1) = LOI: TN(N+1) = HIJ
530  FOR X = 1 TO N
540    FOR Y = X+1 TO N+1
550    IF TN(X) = TN(Y) THEN GOTO 570
560      NN = NN + 1: ND(NN) = TN(Y): X = Y
570    NEXT Y
580  NEXT X
590 REM --------- NODE REDUCTION ------------
600  FOR X = 1 TO NN
610    FOR Y = 1 TO N
620    IF I(Y) = ND(X) THEN I(Y) = X
630    IF J(Y) = ND(X) THEN J(Y) = X
640    NEXT Y
650  NEXT X
660  FOR X = 1 TO N
670    IF J(X) > HJ THEN HJ = J(X)
680  NEXT X
690 REM ----------------- CPM ALGORITHM ----------------
700 REM ------ INITIALIZE ET -------
710  FOR X = 1 TO N+1
720    ET(X) = 0
730  NEXT X
740 REM ------ FORWARD PASS --------
750  FOR X = 2 TO HJ
760    FOR Y = 1 TO N
770    IF J(Y) <> X THEN GOTO 810
780      EX = ET(I(Y)) + D(Y)
790    IF EX  < ET(X) THEN GOTO 810
800      ET(X) = EX
810    NEXT Y
820  NEXT X
830 REM ------ ET/LT WRAPAROUND ------
840  LT(HJ) = ET(HJ)
850 REM ------ INITIALIZE LT ---------
860  FOR X = 1 TO HJ
870    LT(X) = LT(HJ)
880  NEXT X
890 REM ------ BACKWARD PASS -------
900  FOR X = HJ TO 2 STEP -1
910    FOR Y = N TO 1 STEP -1
920    IF I(Y) <> X THEN GOTO 960
930      LX = LT(J(Y)) - D(Y)
940    IF LX > LT(X) THEN GOTO 960
950      LT(X) = LX
960    NEXT Y
970  NEXT X
980 REM ------ CALCULATE ES,LS,EF & LF -------
990  FOR X = 1 TO N
1000   ES(X)=ET(I(X)):EF(X)=ES(X)+D(X):LF(X)=LT(J(X)):LS(X)=LF(X)-D(X)
1010 NEXT X
1020 REM ------ CALCULATE TF & FF -------
1030 FOR X = 1 TO N
1040   TF(X)=LT(J(X))-ET(I(X))-D(X):FF(X)=ET(J(X))-ET(I(X))-D(X)
1050 NEXT X
1060 REM ------ RESTORE ORIGINAL NODE NUMBERS -------
1070 FOR X = 1 TO N
1080   I(X)=TI(X):J(X)=TJ(X)
```

```
1090 NEXT X
1100 REM -------- PRINT RESULTS ---------
1110 CLS:PRINT "ACT I   J    D    ES EF   LS LF   TF FF   CRIT"
1120 PRINT "--- --  --   --  -- --   -- --   -- -- --   --"
1130 FOR X = 1 TO N
1140  PRINT TAB(2) A$(X);TAB(5) I(X);TAB(11) J(X);TAB(18) D(X);TAB(25) ES(X);
1150  PRINT TAB(30) EF(X);TAB(37) LS(X);TAB(42) LF(X);TAB(49) TF(X);
1160  PRINT TAB(54) FF(X);:IF TF(X)=0 THEN PRINT TAB(62) "*"
1170  CT=CT+1:IF CT < 21 GOTO 1210
1180  CT=0:PRINT:INPUT "Hit RETURN to see more Output :;IM$
1190 CLS:PRINT "ACT I   J    D    ES EF   LS LF   TF FF   CRIT"
1200 PRINT "--- --  --   --  -- --   -- --   -- -- --   --"
1210 NEXT X
1220 END
1230 REM --------------- DATA STATEMENTS ----------------
1240 DATA 7, A,2,4,2, B,4,6,4, C,4,8,3, D,6,10,3, E,8,10,4
1250 DATA F,10,12,2, d1,6,8,0
```

PROGRAM CPM-N

This program accepts CPM network data in the node diagram format and performs the network calculations. See (A-5).

Input	Output	
Number of activities	Inputs	
Maximum number of	ES, EF, LS, LF,	
IPAs	FF, and TF	(A-5)
Activities	Critical activities	
Durations		
Number of IPAs		
IPAs		

```
10 CLS:PRINT " ========== CPM-N ==========":PRINT
20 INPUT " Hit K for Keyboard or D for DATA file ";IM$
30  IF IM$ = "d" THEN IM$ = "D"
40  IF IM$ = "k" THEN IM$ = "K"
50  IF IM$ = "D" THEN READ N,M:GOTO 100
60  IF IM$ = "K" THEN PRINT:GOTO 80
70 CLS: GOTO 20
80 PRINT:INPUT " Enter # of activities";N
90  PRINT:INPUT "MAX. # OF IPAs FOR ANY ACTIVITY = ";M
100 DIM A$(N),NIPA(N),D(N),ES(N),EF(N),SS(N),ST(N),LS(N),LF(N)
110 DIM FF(N),TF(N),IPA$(N,M),MAT(N,N),SPA(N,M):PRINT:CT=1
120 IF IM$ = "D" GOTO 240
130 REM ------------- KEYBOARD INPUT -----------------
140 FOR X = 1 TO N
150   PRINT:PRINT "Activity #";X;:INPUT A$(X)
160   INPUT "       Duration";D(X)
170   INPUT "       # of IPAs ";NIPA(X)
180 FOR Y = 1 TO NIPA(X)
190   INPUT "            IPA = ";IPA$(X,Y)
200   NEXT Y
210   CT=CT+1:IF CT > 3 THEN CLS:CT=0
220 NEXT X
230 GOTO 310
240 REM -------------- DATA STATEMENT INPUT -------------
250 FOR X = 1 TO N
260   READ A$(X),D(X),NIPA(X)
270   FOR Y = 1 TO NIPA(X)
280   READ IPA$(X,Y)
290   NEXT Y
300 NEXT X
310 PRINT:PRINT " =========== PROCESSING =========="
320 REM ------------ FIND SEQUENCE STEPS -----------
330   X=1:SS(X)=1
340 FOR U = 2 TO N
350   FOR V = 1 TO NIPA(U)
360   IF IPA$(U,V) = A$(X) THEN SPA(U,V) = SS(X)
370   NEXT V
380 NEXT U
390 FOR X = 2 TO N
400   IF SS(X) > 0 GOTO 460
410   FOR Y = 1 TO NIPA(X)
420   IF SPA(X,Y) = 0 GOTO 460
430   IF SPA(X,Y) > ST(X) THEN ST(X) = SPA(X,Y)
440   NEXT Y
450   SS(X)=ST(X)+1:GOTO 340
460 NEXT X
470 REM ------------- ORDERING ACTIVITIES BY SS ---------------
480 FOR X = 1 TO N
490   FOR Y = X TO N
500   IF SS(X) <= SS(Y) GOTO 560
510   SWAP A$(X),A$(Y):SWAP NIPA(X),NIPA(Y)
520   SWAP SS(X),SS(Y):SWAP D(X),D(Y)
530   FOR Z = 1 TO M
540   SWAP IPA$(X,Z),IPA$(Y,Z)
```

```
550    NEXT Z
560    NEXT Y
570    NEXT X
580 REM ------------ ACT & IPA TO #s ------
590    FOR X = 1 TO N
600    FOR Y = 1 TO M
610     SPA(X,Y) = 0
620    NEXT Y
630    NEXT X
640    FOR X = 1 TO N
650    FOR Y = 1 TO N
660     FOR Z = 1 TO NIPA(Y)
670      IF IPA$(Y,Z) = A$(X) THEN SPA(Y,Z) = X
680     NEXT Z
690    NEXT Y
700    NEXT X
710 REM -------------- FIND ES & EF ------
720    ES(1)=W
730    FOR X = 1 TO N
740    FOR Y = 1 TO N
750     FOR Z = 1 TO NIPA(X)
760      IF EF(SPA(Y,Z)) > ES(Y) THEN ES(Y) = EF(SPA(Y,Z))
770      EF(Y) = ES(Y) + D(Y)
780     NEXT Z
790    NEXT Y
800    NEXT X
810 REM ---------- CREATE FF MATRIX ------
820    FOR X = 1 TO N
830    FOR Y = 1 TO N
840     MAT(X,Y)=-1:FF(X)=99
850    NEXT Y
860    NEXT X
870    FOR X = 1 TO N
880    FOR Y = 1 TO NIPA(X)
890     MAT(X,SPA(X,Y)) = ES(X) - EF(SPA(X,Y))
900    NEXT Y
910    NEXT X
920    FF(1)=0:FF(N)=0
930    FOR X = N TO 2 STEP -1
940    FOR Y = X TO N
950     IF MAT(Y,X-1) < 0 GOTO 970
960     IF MAT(Y,X-1) < FF(X-1) THEN FF(X-1) = MAT(Y,X-1)
970    NEXT Y
980    NEXT X
990 REM ----------------- CREATE TF MATRIX ------
1000   FOR X = N TO 2 STEP -1
1010    TF(X-1) = 99
1020    FOR Y = 1 TO NIPA(X)
1030     MAT(X,SPA(X,Y)) = MAT(X,SPA(X,Y)) + TF(X)
1040    NEXT Y
1050    FOR Y = X TO N
1060     IF MAT(Y,X-1) < 0 GOTO 1080
1070     IF MAT(Y,X-1) < TF(X-1) THEN TF(X-1) = MAT(Y,X-1)
1080    NEXT Y
```

```
1090  NEXT X
1100   TF(1)=0
1110 REM -------------- FIND LS & LF -----------------
1120  FOR X = 1 TO N
1130   LS(X)=ES(X)+TF(X):LF(X)=LS(X)+D(X)
1140  NEXT X
1150 CLS:REM ----------- PRINT RESULTS --------------
1160 PRINT "ACT D   ES EF   LS LF   TF  FF CRIT - IPAS"
1170 PRINT "--- -   -- --   -- --   -- -- ---- - ----"
1180  FOR X = 1 TO N
1190    PRINT TAB(2) A$(X);TAB(5) D(X);TAB(11) ES(X);TAB(16) EF(X);
1200    PRINT TAB(23) LS(X);TAB(28) LF(X);TAB(35) TF(X);TAB(40) FF(X);
1210     IF TF(X)=0 THEN PRINT TAB(47) "*";TAB(55);
1220    PRINT TAB(55);
1230    FOR Y = 1 TO NIPA(X)
1240     PRINT IPA$(X,Y);
1250    NEXT Y
1260    PRINT:CT=CT+1:IF CT < 21 GOTO 1300
1270    CT=0:PRINT:INPUT "Hit RETURN to see more Output ";IM$
1280    CLS:PRINT "ACT D   ES EF   LS LF   TF  FF CRIT - IPAS"
1290 PRINT "--- -   -- --   -- --   -- -- ---- - ----"
1300  NEXT X
1310 END
1320 REM ================ DATA STATEMENTS ====================
1330 DATA 6,2, A,2,0, B,4,1,A, C,3,1,A, D,3,1,B, E,4,2,B,C, F,2,2,D,E
```

PROGRAM TPD

This program accepts CPM network data in the node diagram format, performs CPM calculations, and produces a time-phased bar chart. See (A-6).

Input	Output
Number of activities	Time-phased bar chart
Maximum number of	
IPAs	
Activities	
Durations	
Number of IPAs	
IPAs	

(A-6)

```
10 CLS:PRINT " ========== TPD =========="
20 PRINT:INPUT " Hit K for Keyboard or D for DATA file ";IM$
30 IF IM$ = "k" THEN IM$ = "K"
40 IF IM$ = "d" THEN IM$ = "D"
50 IF IM$ = "D" THEN READ N,M:GOTO 100
60 IF IM$ = "K" THEN PRINT:GOTO 80
70 CLS: GOTO 80
80  PRINT:INPUT " Enter # of activities";N
90 PRINT:INPUT "MAX. # OF IPAs FOR ANY ACTIVITY = ";M
100 DIM A$(N),NIPA(N),D(N),ES(N),EF(N),SS(N),ST(N),LS(N),LF(N)
110 DIM FF(N),TF(N),IPA$(N,M),MAT(N,N),SPA(N,M):CT=1
120 IF IM$ = "D" GOTO 240
130 REM -------------- KEYBOARD INPUT ---------------
140 FOR X = 1 TO N
150   PRINT:PRINT "Activity #";X;:INPUT A$(X)
160   INPUT "    # of IPAs ";NIPA(X)
170   INPUT "      Duration";D(X)
180   FOR Y = 1 TO NIPA(X)
190   INPUT "      IPA = ";IPA$(X,Y)
200   NEXT Y
210   CT=CT+1:IF CT > 3 THEN CLS:CT=0
220 NEXT X
230 GOTO 320
240 REM ---------------- READ DATA STATEMENTS ----------------
250  FOR X = 1 TO N
260   READ A$(X),D(X),NIPA(X)
270   FOR Y = 1 TO NIPA(X)
280   READ IPA$(X,Y)
290   NEXT Y
300  NEXT X
310 PRINT:PRINT " ========== PROCESSING =========="
320 REM ---------------- FINDING SEQUENCE STEPS --------------
330   X=1:SS(X)=1
340  FOR U = 2 TO N
350   FOR V = 1 TO NIPA(U)
360   IF IPA$(U,V) = A$(X) THEN SPA(U,V) = SS(X)
370   NEXT V
380  NEXT U
390  FOR X = 2 TO N
400   IF SS(X) > 0 GOTO 460
410   FOR Y = 1 TO NIPA(X)
420   IF SPA(X,Y) = 0 GOTO 460
430   IF SPA(X,Y) > ST(X) THEN ST(X) = SPA(X,Y)
440   NEXT Y
450   SS(X)=ST(X)+1:GOTO 340
460  NEXT X
470 REM ------------ ORDERING ACTIVITIES BY SEQUENCE STEPS ------------
480  FOR X = 1 TO N
490   FOR Y = X TO N
500   IF SS(X) <= SS(Y) GOTO 560
510   SWAP A$(X),A$(Y):SWAP NIPA(X),NIPA(Y)
520   SWAP SS(X),SS(Y):SWAP D(X),D(Y)
530   FOR Z = 1 TO M
540   SWAP IPA$(X,Z),IPA$(Y,Z)
550   NEXT Z
```

```
560  NEXT Y
570  NEXT X
580 REM ------------ ACT & IPA TO #s ------
590  FOR X = 1 TO N
600  FOR Y = 1 TO M
610   SPA(X,Y) = 0
620  NEXT Y
630  NEXT X
640  FOR X = 1 TO N
650  FOR Y = 1 TO N
660   FOR Z = 1 TO NIPA(Y)
670    IF IPA$(Y,Z) = A$(X) THEN SPA(Y,Z) = X
680    NEXT Z
690  NEXT Y
700  NEXT X
710 REM -------------- FIND ES & EF ------
720  ES(1)=W
730  FOR X = 1 TO N
740  FOR Y = 1 TO N
750   FOR Z = 1 TO NIPA(X)
760    IF EF(SPA(Y,Z)) > ES(Y) THEN ES(Y) = EF(SPA(Y,Z))
770     EF(Y) = ES(Y) + D(Y)
780    NEXT Z
790  NEXT Y
800  NEXT X
810 REM ---------- CREATE FF MATRIX ------
820  FOR X = 1 TO N
830  FOR Y = 1 TO N
840   MAT(X,Y)=-1:FF(X)=99
850  NEXT Y
860  NEXT X
870  FOR X = 1 TO N
880  FOR Y = 1 TO NIPA(X)
890   MAT(X,SPA(X,Y)) = ES(X) - EF(SPA(X,Y))
900  NEXT Y
910 NEXT X
920  FF(1)=0:FF(N)=0
930  FOR X = N TO 2 STEP -1
940  FOR Y = X TO N
950   IF MAT(Y,X-1) < 0 GOTO 970
960   IF MAT(Y,X-1) < FF(X-1) THEN FF(X-1) = MAT(Y,X-1)
970  NEXT Y
980  NEXT X
990 REM ----------------- CREATE TF MATRIX ------
1000  FOR X = N TO 2 STEP -1
1010   TF(X-1) = 99
1020   FOR Y = 1 TO NIPA(X)
1030    MAT(X,SPA(X,Y)) = MAT(X,SPA(X,Y)) + TF(X)
1040   NEXT Y
1050   FOR Y = X TO N
1060    IF MAT(Y,X-1) < 0 GOTO 1080
1070    IF MAT(Y,X-1) < TF(X-1) THEN TF(X-1) = MAT(Y,X-1)
1080   NEXT Y
1090  NEXT X
1100   TF(1)=0
1110  FOR X = 1 TO N
```

```
1120  LS(X)=ES(X)+TF(X):LF(X)=EF(X)+TF(X)
1130  NEXT X
1140 CLS:REM --------------- OUTPUT --------------
1150 PRINT "TIME-PHASED DIAGRAM: XX Duration; == FF; ==+-- TF"
1160 PRINT " - - - - - - - - - - - - - - - - - - - - - - - - - - - - - - - - - - - - - "
1170 PRINT "WORKDAYS--  --  ----  -  ----"
1180  FOR X = 1 TO N
1190   PRINT TAB(2) A$(X);TAB(5) D(X);TAB(11) ES(X);TAB(16) EF(X);
1200   PRINT TAB(23) LS(X);TAB(28) LF(X);TAB(35) TF(X);TAB(40) FF(X);
1210   IF TF(X)=0 THEN PRINT TAB(47) "*";TAB(55);
1220   PRINT TAB(55);
1230   FOR Y = 1 TO NIPA(X)
1240    PRINT IPA$(X,Y);
1250   NEXT Y
1260   PRINT:CT=CT+1:IF CT < 21 GOTO 1300
1270    CT=0:PRINT:INPUT "Hit RETURN to see more Output ";IM$
1280    CLS:PRINT "ACT D   ES EF   LS LF   TF FF CRIT - IPAS"
1290 PRINT "--- -   -- --   -- --   -- -- ---- - ----"
1300  NEXT X
1310 END
1320 REM ================ DATA STATEMENTS ====================
1330 DATA 6,2, A,2,0, B,4,1,A, C,3,1,A, D,3,1,B, E,4,2,B,C, F,2,2,D,E
```

PROGRAM PERT

This program accepts PERT network data in the node diagram format, performs the PERT calculations, and answers questions about the probability of finishing on, before, or after a certain date. It also tells the specified confidence level offered by a completion date. See (A-7). *Note:* This program is limited to networks having only one possible critical path.

Input	Output	
Number of activities	T_E and σ	
Maximum number of	ES, EF, LS, LF, FF,	
IPAs	and TF*	
Activities	Critical activities*	(A-7)
Number of IPAs	Answers to questions	
IPAs		
a, m, and b durations		

*Using expected durations t_e

```
10 CLS:PRINT " ========== PERT =========="
20 PRINT:INPUT " Hit K for Keyboard or D for DATA file ";IM$
30  IF IM$ = "d" THEN IM$ = "D"
40  IF IM$ = "k" THEN IM$ = "K"
50  IF IM$ = "D" THEN READ N,M:GOTO 110
60  IF IM$ = "K" THEN PRINT:GOTO 90
70 CLS: GOTO 20
80 REM ---------- INPUT ------------
90  PRINT:INPUT " Enter # of activities";N
100 PRINT:INPUT "MAX. # OF IPAs FOR ANY ACTIVITY = ";M
110 DIM A$(N),NIPA(N),D(N),DA(N),DM(N),DB(N),ES(N),EF(N),SS(N),ST(N)
120 DIM FF(N),TF(N),IPA$(N,M),MAT(N,N),SPA(N,M),V(N),LS(N),LF(N):CT=1
130 IF IM$ = "D" GOTO 250
140 REM ------------- KEYBOARD INPUT ---------------
150  FOR X = 1 TO N
160   PRINT:PRINT "Activity #";X;:INPUT A$(X)
170   INPUT "    Duration a,m,b";DA(X),DM(X),DB(X)
180   INPUT "     # of IPAs ";NIPA(X)
190   FOR Y = 1 TO NIPA(X)
200   INPUT "       IPA = ";IPA$(X,Y)
210   NEXT Y
220   CT=CT+1:IF CT > 3 THEN CLS:CT=0
230  NEXT X
240 GOTO 320
250 REM ---------------- DATA STATEMENT INPUT -------------
260  FOR X = 1 TO N
270   READ A$(X),DA(X),DM(X),DB(X),NIPA(X)
280   FOR Y = 1 TO NIPA(X)
290   READ IPA$(X,Y)
300   NEXT Y
310  NEXT X
320 REM -------------- FIND te & v ------------------
330  FOR X = 1 TO N
340   D(X)=(DA(X)+(4*DM(X))+DB(X))/6:V(X)=((DB(X)-DA(X))/6)^2
350  NEXT X
360 PRINT:PRINT " ========== PROCESSING =========="
370 REM --------------- FIND SEQUENCE STEPS ---------------------
380   X=1:SS(X)=1
390  FOR U = 2 TO N
400   FOR V = 1 TO NIPA(U)
410    IF IPA$(U,V) = A$(X) THEN SPA(U,V) = SS(X)
420   NEXT V
430  NEXT U
440  FOR X = 2 TO N
450   IF SS(X) > 0 GOTO 510
460   FOR Y = 1 TO NIPA(X)
470   IF SPA(X,Y) = 0 GOTO 510
480   IF SPA(X,Y) > ST(X) THEN ST(X) = SPA(X,Y)
490   NEXT Y
500   SS(X)=ST(X)+1:GOTO 390
510  NEXT X
520 REM --------------- ORDERING ACTIVITIES BY SS ---------------------
530  FOR X = 1 TO N
540   FOR Y = X TO N
```

```
550    IF SS(X) <= SS(Y) GOTO 610
560    SWAP A$(X),A$(Y):SWAP NIPA(X),NIPA(Y):SWAP SS(X),SS(Y):SWAP D(X),D(Y)
570    SWAP DA(X),DA(Y):SWAP DM(X),DM(Y):SWAP DB(X),DB(Y):SWAP V(X),V(Y)
580    FOR Z = 1 TO M
590     SWAP IPA$(X,Z),IPA$(Y,Z)
600    NEXT Z
610   NEXT Y
620  NEXT X
630 REM ------------ ACT & IPA TO #s ------
640  FOR X = 1 TO N
650   FOR Y = 1 TO M
660     SPA(X,Y) = 0
670   NEXT Y
680  NEXT X
690  FOR X = 1 TO N
700   FOR Y = 1 TO N
710    FOR Z = 1 TO NIPA(Y)
720     IF IPA$(Y,Z) = A$(X) THEN SPA(Y,Z) = X
730    NEXT Z
740   NEXT Y
750  NEXT X
760 REM -------------- FIND ES & EF ------
770  ES(1)=W
780  FOR X = 1 TO N
790   FOR Y = 1 TO N
800    FOR Z = 1 TO NIPA(X)
810     IF EF(SPA(Y,Z)) > ES(Y) THEN ES(Y) = EF(SPA(Y,Z))
820      EF(Y) = ES(Y) + D(Y)
830    NEXT Z
840   NEXT Y
850  NEXT X
860 REM ---------- CREATE FF MATRIX ------
870  FOR X = 1 TO N
880   FOR Y = 1 TO N
890    MAT(X,Y)=-1:FF(X)=99
900   NEXT Y
910  NEXT X
920  FOR X = 1 TO N
930   FOR Y = 1 TO NIPA(X)
940    MAT(X,SPA(X,Y)) = ES(X) - EF(SPA(X,Y))
950   NEXT Y
960  NEXT X
970  FF(1)=0:FF(N)=0
980  FOR X = N TO 2 STEP -1
990   FOR Y = X TO N
1000    IF MAT(Y,X-1) < 0 GOTO 1020
1010    IF MAT(Y,X-1) < FF(X-1) THEN FF(X-1) = MAT(Y,X-1)
1020   NEXT Y
1030  NEXT X
1040 REM ----------------- CREATE TF MATRIX ------
1050  FOR X = N TO 2 STEP -1
1060   TF(X-1) = 99
1070   FOR Y = 1 TO NIPA(X)
1080    MAT(X,SPA(X,Y)) = MAT(X,SPA(X,Y)) + TF(X)
```

```
1090  NEXT Y
1100  FOR Y = X TO N
1110   IF MAT(Y,X-1) < 0 GOTO 1130
1120   IF MAT(Y,X-1) < TF(X-1) THEN TF(X-1) = MAT(Y,X-1)
1130   NEXT Y
1140  NEXT X
1150   TF(1)=0
1160 REM -------------- CALCULATE LS & LF ---------------------
1170  FOR X = 1 TO N
1180   LS(X)=ES(X)+TF(X):LF(X)=EF(X)+TF(X)
1190  NEXT X
1200 REM ------------- CHANGE RESULTS TO WHOLE NUMBERS -------------
1210  FOR X = 1 TO N
1220   ES(X)=INT(ES(X)+.5):EF(X)=INT(EF(X)+.5):LS(X)=INT(LS(X)+.5)
1230   LF(X)=INT(LF(X)+.5):FF(X)=INT(FF(X)+.5):TF(X)=INT(TF(X)+.5)
1240  NEXT X
1250 REM ----------- FIND TE & SD --------------
1260  FOR X = 1 TO N
1270   IF TF(X) <> 0 GOTO 1290
1280   TE=TE+D(X):V=V+V(X)
1290  NEXT X
1300   TE=INT(TE+.5):SD=(INT(((V^.5)*100)+.5))/100
1310 REM ---------------- FIND PROBABILITIES -------------------
1320  CLS:PRINT:PRINT "   Project Expected Duration = ";TE
1330  PRINT:PRINT "   Project Standard Deviation = ";SD
1340  PRINT:PRINT "   PLEASE SELECT THE DESIRED OPTION "
1350  PRINT:PRINT "    1 - Network Calculations"
1360  PRINT:PRINT "    2 - Probability BEFORE END OF DAY __"
1370  PRINT:PRINT "    3 - Probability AFTER END OF DAY __"
1380  PRINT:PRINT "    4 - Probability ON DAY __"
1390  PRINT:PRINT "    5 - Find Day to complete with AT LEAST __ confidence"
1400  PRINT:PRINT "    6 - QUIT the program"
1410  PRINT:INPUT "   Enter # of SELECTION ";KD$
1420   IF KD$ = "1" GOTO 1860
1430   IF KD$ = "2" GOTO 1490
1440   IF KD$ = "3" GOTO 1570
1450   IF KD$ = "4" GOTO 1660
1460   IF KD$ = "5" GOTO 1780
1470   IF KD$ = "6" GOTO 2050
1480 GOTO 1310
1490 REM ---------------- BEFORE END OF DAY -----------------
1500 CLS:PRINT:PRINT " Probability BEFORE END OF DAY"
1510  PRINT:INPUT " Enter Day # ";TS
1520   Z = (INT((10*(TS-TE)/SD)+.5))/10
1530 GOSUB 2060
1540  PRINT:PRINT " Probability of completing BEFORE END OF Day";TS;"is";P;"%"
1550  PRINT:INPUT " Hit RETURN to continue ";IM$
1560 GOTO 1310
1570 REM ---------------- AFTER END OF DAY ----------------
1580 CLS:PRINT:PRINT " Probability AFTER END OF DAY"
1590  PRINT:INPUT " Enter Day # ";TS
1600   Z = (INT((10*(TS-TE)/SD)+.5))/10
1610 GOSUB 2060
1620   P = 100 - P
```

```
1630  PRINT:PRINT " Probability of completing AFTER END OF DAY";TS;"is";P;"%"
1640  PRINT:INPUT " Hit RETURN to continue ";IM$
1650  GOTO 1310
1660  REM ------------------ ON DAY ------------------------
1670  CLS:PRINT:PRINT " Probability ON DAY"
1680   PRINT:INPUT " Enter Day # ";TS
1690   Z = (INT((10*(TS-TE)/SD)+.5))/10
1700  GOSUB 2060
1710  P1=P:TS=TS-1
1720   Z = (INT((10*(TS-TE)/SD)+.5))/10
1730  GOSUB 2060
1740   P2 = P
1750  PRINT:PRINT " Probability of completing ON Day";TS+1;"is";P1-P2;"%"
1760  PRINT:INPUT " Hit RETURN to continue ";IM$
1770  GOTO 1310
1780  REM ---------- CONFIDENCE LEVEL ------------------
1790  CLS:PRINT:PRINT " CONFIDENCE LEVEL"
1800   PRINT:PRINT:INPUT " Enter Confidence Level in % ";P
1810  GOSUB 2640
1820   TS = INT(((Z*SD)+TE)+.99)
1830  PRINT:PRINT " Day";TS;"gives a Confidence Level of at least";P;"%"
1840  PRINT:INPUT " Hit RETURN to continue ";IM$
1850  GOTO 1310
1860  REM --- PRINT RESULTS ---
1870  CLS:PRINT TAB(52) "Inputs"
1880  PRINT "ACT D   ES  EF   LS  LF   TF  FF CRIT - a  m  b   IPAs":
1890  FOR X = 1 TO N
1900    D(X)=INT(D(X)+.5)
1910     PRINT TAB(2) A$(X);TAB(5) D(X);TAB(10) ES(X);TAB(15) EF(X);
1920     PRINT TAB(22) LS(X);TAB(27) LF(X);TAB(34) TF(X);
1930      PRINT TAB(39) FF(X);:IF TF(X)=0 THEN PRINT TAB(45) "*";
1940     PRINT TAB(51) DA(X);TAB(55) DM(X);TAB(59) DB(X);TAB(63);
1950    FOR Y = 1 TO NIPA(X)
1960     PRINT IPA$(X,Y);
1970   NEXT Y
1980     PRINT:CT=CT+1:IF CT < 21 GOTO 2020
1990    CT=0:PRINT:INPUT "Hit RETURN to see more Output ";IM$
2000   CLS:PRINT TAB(52) "Inputs"
2010   PRINT "ACT D   ES  EF   LS  LF   TF  FF CRIT - a  m  b   IPAs":
2020  NEXT X
2030  PRINT:INPUT " Hit RETURN to continue ";IM$
2040  GOTO 1310
2050  END
2060  REM ===================== Z TABLE =========================
2070  IF Z = < -2.7 THEN P = 0:GOTO 2630
2080  IF Z = -2.7 THEN P = 1:GOTO 2630
2090  IF Z = -2.6 THEN P = 1:GOTO 2630
2100  IF Z = -2.5 THEN P = 1:GOTO 2630
2110  IF Z = -2.4 THEN P = 1:GOTO 2630
2120  IF Z = -2.3 THEN P = 2:GOTO 2630
2130  IF Z = -2.2 THEN P = 2:GOTO 2630
2140  IF Z = -2.1 THEN P = 2:GOTO 2630
2150  IF Z = -2! THEN P = 2:GOTO 2630
2160  IF Z = -1.9 THEN P = 3:GOTO 2630
2170  IF Z = -1.8 THEN P = 4:GOTO 2630
2180  IF Z = -1.7 THEN P = 5:GOTO 2630
```

```
2190  IF Z = -1.6 THEN P = 6:GOTO 2630
2200  IF Z = -1.5 THEN P = 7:GOTO 2630
2210  IF Z = -1.4 THEN P = 8:GOTO 2630
2220  IF Z = -1.3 THEN P = 10:GOTO 2630
2230  IF Z = -1.2 THEN P = 12:GOTO 2630
2240  IF Z = -1.1 THEN P = 14:GOTO 2630
2250  IF Z = -1! THEN P = 16:GOTO 2630
2260  IF Z = -.9 THEN P = 18:GOTO 2630
2270  IF Z = -.8 THEN P = 21:GOTO 2630
2280  IF Z = -.7 THEN P = 24:GOTO 2630
2290  IF Z = -.6 THEN P = 27:GOTO 2630
2300  IF Z = -.5 THEN P = 31:GOTO 2630
2310  IF Z = -.4 THEN P = 34:GOTO 2630
2320  IF Z = -.3 THEN P = 38:GOTO 2630
2330  IF Z = -.2 THEN P = 42:GOTO 2630
2340  IF Z = -.1 THEN P = 46:GOTO 2630
2350  IF Z = 0 THEN P = 50:GOTO 2630
2360  IF Z = .1 THEN P = 54:GOTO 2630
2370  IF Z = .2 THEN P = 58:GOTO 2630
2380  IF Z = .3 THEN P = 62:GOTO 2630
2390  IF Z = .4 THEN P = 66:GOTO 2630
2400  IF Z = .5 THEN P = 69:GOTO 2630
2410  IF Z = .6 THEN P = 73:GOTO 2630
2420  IF Z = .7 THEN P = 76:GOTO 2630
2430  IF Z = .8 THEN P = 79:GOTO 2630
2440  IF Z = .9 THEN P = 82:GOTO 2630
2450  IF Z = 1! THEN P = 84:GOTO 2630
2460  IF Z = 1.1 THEN P = 86:GOTO 2630
2470  IF Z = 1.2 THEN P = 88:GOTO 2630
2480  IF Z = 1.3 THEN P = 90:GOTO 2630
2490  IF Z = 1.4 THEN P = 92:GOTO 2630
2500  IF Z = 1.5 THEN P = 93:GOTO 2630
2510  IF Z = 1.6 THEN P = 94:GOTO 2630
2520  IF Z = 1.7 THEN P = 95:GOTO 2630
2530  IF Z = 1.8 THEN P = 96:GOTO 2630
2540  IF Z = 1.9 THEN P = 97:GOTO 2630
2550  IF Z = 2! THEN P = 98:GOTO 2630
2560  IF Z = 2.1 THEN P = 98:GOTO 2630
2570  IF Z = 2.2 THEN P = 98:GOTO 2630
2580  IF Z = 2.3 THEN P = 98:GOTO 2630
2590  IF Z = 2.4 THEN P = 99:GOTO 2630
2600  IF Z = 2.5 THEN P = 99:GOTO 2630
2610  IF Z = 2.6 THEN P = 99:GOTO 2630
2620  IF Z = 2.7 THEN P = 99:GOTO 2630
2630  IF Z > 2.7 THEN P = 100:GOTO 2630
2640  RETURN
2650  REM =============== P TABLE ==================
2660 IF P = 0 THEN Z = -3:GOTO 3660
2670 IF P = 1 THEN Z = -2.5:GOTO 3660
2680 IF P = 2 THEN Z = -2.25:GOTO 3660
2690 IF P = 3 THEN Z = -2:GOTO 3660
2700 IF P = 4 THEN Z = -1.85:GOTO 3660
2710 IF P = 5 THEN Z = -1.75:GOTO 3660
2720 IF P = 6 THEN Z = -1.625:GOTO 3660
2730 IF P = 7 THEN Z = -1.5:GOTO 3660
2740 IF P = 8 THEN Z = -1.45:GOTO 3660
```

```
2750 IF P = 9 THEN Z = -1.4:GOTO 3660
2760 IF P = 10 THEN Z = -1.35:GOTO 3660
2770 IF P = 11 THEN Z = -1.3:GOTO 3660
2780 IF P = 12 THEN Z = -1.2:GOTO 3660
2790 IF P = 13 THEN Z = -1.15:GOTO 3660
2800 IF P = 14 THEN Z = -1.1:GOTO 3660
2810 IF P = 15 THEN Z = -1.05:GOTO 3660
2820 IF P = 16 THEN Z = -1:GOTO 3660
2830 IF P = 17 THEN Z = -.95:GOTO 3660
2840 IF P = 18 THEN Z = -.9:GOTO 3660
2850 IF P = 19 THEN Z = -.867:GOTO 3660
2860 IF P = 20 THEN Z = -.833:GOTO 3660
2870 IF P = 21 THEN Z = -.8:GOTO 3660
2880 IF P = 22 THEN Z = -.767:GOTO 3660
2890 IF P = 23 THEN Z = -.733:GOTO 3660
2900 IF P = 24 THEN Z = -.7:GOTO 3660
2910 IF P = 25 THEN Z = -.667:GOTO 3660
2920 IF P = 26 THEN Z = -.633:GOTO 3660
2930 IF P = 27 THEN Z = -.6:GOTO 3660
2940 IF P = 28 THEN Z = -.575:GOTO 3660
2950 IF P = 29 THEN Z = -.55:GOTO 3660
2960 IF P = 30 THEN Z = -.525:GOTO 3660
2970 IF P = 31 THEN Z = -.5:GOTO 3660
2980 IF P = 32 THEN Z = -.475:GOTO 3660
2990 IF P = 33 THEN Z = -.45:GOTO 3660
3000 IF P = 34 THEN Z = -.425:GOTO 3660
3010 IF P = 35 THEN Z = -.4:GOTO 3660
3020 IF P = 36 THEN Z = -.367:GOTO 3660
3030 IF P = 37 THEN Z = -.333:GOTO 3660
3040 IF P = 38 THEN Z = -.3:GOTO 3660
3050 IF P = 39 THEN Z = -.275:GOTO 3660
3060 IF P = 40 THEN Z = -.25:GOTO 3660
3070 IF P = 41 THEN Z = -.225:GOTO 3660
3080 IF P = 42 THEN Z = -.2:GOTO 3660
3090 IF P = 43 THEN Z = -.175:GOTO 3660
3100 IF P = 44 THEN Z = -.15:GOTO 3660
3110 IF P = 45 THEN Z = -.125:GOTO 3660
3120 IF P = 46 THEN Z = -.1:GOTO 3660
3130 IF P = 47 THEN Z = -.075:GOTO 3660
3140 IF P = 48 THEN Z = -.05:GOTO 3660
3150 IF P = 49 THEN Z = -.025:GOTO 3660
3160 IF P = 50 THEN Z = 0:GOTO 3660
3170 IF P = 51 THEN Z = .025:GOTO 3660
3180 IF P = 52 THEN Z = .05:GOTO 3660
3190 IF P = 53 THEN Z = .075:GOTO 3660
3200 IF P = 54 THEN Z = .1:GOTO 3660
3210 IF P = 55 THEN Z = .125:GOTO 3660
3220 IF P = 56 THEN Z = .15:GOTO 3660
3230 IF P = 57 THEN Z = .175:GOTO 3660
3240 IF P = 58 THEN Z = .2:GOTO 3660
3250 IF P = 59 THEN Z = .225:GOTO 3660
3260 IF P = 60 THEN Z = .25:GOTO 3660
3270 IF P = 61 THEN Z = .275:GOTO 3660
3280 IF P = 62 THEN Z = .3:GOTO 3660
3290 IF P = 63 THEN Z = .325:GOTO 3660
3300 IF P = 64 THEN Z = .35:GOTO 3660
```

```
3310 IF P = 65 THEN Z = .375:GOTO 3660
3320 IF P = 66 THEN Z = .4:GOTO 3660
3330 IF P = 67 THEN Z = .433:GOTO 3660
3340 IF P = 68 THEN Z = .467:GOTO 3660
3350 IF P = 69 THEN Z = .5:GOTO 3660
3360 IF P = 70 THEN Z = .525:GOTO 3660
3370 IF P = 71 THEN Z = .55:GOTO 3660
3380 IF P = 72 THEN Z = .575:GOTO 3660
3390 IF P = 73 THEN Z = .6:GOTO 3660
3400 IF P = 74 THEN Z = .633:GOTO 3660
3410 IF P = 75 THEN Z = .667:GOTO 3660
3420 IF P = 76 THEN Z = .7:GOTO 3660
3430 IF P = 77 THEN Z = .733:GOTO 3660
3440 IF P = 78 THEN Z = .767:GOTO 3660
3450 IF P = 79 THEN Z = .8:GOTO 3660
3460 IF P = 80 THEN Z = .833:GOTO 3660
3470 IF P = 81 THEN Z = .867:GOTO 3660
3480 IF P = 82 THEN Z = .9:GOTO 3660
3490 IF P = 83 THEN Z = .95:GOTO 3660
3500 IF P = 84 THEN Z = 1:GOTO 3660
3510 IF P = 85 THEN Z = 1.05:GOTO 3660
3520 IF P = 86 THEN Z = 1.1:GOTO 3660
3530 IF P = 87 THEN Z = 1.15:GOTO 3660
3540 IF P = 88 THEN Z = 1.2:GOTO 3660
3550 IF P = 89 THEN Z = 1.25:GOTO 3660
3560 IF P = 90 THEN Z = 1.3:GOTO 3660
3570 IF P = 91 THEN Z = 1.35:GOTO 3660
3580 IF P = 92 THEN Z = 1.4:GOTO 3660
3590 IF P = 93 THEN Z = 1.5:GOTO 3660
3600 IF P = 94 THEN Z = 1.6:GOTO 3660
3610 IF P = 95 THEN Z = 1.7:GOTO 3660
3620 IF P = 96 THEN Z = 1.8:GOTO 3660
3630 IF P = 97 THEN Z = 1.9:GOTO 3660
3640 IF P = 98 THEN Z = 2:GOTO 3660
3650 IF P = 99 THEN Z = 2.5:GOTO 3660
3660 IF P = 100 THEN Z = 3!
3670 RETURN
3680 REM =============== DATA statements ========================
3690 DATA 7,2, A,4,6,8,0, B,1,7,13,1,A, C,5,6,7,1,A, D,5,5,11,1,B
3700 DATA E,2,4,8,1,B, F,1,5,7,2,C,D, G,7,7,7,2,E,F
```

PROGRAM SIM

This program accepts CPM network data in the node diagram format, runs the forward pass a specified number of times using simulation, and produces an output listing as well as a scaled plot of the resultant distribution. See (A-8). *Note:* Probability ranges are entered as $0 - 99$ instead of $0 - .99$ as in the text; this is to decrease the chance of input error.

Input	Output
Number of activities	Project duration list
Maximum number of	Project duration plot
IPAs for any activity	
Number of iterations	
Maximum number of	
durations for any activity	
Random number seed	
Number of IPAs	
IPAs	
Number of durations	
Durations and probabilities	

(A-8)

```
10 CLS:PRINT "  ============ SIM ============="
20 PRINT:PRINT " NOTE: ACTIVITIES MUST BE IN SEQUENCE STEP ORDER"
30 PRINT:INPUT " Hit K for Keyboard or D for DATA file ";IM$
40  IF IM$ = "d" THEN IM$ = "D"
50  IF IM$ = "k" THEN IM$ = "K"
60  IF IM$ = "D" THEN READ N,M,NI,ND,RS:GOTO 130
70  IF IM$ = "K" THEN PRINT:GOTO 80
80   PRINT:INPUT " Enter # of activities";N
90   PRINT:INPUT " Enter maximum # of IPAs";M
100   PRINT:INPUT " Enter # of iterations";NI
110   PRINT:INPUT " Enter maximum of possible durations for any activity";ND
120   PRINT:INPUT " Enter random number seed (-32768 to 32768)";NS
130 DIM A$(N),NIPA(N),IPA$(N,M),NDP(N),D(N,ND),P(N,ND)
140 DIM ES(N),EF(N),SPA(N,M),RN(N),CP(N,ND),DU(N)
150 IF IM$ = "D" GOTO 290
160 REM ------------- KEYBOARD INPUT -----------------
170  FOR X = 1 TO N
180   CLS:PRINT:PRINT "Activity #";X;:INPUT A$(X)
190    PRINT:INPUT "     # of IPAs ";NIPA(X)
200   FOR Y = 1 TO NIPA(X)
210    INPUT "       IPA";IPA$(X,Y)
220   NEXT Y
230   PRINT:INPUT "     # of durations ";NPD(X)
240   FOR Y = 1 TO NPD(X)
250    INPUT "      duration,probability ";D(X,Y),P(X,Y)
260   NEXT Y
270  NEXT X
280 GOTO 400
290 REM --------------- DATA STATEMENT INPUT -----------------
300  FOR X = 1 TO N
310   READ A$(X),NIPA(X)
320   FOR Y = 1 TO NIPA(X)
330    READ IPA$(X,Y)
340   NEXT Y
350   READ NDP(X)
```

```
360   FOR Y = 1 TO NDP(X)
370    READ D(X,Y),P(X,Y)
380   NEXT Y
390   NEXT X
400 PRINT:PRINT " ========== PROCESSING =============":PRINT
410 REM ---------- RANDOM NUMBER GENERATOR ----------------
420 HIPL = 0:LOPL = 99999!:RANDOMIZE RS
430 PRINT "# of Iterations =";NI:PRINT:PRINT "Now Running #";
440 FOR I = 1 TO NI
450   PRINT I;
460  FOR X = 1 TO N
470   RN(X) = INT(RND * 100)
480  NEXT X
490 REM ---------- CUMULATIVE PROBABILITIES ----------------
500  FOR X = 1 TO N
510   FOR Y = 1 TO ND
520    CP(X,Y) = CP(X,Y-1) + P(X,Y)
530   NEXT Y
540  NEXT X
550 REM ---------- ASSIGN DURATIONS ----------------
560  FOR X = 1 TO N
570   FOR Y = 1 TO ND
580    IF RN(X) < CP(X,Y) THEN DU(X) = D(X,Y):GOTO 600
590   NEXT Y
600  NEXT X
610 REM ------------ ACT & IPA TO #s ------
620  FOR X = 1 TO N
630   FOR Y = 1 TO M
640    SPA(X,Y)=0:ES(X)=0
650   NEXT Y
660  NEXT X
670  FOR X = 1 TO N
680   FOR Y = 1 TO N
690    FOR Z = 1 TO NIPA(Y)
700     IF IPA$(Y,Z) = A$(X) THEN SPA(Y,Z) = X
710    NEXT Z
720   NEXT Y
730  NEXT X
740 REM -------------- FIND ES & EF ------
750 ES(1)=W
760  FOR X = 1 TO N
770   FOR Y = 1 TO N
780    FOR Z = 1 TO NIPA(X)
790     IF EF(SPA(Y,Z)) > ES(Y) THEN ES(Y) = EF(SPA(Y,Z))
800      EF(Y) = ES(Y) + DU(Y)
810    NEXT Z
820   NEXT Y
830  NEXT X
840  EX=EF(N):PL(I)=EX
850 IF EX > HIPL THEN HIPL = EX
860 IF EX < LOPL THEN LOPL = EX
870 NEXT I
880 REM ---------- PROJECT LENGTH DISTRIBUTION ----------
890 RG = HIPL - LOPL + 1
```

```
900 DIM CT(RG+5),PD(RG+5),CR(RG+5)
910 FOR X = 1 TO RG
920  PD(X) = LOPL - 1 + X
930 NEXT X
940 FOR X = 1 TO NI
950  FOR Y = 1 TO RG
960   IF PL(X) = PD(Y) THEN CT(Y) = CT(Y) + 1
970  NEXT Y
980 NEXT X
990 REM --------------- FIND MN ---------------------
1000 FOR X = 1 TO RG
1010  IF MN < CT(X) THEN MN = CT(X):MX = X
1020 NEXT X
1030 REM -------------- PRINT OUTPUT ------------------
1040 CLS:PRINT:PRINT "Days-Freq    Days-Freq    Days-Freq    Days-Freq    Days-Freq"
1050 FOR X = 1 TO RG STEP 5
1060  PRINT PD(X);TAB(6) CT(X);TAB(16) PD(X+1);TAB(21) CT(X+1);
1070  PRINT TAB(31) PD(X+2);TAB(36) CT(X+2);TAB(46) PD(X+3);TAB(51) CT(X+3);
1080  PRINT TAB(61) PD(X+4);TAB(66) CT(X+4)
1090 NEXT X
1100 REM ----------------- SCALE FACTOR -------------------------
1110 SF=1:IF MN > 20 THEN SF=MN/20
1120 FOR X = 1 TO RG
1130  CR(X) = (CT(X)/SF) - .5
1140 NEXT X
1150 PRINT:INPUT "Hit RETURN to see Plot ";IM$
1160 REM ------------- PLOT --------------
1170 CLS:LO=1:HI=RG
1180 IF RG < 19 GOTO 1220
1190 HI=MX+9:LO=HI-18
1200 IF HI > RG THEN HI=RG:LO=HI-18
1210 IF LO < 1 THEN LO=1
1220 FOR X = 20 TO 1 STEP-1
1230  FOR Y = LO TO HI
1240   IF CR(Y) > (X-1) THEN PRINT TAB((Y-LO+1)*4) "X";
1250  NEXT Y
1260   PRINT
1270 NEXT X
1280 FOR X = LO TO HI
1290  PRINT TAB(((X-LO+1)*4)-1) PD(X);
1300 NEXT X
1310 PRINT:PRINT "Iterations =";I-1;" Scale Factor =";SF
1320 REM =============== DATA STATEMENTS ====================
1330 DATA 17,5,10,11,2, ST,0,1,0,100
1340 DATA A,1,ST,2,6,40,7,60, B,1,ST,3,5,20,6,40,8,40
1350 DATA C,1,ST,11,3,1,4,2,5,4,6,9,7,15,8,19,9,19,10,15,11,9,12,5,13,2
1360 DATA D,1,A,4,4,20,5,20,6,40,7,20, E,1,B,2,5,50,7,50
1370 DATA F,1,B,2,6,50,7,50, G,2,B,C,1,5,100
1380 DATA H,3,B,C,D,8,1,3,2,8,3,14,4,25,5,25,6,16,7,7,8,2
1390 DATA I,3,B,C,D,2,6,80,8,20, J,1,E,2,5,75,6,25, K,1,E,2,3,80,6,20
1400 DATA L,2,E,F,1,3,100, M,2,G,J,4,3,40,4,20,5,20,6,20
1410 DATA N,1,H,3,1,20,2,60,3,20, O,1,K,4,1,20,2,20,4,40,6,20
1420 DATA FN,5,I,L,M,N,O,1,0,100
```

DATA STATEMENTS

Syntax for the DATA statement is as follows:

900 DATA 14,25,A,5

910 DATA C,B,2

Following the statement number, write DATA. Following DATA, type the inputs just as if you were entering data using the prompts. Each input must be separated by a comma, and each new line number must start with DATA. *Note:* If, when using data statements, you get a message saying "OUT OF DATA" (or something similar), you don't have enough data points, and if you get a message saying "SYNTAX ERROR," you probably are using the wrong kind of variable (letter instead of number or vice versa). If you have too many data points, you will not get an error message. Be sure to check your input data carefully.

Index

TH438.4.S74 1990
    Stevens, James, 1939-.
    Techniques for construction
network scheduling.

                        15584748

11-16-89